When Women Invented Television

Also by Jennifer Keishin Armstrong

Pop Star Goddesses

Sex and the City and Us

Seinfeldia

Mary and Lou and Rhoda and Ted

Sexy Feminism (with Heather Wood Rudúlph)

Why? Because We Still Like You

When Women Invented Television

The Untold Story of the Female Powerhouses Who Pioneered the Way We Watch Today

Jennifer Keishin Armstrong

HARPER

An Imprint of HarperCollins*Publishers*

HarperCollins books may be purchased for educational, business, or sales promotional use. For information, please email the Special Markets Department at SPsales@harpercollins.com.

FIRST EDITION

Designed by Nancy Singer

Library of Congress Cataloging-in-Publication Data has been applied for.

ISBN 978-0-06-297330-6

21 22 23 24 25   LSC   10 9 8 7 6 5 4 3 2 1

ACTRESS TALLULAH BANKHEAD: Radio is the mother of television.

INTERVIEWER: Who is the father?

BANKHEAD: TV has no father.

CONTENTS

AUTHOR'S NOTE

I tell these women's stories as informed by interviews with surviving witnesses to the era and the women's descendants, as well as by archival documents, press clippings, and archived interviews. I re-create narrative scenes using all of those sources. I've indicated within the text, when necessary, where the accounts come from. I checked scenes using multiple sources when possible; dialogue comes from accounts of those who were present. Full notes on specific sources are available at the end of the book.

INTRODUCTION

Bold Claims

In the fall of 1948, a forty-nine-year-old woman, the absolute prototype of a Jewish mother, marched into the Madison Avenue office of the famous and debonair William S. Paley, the man in charge of CBS, and made a brazen demand. She wanted to write, produce, and star in her own television show. Gertrude Berg believed that she, of all people, deserved a spot on television, and she insisted that one of the most powerful men in media give it to her.

This ultimatum alone would speak to her chutzpah in any TV era, including our own. But she issued it in 1948, not a time we associate with women's liberation.

Five feet five and 150 pounds, the mother of two grown children, Berg proposed an idea that seems radical even today: that she should star in a TV sitcom as the mother of two young teenagers. Of course, she did come with a track record. For the previous two decades, during radio's Golden Age, she'd written and starred in a radio comedy called *The Goldbergs*. Radio had been the default, dominant mode of national entertainment. Families had gathered around their living room radios daily to hear the latest installments of their favorite dramas and comedies as well as news and music. She had reigned supreme in this era. She looked like the prototype of the Jewish mother because she had created it.

In fact, she had already lived an entire situation comedy lifetime: on her show *The Goldbergs*, she had played radio's favorite meddling mother, Molly Goldberg, who had raised her children to adulthood over its seventeen-year course. Now she insisted on starting all over again as *television*'s favorite mother.

And she wasn't the only woman who made such bold claims to the new frontier of television, a discovery I was surprised to stumble upon in the early annals of the medium's history.

I was born in the 1970s, and I grew up with the television on. I watched all the syndicated reruns as a kid, dating back to *I Love Lucy* and *Leave It to Beaver* and *Father Knows Best*, through *The Brady Bunch* and *The Courtship of Eddie's Father*, through *All in the Family* and *The Jeffersons*. I memorized the theme songs to *The Facts of Life* and *Silver Spoons*. I read every *TV Guide* that came to our suburban Chicago home cover to cover. I led the day-after conversations at school about *The Fresh Prince of Bel-Air* and *Seinfeld*. My family communicated in TV catchphrases: "This is Carlton, your doorman." "Not that there's anything wrong with that."

When I grew up to become a journalist, I landed at *Entertainment Weekly*, where I covered the television business for ten years. I specialized in the great women of television, using my deep appreciation for TV history to write stories about Tina Fey, Julia Louis-Dreyfus, *Alias*, and *Grey's Anatomy*; I drew comparisons along the way to Carol Burnett, Mary Tyler Moore, *Murphy Brown*, and *St. Elsewhere*. I transitioned to writing books about television history, chronicling the lives and legacies of *The Mary Tyler Moore Show*, *Seinfeld*, and *Sex and the City*.

Still, I didn't know until recently, and many of even the nerdiest of TV history nerds don't know, that there was a time—a time before, even, Lucille Ball—when women ran television. Not everything, of course: Paley and his buddies occupied the biggest offices. But a surprising number of women pioneered the genres we still watch today, negotiated contracts, directed, produced, and wrote. But their names and contributions have now been largely forgotten.

I got my first hints of this as I researched *The Mary Tyler Moore Show*. Reaching back before its 1970 premiere to understand its history, I ran into Gertrude Berg, who came up as I investigated predecessors to Rhoda Morgenstern, Mary's no-nonsense Jewish friend. Berg played the original groundbreaking Jewish character Molly Goldberg. Unlike Rhoda in the 1970s, who was only implicitly Jewish until the second season of the show, Molly's identity had been explicit since her first radio appearance. I had never heard of her, but *Mary Tyler Moore Show* creators Allan Burns and James L. Brooks assured me that she had been a big deal in her time.

I also learned that Betty White's *Mary Tyler Moore Show* character, a TV hostess named Sue Ann Nivens, was meant as a send-up of White's previous persona, described as "sickly sweet." That baffled me until I looked it up; indeed, White had spent the early years of her career, throughout the 1950s, as one of the first daytime talk show hosts and then a sitcom pioneer, known for her adorable demeanor (and "high necklines").

As I rooted around in this era, I found still more women whose contributions to the medium—not to mention their liberated lives— should have made them household names still known today, but were largely lost to footnotes. Irna Phillips, for example, had conceived the soap opera, including its defining tropes, dramatic organ cues and cliff-hangers that punctuate complicated interpersonal problems. And she did it while she raised two adopted children as a single mother, building an empire along the way that included shows that would run for decades to come. She hoped, she said, that she would eventually meet a man for whom she would give it all up. But she never did; her *Guiding Light*, in fact, holds the record as the longest-running scripted program in broadcast history, ending in 2009 after seventy-two years on radio and television. Decades' worth of soap fans are thankful Phillips never found the right guy.

Hazel Scott, meanwhile, had parlayed a successful career as a jazz musician into hosting a variety show, which made her the first Black person, male or female, to host a national prime-time program. But insidious opposition to her work as a civil rights activist would cut that short and even drive her out of the country.

I wanted to tell the story of a time in television when women's ascendance and equality seemed possible, and their prominence allowed them to set the standards for everything that came after them. They were brave enough to try what hadn't been done before, and in the process found what worked (or didn't), for instance, on a daytime talk show, a TV soap opera, or a family sitcom; they showed us smart, interesting, multifaceted, dignified versions of women of color, single career women, and Jewish mothers. They did all of this seventy-plus years ago, when segregation was still legal and quite the norm, especially in the American South; when women were expected to get married straight out of high school and stay home to feed their husbands, clean the house, and raise the children; when divorced women, single women, and working women were seen as threatening, selfish, failed, used-up, and suspicious.

I found four women, in particular, who represented the different parts of television's, and women's, history of the time: Berg, who played up her motherhood while building an empire; the single mother and daytime soap impresario Irna Phillips; the glamorous political firebrand and variety show pioneer Hazel Scott; and the perky, deliberately single daytime talk show host Betty White.

Television had existed in theory for nine years as these women first entered the business. But it was just growing out of infancy and into toddlerhood in 1948, as television sets' price point crept downward and more people could afford to own one. The number of homes with televisions in the United States reached 1 million, which represented just 2 percent of the population.

Signs indicated that a growth spurt would soon come. The C. E. Hooper Company had just begun tracking television ratings after doing the job for the past fourteen years for radio, the primary means of mass entertainment in the United States. The first nightly newscast, *CBS TV News*, had debuted in May, not long after the radio network had launched its first substantial commercial television programming overall. The other major radio network, NBC, set out to use television to distribute high culture to the masses, bringing its NBC Symphony Orchestra, led by the renowned Italian conductor Arturo Toscanini, over from radio. ABC, which lagged far behind the other two radio powerhouses, launched on television as well, hoping for better fortunes on the new frontier. DuMont, a TV manufacturer, was operating its own network and giving ABC some serious competition. WTVR in Richmond, Virginia, became the nation's first TV station south of the Mason-Dixon Line. The variety show hosts Milton Berle and Ed Sullivan were becoming TV's first superstars.

In that Wild West era of television, no one knew what might work. Broadcasts were live, and anything was worth a try. When Berg did get her television show, she had to layer two or three housedresses over one another on a show night, then run backstage between scenes to strip one off as her quick costume change. Phillips and her directors had to teach the first TV soap opera stars how to play to cameras instead of just speaking into a microphone as they had on radio. (The actors spent Phillips's first TV soap visibly tracking their lines on a blackboard just off camera, making them resemble lookouts rather than soap stars.) Scott had to maintain her trademark cool, fresh beauty while she played piano under broiling TV lights in a silent studio, the opposite of the adoring crowds she was used to. White hosted one of the first daytime talk shows and had to improvise on camera for five and a half hours a day, six days a week, with no writers to help.

The nascent television business included these and other women in a surprising number of jobs, both in front of and behind the cameras. Women hosted daytime music and cooking shows, led industry unions, and even developed new TV news formats, including one of the first public affairs programs, NBC's *Meet the Press*, created and hosted by the broadcast journalist Martha Rountree. It's still on the air as of 2020, making it TV's longest-running show.

In fact, the creative teams behind the handful of scripted, serialized, prime-time shows in 1949–1950 were about 25 percent female, according to my own count, almost exactly where things stand today in television. (Comparable statistics aren't available for the radio industry of the time.) That would drop over the next few decades to a dismal 6.5 percent in 1973—a time when the growing women's movement forced Hollywood's Writers Guild of America to undertake such a count at all; in the years between, no reliable statistics are available. San Diego State University's Center for the Studio of Women in Television & Film began tracking those statistics more closely each year starting in 1997, when women made up 21 percent of behind-the-scenes talent. In 2018–2019, women made up about 25 percent of TV creators across platforms at a time considered to be a high point for women working behind the scenes in the medium—landing us now roughly where we were back in 1949 in terms of gender representation behind the scenes.

Many of the earliest TV stars, female and male, came up through the radio ranks, writing and performing for what was Americans' dominant home entertainment medium until the 1950s. While radio reigned supreme, TV signals reached tentatively across the country, in hopes that someone would be out there to receive them, literally: television was live and broadcast quite similarly to radio, sending

signals out to transmitters, which would beam them to home an-
tennae and produce the picture and sound viewers would experience
as it was broadcast. Every broadcast existed only in the moment.

Crucially for women in the business, television was also still a
speculative business. Resources were scarce and fame wasn't a sure
thing. Women led among the pioneers, willing to try a new field
where men didn't yet hog all the airtime. While male writers, actors, and hosts enjoyed the Golden Age of Radio from the 1930s
through the 1940s, women grabbed the chance to write, produce,
host, and act for TV while it was still an open field.

The most enduringly famous of these women was Lucille Ball,
who came to television from radio in 1951. CBS asked her to bring
her radio hit *My Favorite Husband* to the new medium, and she
agreed to do so only if her real-life husband, the Cuban American
musician Desi Arnaz, could play her spouse. After they proved their
dual appeal with a successful vaudeville act, CBS agreed. Their show
became *I Love Lucy*, the era's defining hit for two major reasons:
Ball's genius for physical comedy and their insistence that the show
be shot on film, which allowed it to live on in syndicated reruns for
decades to come. But Lucy wasn't the anomaly she appeared to be;
many women had come before her in television, with equally important roles both in front of the camera and behind the scenes.

Men flooded the industry and took over many of the jobs women
had been doing when, in the mid-1950s, television became big business and a conservative wave washed over the country. It was the era
that would be idealized as true Americana: idols of white, straight
masculinity, such as James Dean and Elvis Presley, ruled. Marilyn
Monroe was objectified relentlessly as America's biggest film star,
revered for her girlish, feminine wiles. The economy was at full
blast, like the new sounds of rock 'n' roll blaring from a suburban
teenager's car stereo. American life was grand—as long as you were

a white, straight, well-heeled man with a house, a wife, a few kids, and a few cars. TV began to reflect that Father-knows-best patriarchy. As a result, many of those women's contributions, aside from Lucy's, vanished from memory.

I chose these four women—Gertrude Berg, Irna Phillips, Hazel Scott, and Betty White—to tell this story, which encompasses many other female television firsts, because they each represent a different dominant strand of that story. Berg and Scott took on the big leagues of prime time and fought ethnic and racial stereotypes along the way, paving the way for Clair Huxtable and Olivia Pope, *The Nanny* and *The Marvelous Mrs. Maisel*. As a result, they also battled direct attacks on their careers from the supposed anti-Communist crusaders of McCarthyism, who used the Cold War as cover to attack the left. Jews, civil rights activists, and progressives—many of them women—lost their voices and livelihoods in the process. Phillips and White worked in the daytime realm, where female audiences ruled, even though they were often condescended to. Phillips and White pioneered the territory that would later provide fertile ground for the careers of Oprah Winfrey and Ellen DeGeneres. All four women faced an incursion of patriarchal, conservative forces that compelled them to fight for their survival.

I couldn't uncover any direct evidence that Berg, Phillips, Scott, and White knew one another, but they surely knew of one another. The television industry was small at that time, and they had plenty of reasons to cross paths. Berg and Phillips both had a warm, personal relationship with the same advertising representative at Procter & Gamble, a household goods manufacturer that sponsored many programs and thus was a huge force in early television. Berg's television husband, Philip Loeb, worked with Scott and moved in the leftist circles that frequented the nightclub where she headlined, Café Society. Berg and White competed for the first Best Actress award in Emmy history in 1951. Phillips and White vied for the same daytime television audiences, at least once even competing head-to-head.

These four women also shared a common dilemma for high-powered career women in any industry in any time throughout modern history, much less women in such a visible business, during an era of such rigid gender roles: how to balance the expectations of family life with their passion for their work. They came up with four different answers: Berg married a supportive man who didn't seem to mind her fame; he even typed up some scripts for her, likely spent some time looking after their two children during her radio career, and helped manage her career. Phillips never married but adopted two children on her own. Scott wed an equally famous man, the charismatic and handsome Harlem congressman Adam Clayton Powell, Jr. White came out of two short, failed marriages certain that husbands and careers could not coexist. She chose to commit to her career for the foreseeable future.

These kinds of female-centric stories often disappear when history is written, and television history is no exception. Today, when we think of television geniuses, we think mainly of white men: Aaron Sorkin's *The West Wing* and David Chase's *The Sopranos*; Larry David and Jerry Seinfeld's *Seinfeld* and Greg Daniels's *The Office*; Lorne Michaels's *Saturday Night Live*. This book aims to reclaim television history for the women who made it.

I dug through archives, watched footage, interviewed their descendants and surviving colleagues, and pored through old books and articles to get to know these pioneering women well enough to share the forgotten stories of their foundational contributions to television, the medium that now permeates our lives. Their stories are more relevant than ever. They helped to build the foundation of the television we now obsess over, the pop culture touchpoints that drive so many of our conversations. We spend an average of nearly four hours per day watching "television"—that is, video content via a TV, smartphone, tablet, or computer—according to statistics from late 2019. More than five hundred new scripted series were introduced in the United States in that same year. Far beyond a Golden Age, we have reached a Golden Glut.

Imagine how mind-blowing it would be for Irna Phillips to see that her soap opera family dynamics had led to a show such as the addictive drama *Succession*; or for Hazel Scott to see the grounded, loving family of the inventive sitcom *black-ish*; or for Gertrude Berg to see the full and unapologetic portrayals of Jewish families on such lush productions as *The Marvelous Mrs. Maisel* and *Transparent*. Imagine how much more it would blow their minds to know we can also instantly call up video of their own work, at least to some extent, on a number of devices.

Their struggles also echo more modern breakthroughs, like the rise of scrappy, do-it-yourself YouTube and TikTok stars on the Internet. And their technical achievements, working to broadcast live with so few resources, became more palpable as we watched our biggest stars, networks, and producers scramble to make new content during the 2020 coronavirus pandemic—all those involved forced to assemble their own lighting, work with subpar sound transmissions, lob jokes into the void without a live audience, and do their own hair and makeup.

When I investigated the women who invented our television, I found extraordinary stories of ambitious visionaries whose legacies were cut short and erased by that conservative wave of the mid-1950s that reasserted the status quo and reaffirmed that only a white father knows best. These women gave us so much, and it's time that we knew their stories as well as we know our television of today.

1

Yoo-Hoo, Gertrude Berg!

Gertrude Berg

Gertrude Berg entered a room like the prow of a ship, commanding attention to match her ambition. She wasn't arrogant; she just carried her accomplishments with her. She dressed her matronly figure in dark, dignified dresses and furs that showed off her good taste and the fortune she had amassed from her radio program. She had created, written, and starred in *The Goldbergs*, a popular serialized comedy about a Jewish American family living in a Bronx tenement.

She constructed her professional image carefully, her wardrobe tailored, her gloves exquisite, her brown hair always pulled back into an impeccable chignon. She spoke in a practiced mid-Atlantic accent—that distinctive lilt common to 1940s film stars—rather than in the Yiddish accent and patois her radio character was known for. That all reminded the world that Berg was not the hausfrau she played on the radio but a cultured titan of the medium.

Her granddaughter, Anne Schwartz, told me that "she spent money faster than she made it."

Berg looked the picture of empowerment when she walked into Bill Paley's CBS office in late 1948 to demand a television deal. But in fact, she *needed* him to give her a chance on his new television network.

Both had grown to become giants of the Radio Age. Both were approaching fifty years old. Each had aided the other's rise. Not long before, he had done everything possible to win her, and then win her back again, in a series of radio talent-raid wars between his network, CBS, and its main rival, NBC.

Now, though, Berg found herself beseeching Paley to give her a chance on TV. The new medium had debuted at the 1939 World's Fair almost a decade earlier, leaving onlookers mesmerized. It had been licensed to broadcast in the United States since 1941. But it had only recently budded into a viable business—and it was still far from a sure thing. That was exactly why Berg felt it was the perfect time for her to strike, before the market got too saturated, while she could still stake a claim and determine what a Gertrude Berg television show would look like.

Berg had some major factors in her favor. First, she boasted nationwide fame. Second, Paley's wife, Babe, was, according to some accounts, urging him to sign Berg for a television series. But some forces were working against Berg, too: as of 1948, variety shows had been the thing on TV—which was what had made Milton Berle and Ed Sullivan its breakout stars so far. Situation comedies like Berg's had yet to take hold onscreen. They required a more complicated formula: actors, rehearsals, scripts, camera angles. Yet they still had to be broadcast live, as all television was at the time. Thus the looser format of variety shows made the most sense in the early days.

Berg leveled with Paley: she had kept his radio network afloat after the Great Depression and through World War II. She told him she "didn't believe it was fair that a woman who had been so successful with a show on radio, should be shut out from TV without so much as a chance," as she later recalled. She wanted to keep her character, *Goldbergs* matriarch Molly, alive and active in the public imagination at all costs. This goal would drive the rest of her life, and would extract its share of those costs.

Born Tillie Edelstein in 1898 to Jacob and Diana Edelstein and raised in a Jewish section of East Harlem, Gertrude Berg spent most of her life without siblings after her older brother, Charles, died of diphtheria at about age seven. Her parents never recovered: her mother suffered a nervous breakdown, and her father carried the telegram that announced Charles's death in his pocket for the rest of his life. Gertrude referred to herself as an only child. One of her defining qualities was her insistence on moving past tragedy and telling her story as she wanted others to see it. "We lived a life that may have had hardships, but if we had them, nobody told me," she wrote in her autobiography, playing down the family's emotional strife. "All I know is that I was surrounded on all sides by love and affection and very little money."

Her father retained an entrepreneurial spirit passed down from his father, Mordecai. Tillie's grandpa built stills in the family apartment on Rivington Street on New York City's predominantly Jewish Lower East Side so he could make and sell (and enjoy) hooch during Prohibition. "Grandpa Mordecai had been drinking schnapps since he was ten years old," Berg wrote. "By the time he was eleven it was a habit. . . . Grandpa was a great believer in the law. If the government said you couldn't buy schnapps, so all right, you couldn't buy it. But! Where was it written that you couldn't make it?"

Jacob sputtered through several other ventures of his own—a

restaurant, a speakeasy. "I think in that whole Edelstein side there was a restlessness and ambition," Gertrude's grandson Adam Berg told me. "You just don't sit down as a tinsmith and say, 'I think I'll make a still.' You don't say, 'I think I'll run a speakeasy and tempt fate.'"

The Bergs, of course, did. And Jake held his own with his share of schemes. The family lived in a fourth-floor walk-up in the city. But from his various moneymaking ploys, he scraped together enough to buy a resort hotel in Fleischmanns, a village in the Catskills, at a time when the area, also known as the Borscht Belt, was on the rise as a vacation spot for Jewish New Yorkers to escape the city. "When I was in the country I was very glad that my father ran a hotel, but in the city I used to tell all my friends that my father owned a summer estate—it sounded better than a hotel—with fifty rooms and thirty in help," Gertrude wrote. "That wasn't entirely a lie; at least the figures were accurate." She would carry with her into show business this tendency to bend the truth in the name of self-mythologizing.

That hotel would direct the course of Tillie's life. There she began writing and performing, and there she met her future husband, Lewis Berg.

Tillie took it upon herself to entertain the summer guests with comedy sketches and characters she created, leading her to eventually take some writing classes at Columbia University in the city. This biographical detail sometimes inflated depending upon the time and place it was retold: in some interviews, she implied that she had graduated from the prestigious school but offered few details. Later in her life, though, she told *Commentary* magazine that after she had graduated from Wadleigh High School for Girls in Harlem, "I went to Columbia, taking all sorts of courses, but majoring in nothing and not graduating."

Lewis visited the resort when he was twenty-three and Tillie was thirteen. "When I was a very advanced thirteen I met a man with an English accent and I paid hardly any attention to him at all except I loved to listen to him speak," Berg wrote. "He fascinated me because he had really been born in London and he spoke like a Waverley novel. He said 'whilst' and 'hence' and 'shed-yule.'" He had grown up British, then come of age in Paris at the turn of the century—as a "boulevardier," as his grandson Adam recalls from family stories. Adam says his grandpa Lewis told him, "Well, we would walk up and down the Champs-Élysées all day and all night."

On Lewis's first trip to the Edelsteins' resort for a two-week vacation, he impressed young Tillie with his intellect and sophistication. He returned when she was seventeen, and they married when she was nineteen. Lewis, who had studied chemistry, was on a team during World War I that invented instant coffee for use by US troops. He then got a job in the sugar business during the early years of his and Tillie's marriage, which included a stint at a Louisiana plantation. The factory there burned down, which was good news for Tillie, who had no interest in remaining in the South.

They returned to New York City, where she gave birth to their son, Cherney, and then their daughter, Harriet. Lewis—"Lew" to his wife—took up accounting and opened his own practice in Bridgeport, Connecticut, a train commute away from Manhattan.

Meanwhile, Tillie began to pursue what she wanted: a show business career. She changed her name to the more aristocratic-sounding Gertrude and leaned on the writing principles she'd learned at the Fleischmanns resort and in those Columbia courses. She spun her work at her parents' resort into a line item on her résumé about "Jewish art theaters." She got herself hired to write sketches to run between acts at what she later described as an "African revue" before she encountered an opportunity in radio, voicing a Yiddish commercial. She didn't know Yiddish, so Lewis, who did, helped her to rehearse.

As she pursued writing for radio, Lewis often typed up her scripts for her, since he was one of the few people in the world who could read her handwriting—which looked like loopy shorthand but meant little to most readers and got worse when her pencil grew dull or she rushed. She got her first show on the air in 1927, a radio drama called *Effie and Laura*, about two clerks in a dime store. CBS canceled it after just one episode because of Laura's remark that "marriages are never made in heaven."

When Gertrude pitched her next show in 1929, about a Jewish family named the Goldbergs getting through life together in a Bronx tenement, she had written her sample scripts by hand, in pencil, even though she, of course, owned a typewriter. This time, Lewis hadn't stepped in to make them presentable. One version of the story goes like this: The radio executive she met with couldn't read her scrawled script, so he handed the pages back to her. He asked her to read them aloud to him. After hearing her read it in her warm, expressive voice, he accepted her script—and insisted that she play the lead. In a later version of the story, which she told to a reporter, she had planned the whole thing so she could get the part.

Whichever way it happened, she had forged her future stardom.

The Rise of the Goldbergs premiered on NBC Radio in 1929 as a fifteen-minute program that aired weekly. It followed a family headed by two Jewish immigrant parents, Molly and Jake, as they tried to assimilate into New York City life and raise their American-born children, Sammy and Rosalie, with help from Molly's uncle David. The show was based on the older generation of Gertrude's family: "My sense of Jewishness comes not from my father and mother so much as from my grandparents," she explained in a later interview.

The show ran without a sponsor for two years—a practice called "sustaining," in which a network would support a series financially because it showed potential but needed a chance to prove it could find an audience. Sustainers had to eventually attract a sponsor to stay on the air for the long term. NBC executives suggested that the show would be more likely to secure one if Berg toned down her character's Yiddish accent and changed her last name to Smith or Jones. Berg refused. "The show would be nothing if I watered it down," she wrote in an article years later. "I write about middle-class Jewish people because I know them, love them, am one of them."

The production centered Berg's big personality as Molly, whom she herself described as a "plump, dark, and motherly" woman in a 1931 short story collection based on the show. Every episode began with her shouted catchphrase, as if she were leaning out of an apartment window to summon her neighbors to chat: "Yoo-hoo! Is anybody . . . ?" Then announcer Bud Collyer would chime in with some variation of "There she is, folks! That's Molly Goldberg, a woman with a place in every heart and a finger in every pie!" Her character had strong tendencies to meddle, matchmake, and mangle the language just a bit ("Enter whoever!").

Molly didn't merely attract the necessary sponsors; her show became a sensation, rivaled in popularity only by another situation comedy, *Amos 'n' Andy*. Ten million listeners tuned in to every episode. At one point in the show's run, Berg got sick and the series took the week off. NBC, its home at the time, received 37,000 letters of concern. The show succeeded through the Great Depression and aired six times a week by 1931. When it moved to CBS in 1936, it shortened its title to *The Goldbergs*.

The Goldbergs depicted Jews and the Jewish American experience without apology, drawing from Berg's own experiences growing up in a Jewish section of Harlem. "It's hard to say where I get my ideas for the sketches," she said years later in an interview. "You know, how can any writer tell you how he works? From friends I visit—I have very many everywhere—from the family. Sometimes I build the program around an idea, like the problem of an old widower, sometimes around a character type. If I'm impressed by an actor some place, I'll write a part for him that uses his special quality." That included the Broadway musical star Eartha Kitt, whom she wrote a part for on the radio show, and Menasha Skulnik, a Yiddish theater actor who played Molly's uncle David for nineteen years on the radio.

And unlike *Amos 'n' Andy*, which featured two white men acting out racial stereotypes as Black characters, her show had found success with a humor that respected its characters' dignity. She got mainstream audiences across the United States to invest their time, attention, and empathy in a Jewish family who had Yiddish accents, ate gefilte fish, and celebrated Passover. Her radio husband, Jake, was a stubborn, proud man who worked in the heavily Jewish "rag trade," making and selling clothing.

A 1932 editorial in the publication *Broadcast Advertising* confirmed that Berg had made the specifics of a Jewish family in New York City universal, showing that *The Goldbergs*' audience was spread evenly across geographic regions. The report also quoted an executive from the show's advertiser Pepsodent who said, "Although the program concerns a Jewish family, the vast majority . . . of appeals to keep it on the air came from Gentiles."

So did fan letters. In the 1930s, one listener, Mary E. Kelly, wrote from Cleveland, "We love Mollie! [*sic*]—for her tolerance, which she preaches so beautifully—without preaching; for her understanding heart; for her love of her little family; for the many worries she hides so valiantly behind her happy ways; for her patience in achieving the desired end in view, without hurt or unkind speech;—for her sympathy with the views of the younger generation in her family, without relinquishing her gentle authority—in fact, for just being Mollie."

Friends and family knew Berg as progressive, and she supported Franklin Delano Roosevelt as president, but she played coy in public about the potential political power of her show to improve relations between Jews and whites. "I didn't set out to make a contribution to interracial understanding," she said. "I only tried to depict the life of a family in a background that I knew best." That sort of dodge, in fact, became a common tactic, echoing throughout future generations of mass media creators; everyone from *The Mary Tyler Moore Show*'s creators, James L. Brooks and Allan Burns, to *Schitt's Creek*'s Daniel Levy has downplayed their political intentions. It makes sense that they would start with the characters first, not wanting to assume their creations would have a lasting impact. It also makes sense that they wouldn't want to scare viewers away with admitted political grandstanding.

Berg had learned to use that approach in radio because of broadcasting's trend toward keeping politics off the airwaves starting in World War II. The Roosevelt administration began to carefully monitor radio commentary, and networks responded by self-policing to appease both government officials and advertisers. Berg later explained her own take on those unspoken rules: "You see, darling, I don't bring up anything that will bother people. That's very important. Unions, politics, fund-raising, Zionism, socialism, inter-group relations, I don't stress them. And, after all, aren't such things secondary to daily family living?"

So she built the franchise of *The Goldbergs* to be political enough to make a positive difference, but not so political as to alarm radio regulators. As the show reached the end of its natural sitcom life span after nearly two decades on the radio—it was a family story, and the children had grown to adulthood—Berg scanned the horizon for new opportunities. She branched out with an advice column called "Mama Talks" and a spin-off book called *The Rise of the Goldbergs*, as well as a *Goldbergs* comic strip, biding her time until the right next step materialized.

The Goldbergs became radio's second-longest-running program after *Amos 'n' Andy*—which it followed on the air for several years—spending many of its seventeen successful years on Paley's CBS radio network. In the 1930s, a national poll named Gertrude Berg the second most respected woman in America after First Lady Eleanor Roosevelt. Berg's ferocious ambition, backed by talent, had gotten her far, but she wanted still more.

Then the next phase of *Goldbergs* life arrived: Months before she pitched Paley her show for television, she wrote and starred in a Broadway version of the series called *Me and Molly*. It ran from February to July 1948. *Me and Molly* took the Goldbergs back to the beginning, set in 1919 New York City. In this version, Molly, her husband, Jake, and their two young children have just moved into a new apartment as Jake yearns to start his own business. Molly has an idea as to how he can do that: He should, she says, make dresses in half sizes for harder-to-fit body types. That brilliant idea—a very progressive one, indeed—inspires Jake. But for him to strike out on his own, the family will have to scrimp and save for a while. The plot turns on whether they'll be able to afford piano lessons and a piano for eleven-year-old Rosie and how Molly's matchmaking scheme of the moment might help—or hurt—the business plan.

The production demonstrated Berg's critic-proof appeal. Many of the reviewers, in fact, seemed to throw up their hands in mid-review, giving in to her charm while they pointed out the gaping flaws in the work itself. The *Chicago Daily Tribune*'s reviewer said, "Not in a long time has there been so friendly a play as Gertrude Berg's *Me and Molly*, which puts upon a stage the Goldberg family of radio fame. It is generous, simple, and good-natured—and, as a piece of dramatic writing, artless." The *Christian Science Monitor*'s reviewer noted, "As a play, *Me and Molly* seems pretty much of a shambles. But it is almost as endearing as it is untidy."

The play nearly led to a film version: Paramount Pictures assigned a scout to the stage production, who wrote a detailed, scene-by-scene report on its contents that was filed with no record of it being pursued further. Movie stardom wouldn't come for Gertrude Berg, as it turned out, until *after* TV stardom.

What looked like a lark of a Broadway run contained two important seeds that would sprout and then grow, having a massive effect on Berg's life, her work, and the future of television. One would result in the premature demise of her own career and come to a tragic end. One would blossom into her invention of the family sitcom for television and affect every TV comedy to come.

The first of those seeds was her casting of Philip Loeb, an experienced, respected stage actor, as her harried husband, Jake Goldberg. Loeb was good-looking in an accessible, everyday way, with a full head of wavy, dark, often mussed hair, and wire-rimmed glasses. He was charismatic and, offstage, could unleash a filthy—but still witty—sense of humor in front of the right audience. He was a show business labor activist with the Theatre Guild and Actors' Equity Association who had helped fight for rehearsal pay and other benefits for working actors, which allowed many for the first time to make a living at the craft. His acting work thus far had been mostly onstage, though he had appeared on television in 1939 when almost no one was watching as part of *The Ethel Waters Show*, a variety production that starred the Black singer and actress. His stage acting experience was a boon to Berg's production and to Berg herself, who was just learning to act in front of an audience, rather than playing to radio listeners.

The second of those seeds was the inspiration to try television. "It was during the time that *Me and Molly* was running on Broadway that I saw somebody was writing on the wall," she wrote in her autobiography. "The translation was simple: all the writing said was, 'Television!'"

Berg had long before seen the potential of the emerging television industry, placing her well ahead of most of show business. She had written and performed a sketch from her other radio series, *House of Glass*, as part of NBC's first official television broadcast in 1940, billed as "a two-hour gala featuring stars of stage, motion pictures, and radio." The critic Gilbert Seldes later described seeing her appearance on the show as a clear highlight, a demonstration that she, unlike the rest of those who appeared, was "exactly right for television." He wrote, "This was television and nothing else."

Now, in the late 1940s, a successful Broadway run on her side, Berg had perfectly positioned herself to invade television as sets rolled into the living rooms of those forward-thinking souls who could afford them. A twelve-inch console television designed for living room use cost $985 in 1948—more than $10,000 in 2020 terms. Though she tended to depict middle-class life, which television owners of the time had likely left behind, she had other points of appeal: Her material reflected life in a large city, and TV reception was available at the time only in metropolitan areas. Her Jewishness would play well with much of that audience, too, since Jews tended to cluster in such cities.

To solidify her approach, she performed in an anthology series called *The Chevrolet Tele-Theatre*. The writer of the episode, Ernest Kinoy, had attended camp with her now-grown children, Cherney and Harriet, and he sent the script to the distinguished madam of radio through those personal channels. His story was about two matchmaking women, a perfect fit for Berg. She agreed to the part. With that, she saw that TV was every bit as good as she had remembered. TV recalled that the feeling was mutual.

By the time she pitched herself to Paley for television, she had been producing, writing, and starring in some version of Molly Goldberg's story for nearly twenty years—the last ten of them at Paley's radio network, where she had landed for good in 1936 after the bidding wars with NBC. She had written more than five thousand episode scripts as well as the Broadway play.

Things were falling into place for the next phase of Berg's career, perfect timing now that her two children were grown and out on their own. (Cherney was twenty-six; Harriet, twenty-two.) After twenty years of dominating the radio world, Gertrude Berg saw she could have her own niche on television, a family comedy. She envisioned a program that was like her radio show, but visual; like her stage play, but with different episodes every week that would keep people coming back to find out what the characters did next. She intended to conquer the new medium while it was still up for grabs.

Even though she was forty-nine, she was not about to step aside and let a new generation take over. She wrote yet another *Goldbergs* script and pitched it to the television networks: ABC, CBS, DuMont, and NBC. They all turned her down.

But Paley's rejection particularly stung after all they had been through together in her radio days. And perhaps also because they were kindred spirits who, despite their differences, understood each other. Berg loved her expensive hats, furs, dresses, pearls, and pins. Paley saw her glamour and raised it. He had slicked-back dark hair and favored dark suits and ties with white shirts. He appreciated the trappings of show business. Just a year earlier he had married Barbara "Babe" Cushing Mortimer, the divorced daughter of a renowned Boston brain surgeon. Babe was one of New York's most famous and fashionable socialites. Later, her friend Truman Capote would say of her, "Mrs. P. had only one fault: she was perfect; otherwise, she was perfect." Together, Babe and Bill made a stylish "It" couple who loved to throw parties. Their tastes determined trends in media and fashion.

Bill had built CBS from a small radio network into a major radio and TV network. His father, Samuel, a Jewish immigrant from Ukraine who had become a multimillionaire cigar magnate, had given him a significant boost. In 1927, Samuel and some business partners bought a network of sixteen radio stations in the Philadelphia area. Over the next ten years, Bill built it into a national network of more than a hundred affiliates. At the time Berg stormed into his office in 1948, CBS remained a radio juggernaut, the home of such hits as *My Favorite Husband*, starring the movie actress Lucille Ball.

As the two titans, Gertrude Berg and William S. Paley, faced each other, Berg made her message clear to Paley: she had kept his radio network afloat after the Depression and through World War II. He owed her a chance.

She left his office that day without a firm answer as she brooded over the reasons he refused to give her the deal she knew she deserved. Paley may have been resisting her program's Jewish content. He had, for instance, turned down a chance to finance the play *Fiddler on the Roof* because, he said, it was "too Jewish." Despite his own ancestry, he tended to shy away from public support of Jewish programming or causes, concerned, like Hollywood studio bosses before him, that he would be perceived as overstepping and would unnecessarily rile anti-Semitic backlash.

In the case of *The Goldbergs*, the visual aspect of television would only emphasize the characters' ethnicity. In the coming decade, in fact, video's cultural takeover would heavily favor stars who hewed closely to a strict visual standard: conventionally beautiful, thin, and white Anglo-Saxon Protestant. It was a curse that would lock television into depicting an extremely narrow range of experiences, a curse that has begun to lift in recent years but still has a long way to go.

The film industry had similarly shied away from explicit Jewishness onscreen. Even anti-Nazi movies made by Warner Brothers in the 1930s and '40s avoided mentioning Jewishness. The first major films about anti-Semitism had only recently been released: 1947's Best Picture Oscar winner, *Gentleman's Agreement*, starring Gregory Peck as a journalist who poses as a Jew to expose anti-Semitism, and *Crossfire*, a film noir about a bigotry-motivated murder.

After World War II, Judaism was slowly, carefully being recognized as a "third religion" in the United States—along with Catholicism and Protestantism—and blatant anti-Semitism was on a slow decline. A few years later, the Jewish writer Will Herberg's bestseller *Protestant-Catholic-Jew* would reflect that new recognition among Americans. To be anything else besides those three major religions "is somehow not to be an American," he wrote. The fact that Judaism was in the mix was a huge step forward.

And Berg was only one of several Jews who were embracing their identity in pop culture: In 1945, Bess Myerson became the first Jewish Miss America. Rabbi Joshua L. Liebman had hit number one on the *New York Times* best-seller list with his self-help book *Peace of Mind: Insights on Human Nature That Can Change Your Life* in 1946, and it had remained popular since. But paradoxically, the progressivism that many American Jews embraced as part of their culture was slipping out of favor across the country as it rebounded from World War II, which meant that Berg's heretofore successful identity as America's Jewish mother would require an increasingly tricky balancing act between authenticity and crowd pleasing.

Berg headed home from her meeting with Paley unsure whether she had changed his mind about putting *The Goldbergs* on television. But at least she could rest assured that she had done everything she could to fight for her vision of putting her radio family into living rooms across the country.

That evening, she at last got the call she had hoped for: CBS would audition her program for potential sponsors. She had won! She was on her way to television. Her show would be among the first televised situation comedies—preceded only by a lark of a fifteen-minute show about a young married couple called *Mary Kay and Johnny*—and would set the template for the sitcom's predominant form in decades to come, the family comedy.

On Thanksgiving Day 1948, Berg assembled a cast at CBS headquarters. They performed her pilot script before cameras, which beamed the performance via closed-circuit to potential advertisers. Afterward, the trade papers reported that CBS was indeed working out a suitable time slot on its schedule for *The Goldbergs*. The audition had succeeded.

After the tryout, CBS director of programs C. M. Underhill tried to soothe Berg's ego after the arduous pitch process. He sent her a note: "I just wanted to let you know how much we all enjoyed *The Goldbergs*. And how much we appreciated your artistry in writing and performance. It is a charming show and one which we are looking forward to."

Berg's life's work, *The Goldbergs*, would continue on television, presenting a female auteur and star's vision and depicting a proud Jewish family at a time when Jews around the world were just starting to heal from the devastation of the Holocaust.

Of course, getting a spot on CBS's schedule marked only the beginning. It remained to be seen whether Berg could keep viewers interested in her new TV family week after week. There were few examples to follow, so she would make it up as she went, inventing the family sitcom along the way.

And although the audition had been deemed successful by the network, the show still didn't have one crucial element: a committed sponsor. The show was signed as a "sustainer," just as *The Goldbergs* had been on radio. It would get a tryout on television in hopes of attracting a brand to pay the bills.

At the time, television replicated radio's model for handling its production costs: A single advertiser signed up to sponsor an entire series, working closely with the creators and producers, as well as an advertising agency, to make a show and ads that everyone involved agreed upon. The ads might be delivered by an announcer, or, especially in the case of variety show hosts, by the star. Many early shows were even named for their sponsors, such as Milton Berle's *Texaco Star Theater* and the dramatic anthology *Philip Morris Playhouse*. The show was delivered as a finished package to the network that had decided to air it. Often ad agencies even conceived and produced series as a service to their client corporations. Networks' primary functions were agreeing to air a show and finding a time slot in which to do so, not overseeing the minutiae of the show's production, once a sponsor was in place. This system gave advertisers enormous power over content, which would present major problems as television progressed.

Signing *The Goldbergs* as a sustaining show was a common part of the process, but finding a sponsor soon would be crucial to the series' longevity.

Berg worked with CBS's head of program development, Worthington Miner, to prepare the series for air. The time was characterized, Miner said, by "frantic conferences, endlessly ringing telephones, deadlines, and constant crises. It was an [sic] all new and terrifyingly complex. Since until now no one had ever tried to do it before, nobody really knew how to do anything. An 'old hand' was somebody who'd worked on the show last week." Berg went to work to convert several of her fifteen-minute radio scripts into half-hour television episodes—CBS had assigned her a thirty-minute slot on its schedule—while she and Miner consulted on everything else—sets, costumes, sound, lighting, cameras.

The Goldbergs premiered live on CBS on January 10, 1949, as it awaited its savior sponsor.

Even with the move to television, the Goldbergs themselves still lived where radio had left them, in a tenement apartment building at 1038 E. Tremont Avenue in the Bronx. But now, we could see their living room, with its piano, its tufted sofa, its window opening into the air shaft, and a portrait of George Washington hung on the wall. Their decorating instincts leaned rococo, with gilded, striped wallpaper in their entryway; carved wooden architectural details; and a menorah gleaming from the dark, wooden sideboard. The apartment, in fact, looked as if the Goldbergs had been living in it the entire time they'd been on the radio. The layers of aged-looking furniture and tchotchkes precisely mimicked those of a long-inhabited space.

The characters matched the ones Berg had used through all the iterations of The Goldbergs thus far, though she rolled her children's ages back to facilitate a fresh shot at several years of broadcast family life after they had both grown up to adulthood on the radio. On TV, Arlene McQuade played the Goldbergs' preteen daughter, Rosalie, and Larry Robinson was the teenage son, Sammy. Those all-American kids were assimilated in ways their parents could never dream of. Both were even played by Gentiles, though they were based on Berg's own children, Harriet and Cherney.

Uncle David, Molly's live-in relative, served as her loyal sidekick, helping out with household chores, offering philosophical advice, sewing, cooking, and wearing an apron. Eli Mintz, a Polish Jewish actor who had played the role in the stage version, followed Berg to television, bringing Uncle David's wire-rimmed glasses and gray mustache with him. He was, in fact, five years younger than Berg, but extensive makeup aged him into her TV "uncle." Berg also retained Philip Loeb from *Me and Molly* as the Goldberg patriarch, Jake. She had such a connection with Loeb—a natural spark intensified through their months onstage together—that she would have been a fool not to. The two came across onscreen as a real couple, one of TV's first examples of the kind of chemistry that makes viewers believe in the marriage so much that any future cast change would feel like a real divorce.

The TV version retained the iconic radio opening, with Molly calling out the window, "Yoo-hoo! Is anybody . . . ?" Television delivered an instant thrill: Fans could see Molly Goldberg in an actual window. The camera work emphasized this, shooting her from outside the window frame in the opening of every episode, giving viewers the perspective of a nearby neighbor.

The live broadcast required everyone involved in the production to function at top level on show night. That mimicked the forms it was derived from, live theater and radio. And it didn't rack up the costs and difficulties associated with shooting on film, the only other option at the time. That began to change in the mid- to late 1950s with the advent of videotape, which was significantly cheaper and allowed pretaping and editing. In the meantime, the only way to capture and later broadcast a live show was via a kinescope, which meant plunking a film camera down in front of a monitor during a live broadcast. These recordings would then be shipped across the country for rebroadcast, but the quality was as terrible as one would expect from such a process.

For the live broadcast, camera angles were rehearsed ahead of time along with everything else. On show nights, the director would call the shots from a control room. Because it was live, scene and costume changes were challenging, with no downtime once the show was rolling. If a costume change was necessary in an episode, the character would usually layer one change of clothing on top of another, then peel one off quickly off camera when the time came. The cameras might cut briefly to a new set of characters while a switch occurred. Sometimes costume changes were cleverly avoided by showing a character, for instance, lying in bed up to her neck in the covers.

To ready themselves for the rigor of live Monday broadcasts, the cast and crew rehearsed from Tuesday morning—when Berg would have the next script ready—through the weekend, rotating among four different New York City studios: Caravan Hall on East 59th Street, CBS Studios on East 52nd Street, Liederkranz Hall on East 58th Street, and Nola Recording Studios on West 57th Street. Berg often worked eighteen-hour days that encompassed a combination of table reads, blocking, dress rehearsals, wardrobe consultations, and meetings about set design and props. This was on top of her writing duties.

On Mondays, the cast convened in the morning for final blocking, a one-hour break for an early dinner, two dress rehearsals, and then, finally, the live broadcast.

At that time, the stage manager called, "Thirty seconds! Quiet in the studio!"

Berg looked at her costars and instructed, "On your toes, darlings." Then she became Molly Goldberg and greeted her waiting cameras.

Early reviewers loved the results. *Newsweek* called it "a warm, human, humorous show." *Life* described it as "an immediate hit on television ... a classic in the field, *The Goldbergs* employ a basic formula so neatly suited for television it may well be the forerunner of a whole rash of televised domestic serials." And the *New York Times'* Jack Gould wrote, "The Goldbergs came to television last week and the word this morning is that they probably are going to be there for about as long as they choose. Gertrude Berg's account of life in the Bronx with Molly, her family and her neighbors reaches the home with all its warm-hearted and genuine appeal intact."

Accordingly, the show indeed secured its first sponsor, Sanka instant coffee. That would have been a critical moment in any new show's life at the time, but in this case, Sanka and *The Goldbergs* would become inextricably linked, the ad spots as integral to the show as any plotline and at least as enjoyable. It turned out that no one could deliver a television ad like Gertrude Berg.

As of February 1949, Sanka executives were still fussing with the proposed ad format, but they had decided that Berg would deliver the ads within the show, as Molly Goldberg. This would innovate upon the approach used by variety show hosts, ads delivered by a star, by adding another layer: the star would play her fictional character while she advocated for the product, and she would write the ads herself so she could seamlessly transition between the ads and the show.

"While *we* know *what* to say—only *she* can say it in her own charming and individual way," Young & Rubicam ad executive Joseph A. Moran wrote in a letter to CBS executive Miner. "As I explained to you—this is a procedure we've never followed before. But, then, we've never had Mrs. Berg before—and we admire her so much as a warm craftsman and a sincere personality that we want to help, rather than hinder, her show values."

A month later, Moran proposed that the Goldbergs sit down to drink some instant decaffeinated coffee in the middle of an episode—an early version of what we now know as product place-ment. Perhaps the flower on the family's windowsill could find a new pot. "Or what do you think of having the geranium in a Sanka can?" Moran wrote to Berg. "*You* know where and when a Sanka mention in the script is natural—and natural with you," Moran concluded. "And you know how to sell. An unusual, happy combi-nation." The Sanka can was the proud home of the geranium for as long as Sanka and *The Goldbergs* were in business.

After a meeting among the executives at General Foods, San-ka's parent company, Moran wrote, "In effect, we have a first in TV commercial presentation—a show without an announcer . . . with-out slides, film, cartoons—rather with commercials containing the simplicity of the show itself—delivered in character by one of the very few TV stars who can do it."

This proved true, and it proved a key to the show's early success.

An episode of *The Goldbergs* now looked like this: in the open-ing, Molly Goldberg—her dark hair pulled back and her pearls peeking above the neckline of her practical dress—appears in the window of her apartment and looks straight at the camera. "You know, you know something, I can't believe it's already the middle of October." Her words tumble out in a Yiddish accent, with a conver-sational rhythm full of imperfections and repetitions captured by the live cameras. "Can you imagine how time flies?"

Molly transitions into the wonders of Sanka instant decaffein-ated coffee, a modern marvel. On the screen, Molly spotlights Sanka in a way the ad executives couldn't have dreamed of. She's so natural, so convincing—"Ninety-seven percent of the caffeine is removed, but all the sleep is left in!"—that it's impossible to watch without wanting a cup.

Then one of her neighbors calls from a window across the air shaft, "Yoo-hoo, Mrs. Goldberg!" They gossip for a minute; then the show jumps seamlessly into the little domestic problems of family life in a New York City tenement.

It all, quite simply, worked. Critic Gilbert Seldes had gotten it right: Gertrude Berg was TV and nothing else. Her warm charisma wafted straight through the screen and into viewers' living rooms like the smell of freshly brewed Sanka. Just as Sanka coffee managed to take out 97 percent of the caffeine, Berg managed her own impressive percentage: Sanka purchases increased by 57 percent among her viewers, as a brochure that went out to advertisers later boasted.

Berg, who continued to write all of the show's scripts, also displayed her progressive views through her early TV episodes; occasionally, plotlines leaned visibly left, with the Goldbergs, for instance, organizing their neighbors in a collective action against an overbearing landlord.

The Goldbergs wove their specific identities—Jewish, progressive, city dwelling—into a picture of an all-American family. Berg had addressed the family's Jewishness head-on in a number of radio episodes leading up to and during World War II: a 1939 script addressed Kristallnacht and the rise of Nazism in Germany when a rock was thrown through the Goldbergs' window during their Passover seder, while other episodes throughout the war referred to relatives trying to escape the Holocaust. And Berg didn't water down her Jewishness one bit for television, at least not in those days. She and Uncle David spoke in strong Yiddish accents, and Molly and her husband mentioned European relatives. It's hard to overstate how revolutionary this was—the equivalent, these days, to a fluffy American network sitcom about a devoutly Muslim family. Two decades later, CBS executives would shoot down the original concept for *The Mary Tyler Moore Show*—Moore playing a divorced woman—by quoting a maxim of the TV business: "Our research says American audiences won't tolerate divorce in a lead of a series any more than they will tolerate Jews, people with mustaches, and people who live in New York." After *The Goldbergs*, an openly Jewish major character wouldn't appear on network television again until the 1972–73 sitcom *Bridget Loves Bernie*, about a marriage between a Catholic woman and a Jewish man.

As Berg, her cast, and her crew forged ahead with their show, television itself was growing. "The studio was being built around us as we rehearsed and there were no experts who knew what some other experts told them a survey said the public wanted," Berg later wrote. Among the chaos of early television, she built a TV empire atop her radio empire, her husband, Lewis, always there to type up scripts or help make sure their Park Avenue apartment *and* Gertrude's business dealings were running smoothly. In the process, Gertrude Berg built the prototype of the family sitcom form that still endures.

Viewers would grow to love returning to *The Goldbergs'* familiar characters weekly. But nothing would ever prove as easy as the show's first year. Other women who invented television would have an even harder time getting—and keeping—their work on the air.

2

Predicament, Villainy, and Female Suffering

Irna Phillips

Hope flickered on the horizon for Irna Phillips, and it looked like the cathode ray of television. But, to be clear, she felt she offered at least as much hope to television in return.

Phillips had watched from the beginning: she had seen RCA president David Sarnoff present television to the public at the New York World's Fair ten years earlier. Sarnoff had dedicated an RCA Pavilion at the fair in April 1939, his speech televised to hundreds of sets throughout the structure and to the sixty-second floor of Radio City in Manhattan. "Now we add sight to sound," he said, referring to the transition from radio to television. "It is with a feeling of humbleness that I come to this moment of announcing the birth in this country, of a new art so important that is bound to affect all society. It is an art which shines like a torch in a troubled world."

During the decade since witnessing that historic moment, Phillips had realized the medium's potential for her own career.

She, like Gertrude Berg, hoped to follow the uncertain path from radio to television. As the woman credited with inventing daytime radio soap operas, Phillips joined Berg as one of the most powerful women in the medium. Throughout her most successful radio years in the 1940s at NBC's Chicago affiliate station, WMAQ, she wrote 2 million words per year, dictated scripts over six to eight hours per day, and earned $300,000 annually—all while she raised her two adopted children as a single mother.

But at age forty-seven in 1948, she was losing her grip on the radio industry, and TV was looking more and more like a chance at a second life in show business. She needed to figure out some way forward for her stalled career: she was down to just one radio show from a peak of four. And that one, *The Guiding Light*, was struggling. She had just returned to her hometown of Chicago with her young children, seven-year-old Thomas and five-year-old Katherine, having been beaten down by a few rough years of trying to make her way in Hollywood.

Phillips didn't even own a television, but by late 1948, a few clear signs had come to her indicating that TV was the answer to her problems.

First, she had gotten a letter from her friend Bill Ramsey, who was also her longtime contact at household product conglomerate Procter & Gamble, which sponsored many of her radio programs. Ramsey wrote to her with swooning accounts of his recent trips to New York from Procter & Gamble's headquarters in Ohio to visit the live TV broadcasts in Manhattan studios on Friday, Saturday, and Sunday nights. "We're beginning to get really active in television," he wrote in June 1948. The week before, P&G had bought its first program, *Fashions on Parade*, a simple, self-descriptive show aimed at the women who bought P&G products.

Then, executives at a new NBC television station in Chicago, where Phillips lived, approached her about developing a daytime soap opera for them. It would be the first in TV history, and the executives hoped it would establish Chicago as a soap opera hub for television.

Intrigued by NBC's offer, Phillips dictated a letter to her secretary in the two-room suite at the Ambassador Hotel in Chicago where she was temporarily living. In it, she asked Ramsey for feedback on an innovative plan she was formulating. She had ideas about not simply how to transfer her radio creations to the screen but also to advance the way her advertisers used it—which, in a medium run by advertisers, could be game changing. "The intriguing angle of course is the commercial angle where the product could be seen and used but not announced as much as it is announced today," she wrote in the September 1948 letter. "It would be more or less integrating the magazine ad as an integral part of each day's episode." She was proposing true product placement, more subtle than Gertrude Berg's Sanka methods.

This was a typical move for Phillips, whose professional strengths lay in proposing bold new concepts, doing whatever it took to prove herself—and taking adversaries to court when things went wrong. She had short, dark hair, and hooded, weary eyes, which caused her to resemble a mature version of the cartoon character Olive Oyl. She was direct with her criticisms, exacting as a producer, and tough as a negotiator. She had a reputation as harsh and difficult. She did not have the kind of personality that would allow her to pull off the Gertrude Berg trick, building an empire while playing America's favorite mother.

As with many of her ideas, this one was ahead of its time. Ramsey's reply: "To my way of thinking, there is no question that the dramatic serial will have an extremely important place in television eventually." He continued, however, with a hint of caution, and an explanation for why P&G wasn't keen on TV soaps just yet: "Because the medium is infantile, there aren't, to the best of my knowledge, any clearly defined scales of payment for talent, writing, or otherwise."

That uncertainty wasn't about to stop Phillips. She'd overcome far greater difficulties in her career.

Irna Phillips was born in Chicago in 1901. She came last, the youngest of the ten children born to businessman William S. Phillips, whose parents were Polish immigrants, and his wife, Betty, a Jewish German immigrant. The family lived above a grocery store William owned and ran until his death, when Irna was eight. As a single mother, Betty provided for the family with several rental properties they owned. Irna's sister Sadie, sixteen years older than she, became like a second mother to her. Irna later described herself as "a plain, sickly, silent child, with hand-me-down clothes and no friends."

Irna graduated from Senn High School on the city's North Side and earned a bachelor's degree in 1923 from the University of Illinois. She hoped to become an actress, but her college drama teacher told her she had "neither the looks nor the stature to achieve professional success." So she set her sights on a career in education, teaching speech and drama in Missouri and Ohio and getting a master's degree from the University of Wisconsin.

After graduation, she longed to find a reliable husband like her father had been to her mother, but her tumultuous love life instead mirrored those of many of the soap opera characters she would later create: in her twenties, she fell in love with a charismatic doctor eight years her senior while she visited one of her brothers in Dayton, Ohio; she moved there to be with the doctor, then ended up accidentally pregnant and abandoned by her paramour.

Phillips asked her friend Ralph Skilken, a recent law school graduate who had an unrequited crush on her, if there was any legal way to force the doctor to admit paternity. Though Skilken worked in the office of Dayton's assistant district attorney, he offered to represent her in court. He arranged a closed hearing with the doctor and his lawyer. Phillips and her former lover did not speak to or look at each other, but he acknowledged the unborn child as his. The judge awarded Phillips what she had asked for: $500 to help with medical expenses. She had not requested child support.

Six months after her court date, she gave birth to a daughter, who was stillborn.

When Phillips returned to Chicago for a family visit in 1930 at the age of twenty-eight, she was ready for a fresh start. Like Gertrude Berg's, her oft-told radio origin story involved a bit of a mix-up sending her on the path to great fortune: she took a tour of the city's broadcast studios. Someone at WGN thought she was there to audition and gave her a poem to read aloud, Eugene Field's "The Bow-Leg Boy." Her acting ambitions reawakened, she read it. She didn't take that job, but she maintained her relationship with the station.

Smitten with radio, she moved back to Chicago and sold the station on a new program, a ten-minute spot called *A Thought for Today*. On it, she combined bits of poetry, famous speeches, and literature with some of her own experiences, aiming to uplift audiences suffering through the Depression.

Next, WGN wanted her to come up with a program that would appeal to women, a primary target audience for the household product manufacturers that sponsored programs—and the majority of the daytime audience. She would get $50 per week for her trouble. She created a show called *Painted Dreams*, a simple drama focusing on the relationships among four women. It would become known as the first radio soap opera, so named for its ads selling soap to housewives.

The series, which premiered on October 20, 1930, and aired six days a week, told the story of an Irish American widow named Mother Moynihan, her two daughters, and a young female boarder who lived with them, which echoed Phillips's own relationship with her mother and the tenants they rented to. Phillips simply translated her own German Jewish immigrant family into an Irish Catholic household like many in the Chicago area.

Painted Dreams spotlighted distinctly feminine problems. In one episode, for example, one of the young women debates borrowing a dress from the other to serve as a bridesmaid. ("I've never worn that shade of orchid in all my life. I'd look like a perfect washout. Besides, that's your very best special occasion dress. I wouldn't think of taking it.") Phillips wrote every episode and at times voiced Mother Moynihan or one of the Moynihan daughters. She played supporting characters as well.

Painted Dreams set a template for daytime soap operas that has remained remarkably intact throughout the genre's history. It focused on women and their domestic relationships and employed cliff-hangers to keep listeners interested. Phillips, twenty-nine years old when *Painted Dreams* became a hit, had originated those hallmarks. She had found her calling.

Her pay rose to $100 per week. But she wanted more after the success of *Painted Dreams*. Her relationship with WGN soured when its executives refused to try to take her show national. Furthermore, they informed her, she could not do so, either. They claimed they owned the show, its characters, and its plots.

Drawing on her experience suing her former lover, she sued the station for rights to *Painted Dreams*. This time, however, she lost. Her suit set a precedent for the now well-known concept of "work for hire": creative works made for an employer belong to the employer, not the creator.

So in 1932, Phillips left behind WGN's studios at the lakefront Drake Hotel and took her soap opera vision to a rival station, WMAQ. There she created the hilariously similar series *Today's Children*. The character names alone made only a half-hearted attempt to distinguish themselves: the show followed a Mother Moran and her daughter, Frances, rather than Mother Moynihan and her daughter, Sue.

The show succeeded, running until 1938, when Phillips chose to end it because her mother fell ill. She found it too painful to continue the series that had been so inspired by her mother. She in fact lived at the time with her mother, her brother Phil, and her sister Sadie.

Phillips's breakout hit came next, with *The Guiding Light* on NBC. The series drew on her experience earlier in life when she had given birth to her stillborn daughter and took comfort afterward in the sermons of Dr. Preston Bradley at the Peoples Church of Chicago, a Unitarian church. The show centered on an inspiring religious leader, the Reverend John Rutledge, the "keeper of the guiding light," and the stories of those who came to him for advice. It was successful enough to spawn a novel called *The Guiding Light*, written by a ghostwriter from the perspective of the character of the reverend.

With *The Guiding Light*, Phillips also added perhaps her most distinctive, and mocked, feature to the soap opera form: dramatic organ cues that would become the telltale sign for soapiness. She used them on *The Guiding Light* because of its church setting, but they stuck around as a convention for many soaps to come. "A soap opera is a kind of sandwich, whose recipe is simple enough, although it took years to compound," James Thurber wrote in a wry 1948 *New Yorker* retrospective on the form. "Between thick slices of advertising, spread twelve minutes of dialogue, add predicament, villainy, and female suffering in equal measure, throw in a dash of nobility, sprinkle with tears, season with organ music, cover with a rich announcer sauce, and serve five times a week."

Phillips expanded her empire to include *The Road of Life*, *The Right to Happiness*, and *Woman in White*, which were all on the air concurrently by 1939. She was known to dictate up to six scripts per day to keep up with the demand.

Throughout the 1940s, she worked with a staff to produce five daytime serials. She had to develop an elaborate chart system to keep her plotlines straight. Phillips no longer acted in her radio series, but she continued to act out the parts as she dictated scripts to her secretaries. She remained the clear voice of all of her creations. Her $300,000-per-year pay put her into the upper echelons of all American earners at the time but was particularly astonishing for a woman. (An average nonfarm family took in about $3,000 per year in 1946, for comparison. In 2020 terms, she was pulling in nearly $4 million a year.) *Time* magazine called her "America's highest-paid serial litterateuse." She told *Time*, however, that she'd give it all up if she met the right husband.

The Road of Life featured a doctor as a main character, another major innovation on the form—most radio shows before it focused on working-class characters, but the addition of doctors and ministers like those in Phillips's shows opened up possibilities for endless new story lines as they cared for patients and parishioners. It also allowed for further upward mobility among soap characters, which would eventually allow them to become the wealthy and glamorous characters most associated with the genre now.

During that time, the idea of the soap opera as we know it, as a bastion of absurd interpersonal drama, started to crystallize: the heroine of *The Right to Happiness*, for instance, began the show in love with her boss, even though she was still married to a man who was confined to a hospital with a terminal illness, and her boss was in love with her daughter. If Phillips did her job right, she believed, the story would be actor-proof. All of the plot excitement left little time to consider the actors' subtleties, or lack thereof.

Though many plotlines focused on traditional values—the exaltation of heterosexual marriage above all else—Phillips's scripts contained radical strains as well. Her soaps portrayed the complex choices modern women faced when it came to balancing career ambitions and family pressures, territory she knew well. She focused on other socially significant issues of the time, too, such as juvenile delinquency during World War II and life for veterans after the war. On *The Guiding Light*, when the actor Arthur Peterson, Jr., joined the army in 1944, his character, Reverend Rutledge, joined the army, too, as a chaplain, leaving his church in the care of another pastor while Peterson was away.

When Phillips noticed that the radio show *Amos 'n' Andy* featured only men, she decided to include mostly female characters in her earliest series. That cut down on budgets, as she and other actresses played multiple parts, but mostly, it allowed her to speak to those who mattered most. "In time my use of women as central characters became a formula," she later wrote. "To be sure I was still drawing on my own life, especially on memories of my mother, but I was also consciously appealing to the largest segment of the audience—women." Thus some of her earliest creations would live up to the modern standard of the Bechdel Test, first articulated in 1985: to pass, a work must feature at least two named women who talk to each other about something other than a man. Many, many works since then have failed.

Phillips would spend the rest of her career defending the intelligence and potential power of her female audience. Her genre was regularly maligned in critical circles for its slow pacing, histrionic plots, and what was seen as frivolous subject matter: the domestic concerns of women. Most of these key elements of the genre were, of course, deliberate: she developed her plots at a slow pace, for instance, so the housewives who listened could continue with their housework while the show was on "without missing a word, tear, or heartbreak," as she told *Fortune* magazine in 1938. Women were a prime target for radio overall until 1945, with many American men away overseas serving in World War II. And during the day, women were always, and would remain, the primary audience.

Phillips would dedicate the rest of her life to maintaining and advancing the genre in which she had staked her claim, the soap opera, even as its audience was constantly maligned and underestimated by the radio and TV industries.

Phillips had become famous, a role model for young women who wanted to get into the radio business. After Agnes Eckhardt graduated from Northwestern University in 1944, her dreams came true when she landed a job interview with Irna Phillips. She had managed it through a friend of her father. Eckhardt had heard of Phillips, of course; she had "heard like one hears about the president of the United States or something," as she later recalled. She wanted to be an actress or a writer. Her father offered to help set up the interview, though he warned her that Phillips would probably turn her down.

Eckhardt figured her father was probably right, but she wanted to take the chance. She was in awe of Phillips, who she knew was successful and unmarried. For the meeting, Eckhardt brought a script she'd written at Northwestern. Phillips took it from her and read it aloud as her secretary sat in the room with them. Eckhardt wished she could disappear.

But Phillips read it straight through, for its full half-hour duration. Then she put it down and asked if Eckhardt would like to work for her. "She wasn't an actress, but I did see in her a potential writer," Phillips wrote. She hired Eckhardt to write and produce radio shows for her, including *The Woman in White*.

After the interview, Eckhardt's father ran into Phillips in the waiting room of their mutual friend, a doctor. He said, "Miss Phillips, I want to thank you for what you did for my daughter."

"Mr. Eckhardt, I'm a businesswoman," she replied. "I hired your daughter because she's good, and for no other reason."

Agnes Eckhardt appreciated Phillips's drive and honesty. "A lot of people think Irna was very difficult," she said. "But she was a woman ahead of her time. She could be tough and drive a bargain, but she was totally honest and kind to me."

In 1943, Irna Phillips added another responsibility on top of her massive workload: she adopted a baby boy, whom she named Thomas Dirk. She had always wanted children and did not anticipate getting married any time soon, so she decided to become a mother on her own. Less than two years later, she also adopted a daughter, Katherine Louise. This was possible under adoption guidelines at the time, though that would change with the 1950s' wave of conservatism that brought with it a worship of two-parent families. Phillips's children, by then in their teens, would later point out to her that she would no longer be allowed to adopt them when they wanted to lash out during a fight.

Soon after she adopted Katherine, Phillips began craving new career challenges and sent telegrams to all of the major advertising agencies' heads of programming, asking for work in nighttime radio. She hoped to learn a new area of the business. She received offers from two of the largest agencies, the better of which was from Robert Colwell at J. Walter Thompson Company. The agency was preparing to premiere two new variety shows, one with the crooner Frank Sinatra as a host and the other an ill-defined show called *What's New*. She would get $15,000 a year to help. She would have to relocate to Hollywood, which intrigued her, since it was a national hub of nighttime radio production.

She would also have to leave her hometown and her siblings behind. That was particularly difficult in the case of her older sister Sadie, whom she found both difficult and comforting. Sadie had served as a second mother figure throughout her life, while their mother had tended to the family rental business, and the two had lived with their mother as adults until their mother's death.

Planning to stay in Los Angeles for at least a year, Phillips left her Chicago apartment and moved west with her children, secretary, and three other staffers. They stayed in a hotel until they found a furnished home with a large yard to rent in Los Angeles's Brentwood neighborhood.

That was when her life and radio career began to unravel.

Phillips spent her mornings working on her ongoing radio shows with her staffers, then headed to the J. Walter Thompson office in Hollywood for the second half of her day. When she reported for her first day, she found that her office space was a mess, and she was snubbed by her coworkers. Later, she learned why: the trade paper *Variety* had run an article about her new job—and its salary. She made more than nearly everyone else at the agency. "During the time I was there only a few of the men changed their minds about me," she wrote.

She grew more agitated when Sadie visited. Sadie offered to

move there to help care for the children. But Irna said no, beginning a pattern that would last for the rest of her child-rearing years: as a single mother, she seemed determined to make up for her children's lack of a father figure by being hypervigilant about the influences she allowed into their lives. In that case, she said, she preferred that the children have a younger caretaker and she didn't want another older person around the children all the time. (Sadie was in her late fifties.) Irna had begun to wish she'd adopted the children at a younger age herself and was perhaps overcompensating now. Sadie got angry. "You've lost the human touch," she told Irna. "All you've given me is money—nothing of yourself."

After Sadie left, Irna's new job grew still worse. Her task was to find "dramatic material" to use as part of *What's New*, though she couldn't seem to get any clear answers from the agency as to what the format of the series would be. So she worked anyway, contacting writers she knew and asking for self-contained ten-minute dramatic scripts. At the show's first rehearsal she hoped to get help from the host, Don Ameche, whom she'd worked with in Chicago when he was a young actor. Not much luck; now that he was a film star, he ignored her for the first fifteen minutes she was there, then offered a perfunctory greeting and little else.

Phillips became friendly with one person at the agency, a man named Caroll, who told her to, she later recalled, "keep my eyes closed and my mouth shut." She couldn't do it. She fired off a string of memos to Colwell that detailed her difficult working conditions. But because he was a continent away in New York, he had little sway over daily operations in the Los Angeles office.

Colwell did eventually visit, and he asked Phillips to switch to supervising two new dramatic serials. But she felt that assignment would bring her too close to conflict with her other work on her own soap operas sponsored by General Mills. Next, Colwell asked her to write promotional materials for Ford Motor Company. But that didn't work for her, either. "It was well-known in the trade that the Ford people, and especially Henry Ford, were not overly fond of Jews," she wrote. "In fact, Henry had never kept his antisemitic feelings a secret."

She was, perhaps, no longer suited for corporate office life.

Soon her office life was beside the point. She got word that her sister, Sadie, was seriously ill back in Chicago. Phillips dropped the job and headed to Chicago, leaving the kids with caretakers in California, as her sister's last words to her—"You've lost the human touch"—replayed in her head throughout the train ride. But before she even arrived, she received a telegram on the train: Sadie was dead.

Things grew still worse for Phillips when she returned to California after grieving her sister.

She visited Page Military Academy in Los Angeles's Larchmont neighborhood on a Friday to see her son's kindergarten class perform their weekly "full dress parade," a demonstration of the tiny boys' marching skills. She had enrolled him there because though he didn't like the idea of school, he did like the idea of wearing a uniform and carrying a wooden gun.

She watched as his class, the youngest of the bunch, wandered in, hardly in military formation but making an effort.

Her son, Tom, was nowhere to be seen in the group. That was a sign of things to come.

Though Phillips was ambivalent about Los Angeles, her children had so far seemed to love their new home. Thomas had grown into an active, redheaded toddler and taken to playing outside. But he'd had difficulties as well. He had been ignoring his sister, Kathy, since Phillips had brought her home from the hospital, upset by the competition for attention. As he neared age five, he had developed temper problems. "For the first time I became more aware of the problems of trying to rear two children in a one-parent home," Phillips wrote. "I couldn't be both mother and father, particularly to a boy." She worried a lot about the lack of an adult male presence in her home.

She had hoped the military academy would remedy that. She wrote, however, that "as the weeks went by I never could get Tom to talk about school. Often when he came home he would sit in the corner of the den and sulk." Eventually, she figured it out: he didn't want to go to school while his two-year-old sister got to stay home. Phillips, desperate to please him, enrolled Kathy in preschool.

So his failure to appear in the Friday parade when she was there to watch disappointed Phillips, but it didn't surprise her.

When she went looking for her son, she found him back in the "barracks," refusing to march. She wondered if he needed a different kind of school.

But the military academy's director, Colonel Page, advised Phillips against moving Tom to public school. "Miss Phillips, you're making a big mistake," he said. "That young man needs a thumb right on him at all times." Though she didn't heed his advice, she later felt he was right.

Soon afterward, Tom stoked her worry even more.

She threw an Easter party for him and about twenty of his classmates. One of the boys asked Tom, "Where's your dad?"

Tom looked up at Phillips, who was standing right next to him. "He was killed in the war, wasn't he, Mom?"

Devastated and startled, she answered, "Yes."

Caught off guard, she had reinforced his hurtful and telling lie. A pattern had been set. For the first time, Phillips wondered if she had made a terrible mistake when she had adopted two children.

As she struggled with these feelings, she decided to move her soap opera operation, still based in Chicago, to the West Coast so she could oversee daily affairs and keep the kids in the same schools. She did so begrudgingly, though many shows at the time were relocating to either New York or Los Angeles, where most of the actors were. "It was difficult for me to reach a decision," she wrote. "I didn't like southern California nor most of the people I had met. There was also a bit of provincialism in me. I had been born and raised a Midwesterner, loved Chicago and felt at home there. Too often during my . . . stays in California I had felt like a stranger. There was and still is a tendency for many people in the entertainment business on the West and East coasts to look down their noses at Midwesterners. Although it meant a complete uprooting, in the end I agreed to make the move."

She put down roots in Los Angeles now, despite her reservations. Though housing prices in LA were high at the time, she paid cash for an eight-room Colonial in the Westwood neighborhood. It was a charming two-story with a sloped front yard, an unassuming classical home at 503 Dalehurst Avenue located in a posh, growing neighborhood. She had her furniture shipped from Chicago, where it had been stored for some time, and filled her new rooms.

Phillips established a work routine from the house, with writers often stopping by to go over outlines. Several of her regular actors even made the move west with her. In fact, the industry saw her move as "the death knell of daytime radio serials in Chicago," she wrote. "I felt somewhat like a traitor and have never forgiven myself for this. In their heyday in the late thirties and early forties, dramatic serials had provided work for hundreds of men and women."

But now even her soap opera work was experiencing difficulties. *The Guiding Light* was pulled off the air for about six months because of a lawsuit in which a former writer claimed credit for the series's premise. Then, the writer won. He persuaded a court that he had contributed enough to the show's concept, through his scripts, that he deserved credit. Phillips, who adamantly denied his allegations, had to pay him $250,000 in damages and add his name to the credits.

The show returned to CBS in June 1947, sponsored by Procter & Gamble, in a slot just fifteen minutes before Phillips's *General Mills Hour* on NBC. Though that didn't violate any agreements, General Mills threatened to cancel all of the Phillips programs it sponsored if she continued to make *The Guiding Light*. Phillips refused to break her word to Procter & Gamble and her longtime contact there, Bill Ramsey. So General Mills decided to trigger a contract clause that allowed them to buy the shows they sponsored from her for $50,000 each. *The Woman in White* and *Today's Children* no longer belonged to her.

In just eight years, the mother of soap operas had watched her empire shrink from four shows to one. *The Guiding Light's* return on June 2, 1947, had not shown much promise, either. The episode was messy and clumsy, and Phillips knew it.

She had gone from a high of more than $300,000 per year to about $44,000 for *The Guiding Light*, which fell to the bottom of the ratings charts because of its time off the air. She had the General Mills money coming, but the larger issue was her professional pride—and her creative life. She had no choice but to throw herself into production of the new *Guiding Light* from California, even as she heard rumors that it might be canceled soon.

Six months later, as 1948 began, Phillips was contending with ominous spring winds in Los Angeles. For a Chicago transplant, southern California weather phenomena—aside from its famous 72-degrees-and-sunny norm—can feel alien. Cold air whipping through Chicago, the city known as "windy," makes sense in your bones; warm but forceful winds that mess with California's perfect-weather veneer do not. Phillips tried to put a positive spin on it, as in a May 1948 letter: "I choose to think of these semi-windstorms as a very favorable omen. As the breeze breezes and the tree treeses I hear a whisper, an echo perhaps . . . remember Chicago? . . . re-member Chicago?"

The cracks had begun to show in the foundation of her life after a few years in LA, and she was scheming to get back home to the Midwest.

But in another exhausting turn of events, she fell ill before she could do anything about it.

Phillips was hospitalized at Cedars of Lebanon Hospital for weeks under the care of a Dr. Friedman because of a bout of the digestive distress that had plagued her throughout her life—"Spasmodic turmoil," as she later described it in a letter. When it was time for her to check out, Dr. Friedman stood over her as Phillips sat in a wheelchair in a "foreboding corridor," she wrote. The doctor said, "You can leave now." Then he added, "There is nothing wrong except up here." He pointed to his head.

It was time to reset by skipping town, back to her beloved Chicago, preferably before any more bad luck could befall her. There was not a moment to waste.

Phillips and her secretary, Rose Cooperman, traveled back to the Midwest to look for apartments, but the outlook was discouraging. "Apartments in Chicago were either exorbitant or restricted," Phillips wrote. "This was the first time I personally encountered anti-Jewish sentiment. I wasn't disturbed, but Rose was angry. My attitude has always been if somebody doesn't want me then I certainly don't want them."

Phillips did still own her family's old three-flat apartment on

Winnemac Avenue. Tenants occupied all three floors, but, with few other options, she asked the first-floor tenants to move. They did not hurry, but she could not wait. She would find her family temporary housing if she had to, but she would return to Chicago immediately.

In spring 1948, she sold her Westwood house at a $20,000 loss, but that hardly mattered to her anymore. "Yes, the grass is green, the patio is a profusion of color and the sun is shining—but mama is going home," she wrote to her friend Bill Ramsey in May 1948. "To drab, colorless, dirty, windy Chicago? Maybe, but as I approach my 47th year I know I am definitely Midwest and that I will welcome solid ground under my feet once more."

That was step one of her recovery plan.

She fled back to Chicago at the start of summer. She didn't even have a chance—or bother—to see many of her Los Angeles acquaintances before she departed.

As she waited for the tenants to leave Winnemac Avenue, Phillips booked a two-bedroom suite at the Ambassador West Hotel and put her furniture in storage. She and her two children would live there for six months.

Variety columnist Jack Hellman covered her cross-country move: "Back in her beloved Chicago, where 19 years ago she wrote her first chapter play, Miss Phillips calmly surveys the past and with equal equanimity appraises the future—'radio in a state of flux and the flickering of television'—and with the pressure easing." She had a flawless track record, he noted: during her nineteen years in the business, she had never had a show canceled on her; she had ended her shows when it felt right to her. (General Mills had recently taken two shows from her but had not canceled them.) Surely someone would give her a chance again, whether in radio or in television.

Phillips struggled to help her children adapt to their new home. They had returned to Chicago in the summer of 1948, with no school to keep them occupied. She enrolled them in Blackhawk Day Camp, but weekends cooped up in the hotel were still trying. She took them to the zoo, the park, and museums. "But I was too much a teacher not to know that children want to be with their own age group," she wrote.

For the fall, she chose the nearby Latin School both for Tom, who was going into second grade, and Kathy, who was starting junior kindergarten. Tom would remain there through seventh grade and Kathy through tenth grade.

The winter after they returned to Chicago, the family moved into the Winnemac Avenue apartment. Phillips had to sell a lot of her furniture, it was so small. But each of the children had a bedroom, and Phillips could house a live-in nanny as well. Phillips slept on a springless sofa in the living room to do so, which resulted in a persistent backache. She called it "going to couch" instead of "going to bed."

The move back to Winnemac Avenue felt like time travel for Phillips. The neighborhood looked just the same as when she had grown up there, full of working-class German and Eastern European families. Trees, single-family homes, and two- and three-floor apartments lined the street. Children roamed everywhere; however, much to Phillips's chagrin, they all seemed to be girls. Tom had no boys to play with. At first, she had considered kicking the upstairs tenants out of the building and taking both floors for her family. This plan had run into trouble when Tom, now seven years old, had "fallen in love" with a girl a year and a half older who lived upstairs; though that might have been because her family owned a television, while Phillips did not.

Between the couch sleeping and the lack of male companionship for Tom, Phillips decided that yet another move was in order. She shopped for a new apartment near the Latin School and purchased one that was being built in one of the North Side's first high-rise buildings. They had finally found their Chicago home; it was spacious, with high ceilings and thirteen closets. Phillips could sleep in a bed in her own bedroom again.

Meanwhile, *The Guiding Light*'s production had moved from Los Angeles to New York, with Phillips providing scripts from Chicago and visiting regularly. The show's ratings began to climb again. Life was finally trending in the right direction, though Phillips had yet to fully recover emotionally or professionally.

Hope soon arrived. In late 1948 executives at NBC's brand-new local Chicago TV station, WNBQ, expressed interest in Phillips developing a soap for them. They believed she could invigorate the Chicago television production market the way she had once done for its radio market. Owned and operated by the NBC network, not an affiliate, WNBQ had a direct connection to the national office. This could smooth the path to national distribution.

She pitched a dramatic serial called *These Are My Children*. She conceived the series as a variation on one of her earliest radio hits, *Today's Children*. On the radio version, most of the action had taken place in Mother Moran's kitchen—which was fine, since the audience couldn't see the characters and didn't much mind where they were.

She knew she had to think of the television version differently, but she also understood it had a much greater power when it came to displaying the products made by her sponsors. "Of course one couldn't concentrate on a kitchen—looking at one set even twice a week might become a bit boring—it would depend entirely on the ingenuity of a writer to indirectly show the product and its use," she wrote to Bill Ramsey in September 1948, as she brainstormed by letter. "Offhand I can see two girls washing out sheer hose in a hell of a dramatic scene. On the other hand I can see making an announcer more than an announcer by becoming almost part of the cast."

Ramsey agreed: "To me, one of the most ridiculous aspects of the present eastern television operation is the failure of many advertisers to take full advantage of what television actually offers them. You'll see for yourself how many television advertisers are simply using good old-fashioned radio commercials." He'd seen it during *Fashions on Parade*, which Procter & Gamble planned to sponsor soon. "The all time high was when they put the television camera on our announcer while he actually read off a straight radio commercial. It was preposterous." *The Goldbergs*, with Gertrude Berg's ingenious ad delivery in character, had not yet premiered.

Phillips had not seen much recent television beyond glimpses on her neighbors' set, but she understood the potential business implications for herself. She was still working out how to get housewives to tune in and remain engaged without worrying them about taking too much time out from their daily chores. Radio had been different; they could listen while they cleaned. Now she had to be visually interesting, but not *too* visually interesting, and not so visual that they'd miss a key plot point if they were looking away from the screen at their ironing or dirty dishes.

But a job was a job and a challenge was a challenge. She and the NBC executives she worked with disagreed on the solution: They thought she needed more action and less dialogue than on radio. She thought there should be "even more dialogue, but pertinent dialogue, then action. She wrote, "A great many of the 'oh's' and 'I see' and 'what do you mean' and 'I don't understand' would have to be eliminated. Of necessity one would have to write only lines that made for sheer drama whether you looked or whether you listened."

By October 1948, she had gone deep into the planning with NBC. "The TV Department and I have seen eye to eye on everything but money," she wrote to Ramsey. She asked his opinion on payment, whether the show was unsponsored ("sustaining") or sponsored: "What do you think the TV serial is worth on a sustaining basis, writing only of course, and on a commercial basis?" The Pepsi-Cola Company and a company called Armour were considering a sponsorship, but they had yet to commit, and might not until they saw the show succeed on the air.

Like Gertrude Berg, Phillips would have to prove herself on television before anyone would sign on to sponsor the show. The next phase of her career—and her recovery from the turmoil of the past few years—would all come down to that moment.

Once she got into the studio with her cast and crew, it became apparent how hard it was going to be. No one knew what to do, exactly, at any given time. The low-budget production of Phillips's *These Are My Children* proved to be truly experimental from start to finish.

Phillips and the show's director, Norman Felton, had to re-envision soap operas for TV. In addition to adding action to the dialogue, they also had to think about casting differently. She wrote, "Television also brought another major change to the dramatic serial. It was now of paramount importance how actors looked."

The show had a classic Phillips setup: an Irish immigrant, Mother Henehan, would deal with the entanglements of her grown children: her daughter, Pat, a neurotic career woman who works in a law office, and John, a perpetually immature adult. During Phillips's prolific radio days, she had developed some ways of working that she brought with her to television. She preferred to work from her apartment and often spent large portions of her day in bed. There she would work on plot breakdowns and sometimes scripts. She dictated those scripts to Rose, her ever-present secretary.

The industry was watching closely. "New show will be eagle-eyed by the trade to see if Miss Phillips comes up with the tele equivalent of the radio serial," *Variety* reported.

Early rehearsals went well, and word spread. Even so, many in the industry remained cautious in their optimism, given the experimental nature of the operation: "I hope Irna does not run into the headaches that everyone in New York runs into once they get their feet wet in television," ad executive Lewis Titterton wrote to her confidant Bill Ramsey. "But I am afraid that it is almost inevitable." He was not mistaken.

These Are My Children premiered on January 31, 1949, a few weeks after *The Goldbergs*. It was at first intended only for the local station, WNBQ, but the promising rehearsals with the six-member cast inspired NBC to take it national, airing at 5:00 to 5:15 p.m. Monday through Friday. As television's first daytime soap opera, the odds were stacked against it: the genre arrived on TV just as derided as it had ever been on radio. "Last week television caught the dread disease of radio," *Pathfinder* newsmagazine sneered. "Soapoperitis."

These Are My Children, which was broadcast live, required the actors to memorize their lines now that the audience could see them. To help aid their memories, they scrawled key lines on a blackboard that was within their field of vision. The actors, all experienced only in radio, had to learn to follow stage directions.

"Television dived into the corn last week, presenting without advance warning the first soap opera to be seen before the cameras," wrote the *New York Times'* Jack Gould. "The title of the precedent-making cliff hanger is 'These Are My Children' and it has everything: problems, crises, hysterics, clichés, sobs, tensions and the inevitable little joys." Gould also noted that the actors "looked as though they were gazing off into the horizon, expecting a plane to come in on a three-point landing right in the middle of Mom Henehan and all her troubles." They hadn't mastered the blackboard reading just yet.

Variety piled on, homing in on every one of Phillips's fears and pronouncing her every decision incorrect: "*These Are My Children*, of Irna Phillips authorship, is a visualization of an ordinary actionless daytime drama, designed along the theory that the lady of the house is too busy to sit down and look at any tale of travail. Consequently words do everything—just as in radio. There are several flaws in this type of thinking. So long as television tubes cost around $75 to replace, any housewife who shortens the life of the tube when there's no visual interest just doesn't know her economics." The reviewer added, "The only difference in video is that the actors have memorized lines and have to look sad most of the time."

Problems mounted within the production as well. The actors were still learning to play to the cameras and to work with the boom mics. They had no union and had to negotiate their own individual contracts without guidelines. They received about $20 per episode ($216 in 2020 dollars). Phillips made $200 per month ($2,169 in 2020 dollars) to write the scripts. No sponsors signed on.

These Are My Children lasted just five weeks. Nonetheless, Phillips had made the record books: she had created television's first soap opera.

Phillips was determined to press on. In March 1949, in a letter to Bill Ramsey, she called the end of *These Are My Children* "my temporary, I hope, retreat from television." NBC received a barrage of letters and phone calls protesting the cancellation, a hopeful sign.

She met with a writer for *Variety* during one of her regular trips to New York; the publication was investigating why *These Are My Children* had gone off the air "as silently as it had appeared," as Phillips wrote in the same letter. Apparently it didn't occur to the reporter that perhaps his savage review had contributed to its demise. She cross-examined him about his industry credentials: What was his background? How long had he been reviewing radio and TV? Did he have any special training in dramatics? She also had a less contentious conversation with Jack Gould of the *New York Times*, even though he, too, had made a joke of *These Are My Children* in his review.

But she retained her sense of hope. She hadn't lost her creative touch as much as she'd feared, and she was settled back in her hometown as the seasons changed from winter to spring. "Was it only yesterday that the trees were barren, and the ground drab?" she wrote to Bill Ramsey in April 1949. She described her son, Tom, now eight, as he gazed out their apartment window for fifteen minutes straight. When she'd asked what he was doing, he'd said, "Looking at the scenery, Maw."

She continued in her letter, "Very small green sprouts are evident on the trees, bushes have turned green and yellow, grass is coming up here and there, and the change has all been so imperceptible. This is so much more gratifying, Nature reawakening the earth here in the Middle West, so unlike the monotony of the almost sensuous 'scenery,' as Tom would say, of California—one woman's opinion to be sure."

She seemed content with her decision to move back and raise her children in her midwestern hometown. She was, however, clearly already feeling a pressure that would increase as the 1950s progressed: a sense that she would never be enough for her children without a husband. Postwar prosperity and the looming Cold War with Russia, which was on its way to becoming a major nuclear power, led to the rise of the two-parent, multiple-child family as the American ideal. These families, with their exquisite balance of breadwinner and homemaker, were presented as the desirable American alternative to communism, with its sad, factory-working women and day care center children. Working women were selfish, media images said. Phillips couldn't help but buy into this pervasive propaganda, and it would infect her work as well as her personal life.

But for now, she had reached a state of equilibrium.

Phillips continued her trips to New York as she looked for new opportunities and took in plays, including a new Broadway sensation in the spring of 1949, Arthur Miller's *Death of a Salesman*. Phillips's private review in a letter to Bill Ramsey said it was "superbly produced, but I found myself replotting the last set." A soap opera queen is always plotting and replotting.

At the start of summer, an ad agency and sponsor expressed interest in her new proposal for a TV soap called *Challenge to Spring*, and she hoped to have it running by fall on CBS's New York station. She continued to court Ramsey as a sponsor and friend. She hosted him for an elaborate dinner in Chicago that included his favorite dishes: oysters, squab, asparagus, and watercress salad.

Nothing came of the *Challenge to Spring* proposal, but *The Guiding Light* was doing better than ever on radio in the fall of 1949. The new cast now inhabited their roles, and the show's sponsor, Procter & Gamble, was thrilled with Phillips's scripts. "I may be wrong in believing that you have taken unusual pains to make the show foolproof during this critical transition period," company executive A. H. Morrison wrote to Phillips. "But, right or wrong, I feel that you have turned in some of the finest work on the air."

No one had better positioned herself to master the women's realm of daytime television than Irna Phillips—even if she hadn't done it just yet.

In fact, success in television eluded Irna Phillips for good reason. Her soap was not only the first of its genre, it also pioneered new

schedule territory for television: daytime. The upstart network Du-
Mont had just introduced the country's first all-day schedule on its
New York station, WABD, in November 1948, and Ramsey suggested she visit to see how they did things. DuMont was a wild card
network launched by the TV manufacturer DuMont Laboratories
without a radio network to feed it cash, talent, and experienced
broadcast executives. (Think of it as the equivalent of Netflix, for-
merly a video-rental-by-mail service, wading into original programming in the 2010s with no track record in television.) To compete
with the established CBS and NBC, DuMont tried to make waves
by experimenting with TV firsts. It couldn't make shows with the
biggest stars or the best production values, but it could be unique.
In this case, it was the first to program the daytime hours.

DuMont's new daytime lineup included another of early TV's
female breakouts, Amanda Randolph, who was the first Black
woman to star in her own daytime show. She had built her career
in film, Broadway, and radio, including a regular role on Phillips's
radio soap *Kitty Foyle*. Randolph also starred in a short-lived prime-
time comedy called *The Laytons* on DuMont as the family maid,
which may have made her the first Black woman to be a regular on
a network TV series. (The series was also written by a woman, Barbara Boothe.) Randolph specialized in the kind of folksy wisdom
that endeared white audiences to Black characters. A typical line
for her character, Martha: "Yessir, it sure is the truth! Neither fish
nor guests oughta be kept around the house longer than three days."

She proved a natural for the living room medium: approachable
and pleasant. She was described in the *New York Times* as an "actress, singer, and genial back-fence philosopher."

Her DuMont daytime variety program, a simple affair, consisted mostly of the warm, apple-cheeked fifty-two-year-old, who
often wore her hair pulled back in a bun, as she sang and played

piano for the fifteen-minute duration. She occasionally interviewed guests such as *Porgy and Bess* star Etta Moten, many of them prominent residents of Harlem, where her husband, Harry Hansberry, ran a speakeasy called Hansberry's Clam House. The idea was that "television can help rid the world of intolerance simply by getting people acquainted with each other," as the *Pittsburgh Courier* said in its review. *Amanda* aired from noon to 12:15 p.m. Monday through Friday.

Amanda highlighted another major aspect of DuMont's willingness to experiment: the network seemed more eager than others to work with Black artists, though perhaps not from high-mindedness; Black artists were paid less. Randolph, in fact, quipped about her low pay on the show: "For eight dollars a week, what could they expect—Hazel Scott?" She was prophetically referencing the popular and refined Black musician known for "swinging the classics." A few years later Scott had her own variety show on DuMont, which made her the first Black person to host a national show in prime time, a watershed accomplishment that overshadowed Randolph's legacy—though ultimately Scott's show was widely forgotten, too.

On *Amanda*, Randolph acknowledged the problem Phillips had anticipated for her soaps: that the female target audience for daytime shows wouldn't want to pause their housework to watch TV. The *New York Amsterdam News* described how she spoke directly to her viewers: "Amanda Randolph is herself, chatting, playing the piano, singing a song, and giving encouragement—and urging the ladies to go right on working."

The show lasted for only a year, but Randolph was officially a TV star. She played core roles on a number of 1950s hits, including *Amos 'n' Andy*, *Beulah*, and *Make Room for Daddy*. Black women faced difficult choices in the industry at a time when much of the country was still segregated: the road to reliable, regular work was paved with maid roles and racist stereotypes shaped by white creators.

For the networks, daytime television was a potential cash-flow spigot if they got the programming right. Housewives who were home during the day wielded massive purchasing power that intrigued advertisers, if those advertisers could crack the code to tear those women away from their wifely duties. Female stars and creators knew best how to reach them, so more contenders entered the fray every day. Irna Phillips would eventually be one of the most successful among them, but not yet.

Meanwhile, in Los Angeles, one young radio actress was, in fact, already charming daytime audiences with a quick wit and loads of pleasant personality. Her name was Betty White.

3

Women's Realm

Betty White

Betty White never knew what crazy idea she'd come up with next as she applied powder to the face of her TV co-host, Al Jarvis. Jarvis was "a chunky man of medium height, pushing forty—from one side or the other," as White later described him. As she tended to his shiny forehead, she had already finished her own preparations, arranging her chin-length dark curls just so and highlighting her flawless ivory skin. That constituted her daily morning routine circa 1949 backstage at a studio in Hollywood, a building on Cahuenga just south of Santa Monica Boulevard that had recently been converted from a radio to a television operation. White, then twenty-seven, served as the makeup department while she and her cohost planned their episode. There was no writers' room, just makeup time.

That was what Betty White had to offer television: her crazy ideas, her willingness to do whatever it took to succeed, and her outrageously charming personality.

Betty and Al's chats during makeup application were as close as they'd get to rehearsing for the five and a half hours they were about to spend in front of cameras broadcasting live. To be clear, that's 330 minutes of uninterrupted airtime nearly every day, with no live audience to play off of and no commercial breaks—just pitches for sponsored products that they themselves delivered.

As Betty primped Al, they'd come up with a few loose ideas about how to keep their audience entertained for all of those daytime hours—sketches that would provide a bit of structure to their ad-libbing. They'd wing the rest. This was how they got through six days a week for *Hollywood on Television*.

On one such day, Jarvis pitched a rough idea for a conversation starter they'd use on the air later: "Let's talk about how you're going to take dramatic lessons." He didn't have much else to go with for now, but that was standard for them. White knew what to do. Her motto was: *Always say yes*. Improv came naturally to her.

A few hours later, as cameras rolled, White came up with a fictional drama teacher in response to his prompt. They made up the details as they went. The teacher's name: Madame Fagel Bagenhacher, who had, of course, changed her name from Madame Fagel Bagelmaker. (She was, presumably, a Jewish immigrant.) Details continued to emerge over several days of sketches: Madame Bagenhacher lived in an apartment with beaded curtains and would sometimes send White out to fetch her medicine. Once, White explained, Madame Bagenhacher spent a whole lesson teaching how to get into and out of a carriage, because, she said, you never knew when you might be cast in a period movie.

As Betty and Al kept up the ruse over many shows, Madame Bagenhacher even began to get fan mail.

White would eventually rise to Gertrude Berg's level of sitcom stardom. But she would get there by first competing with Irna Phillips for the daytime audience full of housewives, and she would do it by helping to invent a new form of her own: the talk show.

By the age of twenty-seven, White had followed her acting dreams through various small parts on radio shows to the new frontier of television, where her charming personality was needed as a hostess. She could look into a camera, her eyes sparkling, then flash the warmest of smiles that made viewers watching her on their living room television screens, strewn across the greater Los Angeles area, feel as though they were right there with her, as though they were the only one she cared about. That charisma of hers alchemized into a superpower in 1949 as television came into its own.

Betty White was born on January 17, 1922, in Oak Park, Illinois. About two years later, her parents, Christine Tess and Horace White, moved with infant Betty from the Chicago suburb to Los Angeles. Tess was a stay-at-home mom with dark hair and an easy smile, and Horace, a balding man who had passed his dimples on to Betty, was a lighting company executive. They made a small, loving family: Tess and Horace adored each other, according to Betty, and they doted on their one child. She felt loved but not coddled. Betty had lots of friends, but she considered her parents her best friends.

She grew up in the Los Angeles area, which perhaps helped to spark the show business ambitions that would drive the rest of her life. Young Betty first thought she wanted to be a writer, so she scripted an eighth-grade graduation play at Horace Mann Grammar School in Beverly Hills. She also played the lead. Because her class had studied Japan, the WASPy preteen wrote a Kabuki-style piece in which she played a princess who talks to a nightingale.

She fell in love with the stage right there as she looked out at the audience, all rapt in her performance. As every person in the room paid attention to her and only her, she thought, "Well, isn't this fun?"

Just four years later, she sang "Spirit Flower"—a melodramatic number about a flower that bloomed on a former love's grave—at her graduation from Beverly Hills High School. A man who attended the ceremony, an investor in the fledgling technology known as television, saw her performance and offered her a role that would set the course of her life. He asked if she'd like to appear in a signal test he was running in downtown Los Angeles a few months later.

On a February day in 1939, Betty found herself at the six-story Packard Motor Car Company building in downtown Los Angeles. The stylish structure sat at the corner of Hope Street and Olympic Boulevard, the entrance welcoming potential car buyers with the Packard logo in cursive, lit up with neon—one of the first neon signs in the United States. A row of windows allowed passersby to see the gleaming vehicles inside as cars chugged by on the downtown streets.

Los Angeles Packard dealer Earle C. Anthony was a pioneer in broadcasting, having established his own radio station in 1922 to facilitate internal communication between the Hope Street building and his other area dealership. The station, KFI, was Los Angeles's second, and its reach grew from 2 to 50,000 watts at 640 AM on the radio dial, where it became a public commercial station and remains in operation as of 2020.

Now Anthony was again at the forefront of another new medium, his Packard dealership serving as laboratory. A small crowd gathered on the ground floor, buzzing with excitement. They would see a demonstration that movielike images could be transmitted live to audiences from a distance—that is, a few floors away.

Two months before television would be unveiled at the New York World's Fair, Betty stood in front of one of the first television cameras ever used, set up on the top floor of the Packard building.

She was joined by her school's student body president, Harry Bennett, to perform for the experimental broadcast at the building.

In a makeshift TV studio, Betty and Harry prepared to perform songs from the operetta *The Merry Widow* in front of the camera. That thrilled Betty because her idol, Jeanette MacDonald, had starred in a movie production of it. Betty had short, dark hair that she wore in curls, and thin, carefully tended eyebrows like all the movie stars had. She was clad in her graduation dress, which she described as "a fluffy white tulle number held up by a sapphire blue velvet ribbon halter." They had to wear deep tan pancake makeup on their faces and dark brown lipstick "so we wouldn't wash out," she later said. The hot lights necessary for the early cameras coaxed sweat from their pores.

Soon their moment came. The camera switched on. They waltzed and sang for the watching lens.

Success: the signal beamed down to a monitor on the first floor of the building, where the audience, including Betty's and Harry's parents, stood among the Packard cars and watched the teenagers waltz and sing. This "broadcast" on one of the earliest TV systems had reached its viewers. Betty and Harry had appeared on a television before almost anyone else in the world, albeit on a test channel seen by just a handful of people.

After the experiment, White began to consider what kind of performing career she wanted to pursue. At first, she believed her calling was music. Instead of going to college, she opted for classical voice training. Her instructor, the opera singer Felix Hughes—the film and aircraft tycoon Howard Hughes's uncle—encouraged her in her hope of becoming an opera singer herself. But as White's mother, Tess, later wrote, a bout of strep throat that lingered for several weeks devastated Betty's vocal cords and ruled out a life of divadom. White herself later described it differently: "I had been studying singing diligently, and my mind and heart were set on an operatic career," she wrote. "Unfortunately, my voice had no such plans. This didn't deter me one iota: I was sure that if I worked hard enough, I could whip my voice into submission. Wrong."

As World War II took over Americans' lives, Betty set her career plans aside to join the American Women's Voluntary Services, helping to transport military supplies—toothpaste, soap, and candy—to gun emplacements in the hills of Hollywood and Santa Monica. Her uniform was a garrison cap that sat to the side of her head atop her styled curls, a jacket, and a skirt. In the evenings, she attended dances and activity nights at military rec halls with soldiers who were stationed nearby. She met several boys there and continued to write letters to them after they shipped out.

At first she was saving herself for a young man named Paul whose marriage proposal she had accepted before he had left for service overseas in November 1942. They wrote each other every day. But after two years, she sent him a letter that ended things and returned the engagement ring to his mother.

While she volunteered, she met another young man: a P-38 pilot named Dick Barker, whom she married in 1945. But then, to her surprise, she found herself driving back with him to his home state of Ohio to live on a chicken farm. She divorced him after six months and returned to Los Angeles. As she later explained, "Back in those days, you didn't sleep with a guy until you married him."

With the war and her brief marriage behind her, she wanted to find her place in show business. She enrolled at the Bliss-Hayden Theatre just outside Beverly Hills. Run by a husband-wife team of film actors, Harry Hayden and Lela Bliss, the school provided practical experience onstage, with a production every four weeks. The $50-per-month tuition earned students the chance to audition for a role and, if they didn't get one, to work in the stage crew. Betty landed the lead in her first audition, for Philip Barry's *Spring Dance*.

After eight performances, the school tackled the wartime romantic comedy *Dear Ruth*. Betty played the lead again; she was on a roll.

During the performances of *Dear Ruth*, she met another man. Lane Allan worked as a talent agent and had come to scout the show. He was movie-star handsome, with strong eyebrows, a Roman nose, and a sculpted jaw. In fact, he had done some acting and had changed his name from Albert Wootten to Lane Allan for the stage. He had since decided to become an agent for more career stability.

He returned for the closing-night performance. Betty almost blew her line when she saw his face in the front row again. This time, he came backstage and asked her to join him and his friends for an after-show drink. They began dating.

Lane suggested that she pursue a new line of acting work: radio programs. She made audition rounds, and soon developed a job-seeking routine. She went from station to station and sat in offices, even if there was no particular part on offer. She figured the executives would have to give her something if she hung out long enough.

But even as the rejections continued, she made the most of her wide-open schedule, going to the beach, horseback riding, swimming, and dating Allan. She maintained a close group of friends who were classmates from Horace Mann. Many of them had grand ambitions like her; they included a future New York stage set designer, a film editor, and a newspaper columnist. They discussed their dreams together, though it's notable that the others were all young men.

Finally, on one of White's casting visits to the fifth floor of the Taft Building at Hollywood and Vine, a producer of the popular comedy *The Great Gildersleeve*, Fran Van Hartesveldt, brought her into his office. She couldn't get a job, he explained, unless she was in the union.

She found the advice helpful but disheartening. She couldn't get a job unless she was in the union, but she couldn't get into the union unless she booked a job. Feeling hopeless, she left his office and headed for the elevators with the lunchtime crowd. The wait stretched for minutes and minutes as the busy elevators tried to get everyone off to their lunch hours.

White turned to head for the stairs instead just as an empty elevator finally showed up. She got in, and right before the doors closed, another passenger hopped in with her. It was Van Hartesveldt. They shared a silent ride down together.

As they stepped out on the ground floor, he piped up, "Listen, I know the spot you're in. It would help you one hell of a lot to get that union card, so here's what I'll do. I'll take a chance and give you one word to say in the commercial on this week's *Gildersleeve*. You won't break even, but it will get you your card. Think you can say 'Parkay' without lousing it up?" Her mouth gaped wide open in response. "Come back to our offices after lunch and the girl will send you over to the union," he said.

White in fact got to say "Parkay" twice: once for the Eastern Time Zone broadcast, and once for the West. She earned $37.50 total. She had to pay $69.00 to join the union. Her father loaned her the money to make up the difference.

She worried that she would screw up her line, saying "parfait" instead of "Parkay," but she made it through just fine.

She performed several other uncredited, small speaking roles on the program, delivered a Christmas message on the air, and provided a few sound effects. She even sang a song in a questionable "Mexican" accent for an American Airlines ad. ("Why not fly to Meheeco Ceety/You weel like the treep, ee's so preety" is how she later described it phonetically.) This led to other bit parts on the radio comedy *Blondie* and the crime drama *This Is Your FBI*.

She even landed a role in a movie produced by Ansco camera company to show off its new color film. She would have to shoot on location in the High Sierra in eastern California for six weeks. That prompted tense discussions with Allan, who hadn't quite counted on her career taking off even to that low altitude. They were still only dating, but they spent hours discussing the difficulties of two-career families. That brought White face-to-face with her conviction that career and marriage didn't go together. "There are some outstanding examples to the contrary," she later wrote, "so let me clarify by saying I just don't feel it's feasible to *start* them at the same time and still expect to give full attention to both. The fact that I'm compulsive explains a lot."

And, she had to admit, she wanted a career more than anything. She took the film shoot as an opportunity to break up with Allan. She figured she'd be more likely to stick to the breakup if she wasn't near him.

In the movie, called *The Daring Miss Jones*, an actress named Sally Forrest plays a young woman who gets lost in the woods and befriends two orphaned bear cubs. White—her now shoulder-length hair in huge, looped curls—plays Feeney's best friend back home who worries about her so much she flies a plane in to rescue her.

White did a little bit of everything on the set. She worked as the de facto script girl, tracking shots and continuity. She often wrangled the cubs because their "trainer" was drunk. That became more difficult as the cubs doubled in size over the length of the shoot.

She developed a friendship with Forrest, who soon became a successful film noir actress, appearing in such movies as John Sturges's *Mystery Street* and Fritz Lang's *While the City Sleeps*.

White returned to the safety of home and realized how much she had missed Allan. The feeling turned out to be mutual: a package from him waited for her at home, containing a Carl Ravazza record of "their" song, "I Love You for Sentimental Reasons." When they reunited, he professed total support for her career ambitions. They married two months later.

Soon after, Allen's agency, National Concert and Artists Corporation, went out of business and left him without a job. He had to take a position selling furniture at the May Company, and he squeezed in film roles when he could. The couple's budget shrank so much that they considered it a grand night out if they went to get a 25-cent hot dog and Delaware Punch at a stand on the corner of La Cienega and Beverly called Tail o' the Pup, which was shaped like a giant hot dog on a bun. Once, White had to collect some empty Coke bottles around the house to return for their 50-cent deposit so she could pay for her dry cleaning and have a decent dress to wear on her casting rounds.

She really needed to get some more reliable work.

White didn't care whether she did radio, movies, or even television, a market that looked increasingly promising, or at least like one more possibility, by 1949. Gertrude Berg's *The Goldbergs* was flourishing as TV's hottest new thing, and Irna Phillips was still struggling to crack the code for bringing soap operas to the small screen during the daytime hours. Despite the uncertainties, White saw a market just beginning to open up, and she needed to find a job wherever she could get it. And indeed, TV would be the one to embrace White, in contrast to film's cold repudiation and radio's shrug.

On one of her casting rounds, a receptionist surprised her by asking if she would like to speak to a producer who was working on a television show. She said yes, of course. As she later explained, there is one rule for show business success: *Whatever they ask you, always say yes.* When she went in to meet with the producer, Joe Landis, he asked, "Can you sing?"

She said yes again. Besides, she *had* studied opera. Just because her voice was no longer suitable for *Tosca* didn't mean she couldn't carry a tune on TV. He hired her on the spot, without even asking to hear her sing. He offered no pay. She said yes anyway.

The special starred Dick Haynes, who was locally famous as a KLAC radio disc jockey with a show called *Haynes at the Reins*. Landis told White to pick two songs, put on a nice dress, and show up Tuesday ready to sing.

White fretted over her one major job: choosing songs. She spoke of nothing else for the next few days. She asked her husband, her parents, her husband's parents. Finally, consensus emerged: Landis had asked for something bright, and White didn't want to stretch herself beyond her vocal capabilities. She would sing "Somebody Loves Me" and "I'd Like to Get You on a Slow Boat to China."

She arrived at the studio at the appointed time, wearing a black taffeta skirt and a white blouse with sequin flowers on one shoulder. That proved to be all wrong: the taffeta skirt rustled in the microphones wherever she went; the white and the sequins wreaked havoc under the intense lighting, reflecting the light and casting spots on her face.

Nonetheless, she got through the performance, buoyed by the support of the bandleader, Roc Hillman, and the generosity of Haynes himself. She appreciated that she could never see the show, since it was live.

Her career began to flourish, at least as much as it could in television's small market at the time. Haynes recommended her for a new fifteen-minute comedy show on KLAC called *Tom, Dick, and Harry* that starred three vaudevillians. Barely a sitcom, the series featured three characters who ran a hotel. It had one set: the hotel desk. Every episode opened with Tom, Dick, and Harry singing their names and popping out from behind the desk. Then White would emerge, feather dusting everything in sight.

That lasted only a few weeks before Tom, Dick, and Harry gave up and left television.

But White had become a KLAC favorite, and soon she found herself sitting at the end of a line of three other young women like herself answering phones, a made-for-TV switchboard operation. They were appearing on KLAC's *Grab Your Phone*, which featured four "girls" picking up ringing receivers live on the air. The host, Wes Battersea, asked the audience questions, and viewers called in with the answers. White and the other women received those calls. "It must have looked like a tiny telethon," White wrote in her memoir. "But we weren't taking pledges—we were giving out five whole dollars for each correct response!"

In the clattering chaos, Betty had an idea: Wouldn't it be so much more fun if, instead of simply relaying the information about her caller to the host, she delivered it with a little flirtatious smile, some extra sweetness in her voice, maybe a flattering aside, maybe a little banter? She had an instinct for the new medium: no one wanted to see regular old phone answering. She couldn't—nay, *shouldn't*—pretend the cameras weren't there.

The producer loved it. He pulled her aside and told her, "Betty, I must ask you *not* to mention salary to the others. We are going to pay you twenty dollars a week because you sit on the end and ad-lib with Wes, but they are only getting ten a week."

She wondered if he had said the same thing to the others. For all she knew someone else got $20 or even more. But she accepted the bump up, and she understood that she was different from the others, maybe even special. It seemed that even the right kind of phone answering could be scintillating on the small, flickering living room screen. At least when Betty White did it.

Soon another DJ with his eyes on a television career wanted to cast White. Al Jarvis, having seen her other performances, rang her at home, at the apartment she shared with her husband in Park La Brea, a sprawling new complex in West Los Angeles. When she picked up the phone, she recognized Jarvis's voice from the radio. She had listened to him forever. Everyone had: he was Los Angeles's biggest DJ with his show *Make Believe Ballroom*. She could not fathom why the man was calling her.

It turned out he was preparing a daily daytime TV show to be called *Hollywood on Television*. He planned to play records on the air, similar to his radio show. "Would you like to be my Girl Friday?" he asked.

She thought, Gee, another job! Maybe I'll make another $20!

But the job proved much bigger than that. As she told the story, "not only would I be his Girl Friday, but I'd be his Girl Monday, Tuesday, Wednesday, and Thursday as well." And she would do so for hours and hours: he went on the air five hours a day on radio, so why wouldn't he do the same on TV?

"I like the way you kid with Wes Battersea, and since we are going to be on the air for five hours every day, I thought that might come in handy," Jarvis told White. "The job pays fifty dollars a week. What do you say?"

As usual, she said yes.

She couldn't wait to tell her husband and her parents: she had landed a huge part on television! She would make more than twice as much per week as she had on *Grab Your Phone*! She would appear on TV every day! Everyone celebrated, though she noticed Lane was the tiniest bit less excited than her parents were on her behalf. He seemed to like the money part, but he focused right away on how much time she'd spend at the studio. "I should have heard the first faint warning bell," she wrote; "could it be that my taking a job when I could get one was okay, but an actual career for me was not high on his list of long-range plans?"

Startlingly minimal preparation occurred to get *Hollywood on Television* onto television. A few meetings with some advertising reps, nothing more.

As a start-up operation the show had sparse production resources, and White did a little bit of everything: applying makeup, booking guests, and hauling props around as necessary. Jarvis was a mentor from the start. "All you have to do is respond when I talk to you," Jarvis said, explaining the job she was taking on. "Just follow where I lead."

She was in heaven. When she looked back on the time she spent there, from ages twenty-seven to thirty-one, she considered it her college, four years packed with fun and learning experiences that would set the tone for the rest of her life.

Jarvis and White shot on a simple set just below the radio tower atop the station's Hollywood building. White had spent some of her childhood with her parents in a small white house just two blocks north of there. Her father had sold floodlights to KMTR, the radio station that had been in the exact same building before it had switched over to KLAC.

The broadcast started at 12:30 p.m. so Jarvis could do his popular radio show in the morning. This gave White the morning to do chores around the apartment. She could even walk their Pekingese, Bandit—or "Bandy"—who was a wedding present from Allan to White. The complex didn't allow pets, so she had to sneak the dog out, riding on her arm under a coat, past the security guards who watched over the eighteen high-rise towers. Once they had made it across the street to the park that housed the La Brea Tar Pits, she and Bandy walked freely.

However, she hadn't been as sneaky as she'd thought: one day, a security guard called out to her, "Mrs. Allan, your tail is wagging." Indeed, Bandy's tail was waving hello from beneath her coat. Blessedly, the security guard then went about his business as if he hadn't seen a thing.

After walking the dog, she headed three miles northeast to the studio and put in her five hours. The show wrapped up by 5:30 p.m., which gave her enough time to get home and start dinner for Allan. It all seemed as though it would work out, with minimal disruption to her marriage.

Hollywood on Television premiered in November 1949, right around Allan and White's second wedding anniversary.

Recordings of the show don't exist, but accounts of its production indicate that it evolved before viewers' eyes. At first, *Hollywood on Television*—known as *H.O.T.* behind the scenes—simply transferred Jarvis's radio show to the screen. He sat behind a small desk, with White on one side of him and his record player on the other. He opened each show with a brief welcome to the audience, then introduced White, then played a record. Between each song they chatted briefly to the camera.

While the songs played, the audience heard only the music, but they saw Jarvis and White hanging out on the set and talking to each other, their microphones off. Occasionally, the lone cameraman panned to the tank filled with tropical fish, the set's one distinctive feature, for some visual variety.

Viewers did not care for any of that. By the second week, complaints began to roll in, and what they hated most was that Al and Betty talked to each other and said things that *the viewers couldn't hear*. It drove the audience crazy not to know what Al and Betty were saying. So it was decided that Al and Betty would talk for five hours on the air and say whatever they wanted. The turntable was gone, though the fish stayed.

Jarvis and White developed an on-air bit about her being his "Girl Friday"—and Monday, and Tuesday, and Wednesday, and so on. Jarvis often referred to her on the air by the day of the week. As an inside joke, White's mother bought her pairs of silk panties embroidered with the names of each day. White dutifully wore the proper panties throughout the week.

Three weeks into their run, on Thanksgiving Day, they broadcast as usual, despite the holiday. After they signed off, Jarvis called White into his office. She recognized the situation: after three glorious weeks, the fun was probably over. Their show must be ending, as all of her shows so far had done.

She entered his office already dejected and was struck by how official Jarvis looked behind that desk. He made things worse when he opened with an apology. This is it, she thought. Then he finished: He was sorry, he said, for keeping her from the holiday with her family. But he wanted to tell her that the station's manager, Don Fedderson, loved the work they were doing. KLAC would soon launch a big promotion to get the word out about *Hollywood on Television* to even more viewers. And the station wanted to add a half hour to each day's airtime, plus an entire five and a half hours on Saturdays.

Granted, only one other station broadcast in Los Angeles at the time, so viewers didn't have a lot of choices. But viewers did choose *Hollywood on Television* more often than not. Al and Betty would now ad-lib for a total of thirty-three hours per week. White got a raise, from $50 to $300 per week. She could not believe her good fortune.

Jarvis laughed. Meeting adjourned, happy Thanksgiving.

Viewership grew by the day, driven in large part by the growth of television. The station office expanded. Construction began on a new *Hollywood on Television* studio on the other side of the lot.

Meanwhile, the station threw a tentlike roof over the building's patio and drained the fish pond that sat in the middle. *Hollywood on Television* broadcast from here for the next few months until the new set was finished.

They were on the air. Always. White loved it. She never felt tired out by her exhausting schedule. "For whatever reason, be it workaholism, lack of good sense, emulating a father who loved working above all else, the truth of the matter is, it was plain, flat-out *interesting*," White wrote.

They came up with sketch ideas such as Madame Fagel Bagenhacher to entertain their expanding audience. The parade of guests further helped to fill time and inject some celebrity glamour into the show, not to mention spectacle and fresh excitement: the audience could now see their favorite singers and musicians instead of just hearing them, and they could discover new favorites as well. The jazz musician Herb Jeffries, known for his appearances in Western musical films for Black audiences, appeared before the cross section of KLAC's daytime viewership. The French singer-actor Robert Clary, who had survived a concentration camp by performing for SS soldiers, appeared on the show early in his American career, singing songs in French. Billy Eckstine and Nat King Cole were also among the guests.

The blond singer Peggy Lee stopped by to do a number. When White returned home that night, she found her father was smitten. "That girl in the green suit," he said. "She's really something."

The on-air proceedings had a frontierlike atmosphere in which anything could happen. Anxiety could erupt into laughter. Impending disaster could lead to high comedy. Jarvis and White had to appease their sponsors and keep KLAC's entire daytime schedule afloat, so the stakes were high, but no one was sure how to measure the quality of their work or their success. They didn't aim for a seamless show. They just worked to keep viewers interested. And, of course, to keep the commercial spots flowing.

Sometimes those two goals conflicted, particularly when Jarvis's friend Buster Keaton stopped by for occasional appearances. Keaton, a genius of the silent film era, combined physical comedy and deadpan expression to brilliant effect. (The critic Roger Ebert would later call him "the greatest actor-director in the history of the movies.") Keaton, too, had a syndicated half-hour show in 1950.

Once, as he and Jarvis schmoozed and bantered and schmoozed some more on camera, the required commercial spots, to be delivered by White, continued to stack up. The men seemed oblivious. White grew nervous. After all, the show existed through the beneficence of Thrifty Drugstore. Commercials were the real point of the program; the "entertainment" portions were incidental. "As our audience multiplied, our commercial load increased proportionately, and if an interview ran a little long or Al happened to get carried away on a subject, or if we began having a little too much fun, we knew we would have to pay for it," White wrote. "Once we slipped behind, we'd face having to do three or four spots in a row to catch up."

Finally, time had run out, even as Jarvis and Keaton prattled on. White cut in with her pitch for Thrifty, displaying the products available at the store. Keaton, sensing a comedic opportunity, wandered into the spot.

First he watched from the sideline. Then he went in. As White spoke about toothbrushes, he picked one up and pantomimed brushing his teeth. With each product, he followed her, miming with the drugstore items one by one.

Committed to professionalism, White breezed on, touting the wonders of each product and allowing Keaton's comedic genius to take its course. She knew she was the straight woman to his deadpan physical bit. For ten minutes, *Hollywood on Television* became high art. Luckily the Thrifty executives loved every minute.

White delivered many of the ads on the show, and there could be nearly sixty in a given five-and-a-half-hour episode. (The longer format of the show required multiple sponsors, unlike shows that were sixty minutes or shorter.) Adding to the challenge, both she and Jarvis refused to read off a script on camera or even use cue cards. They memorized what they needed to know about the products and delivered as best they could while broadcasting.

That didn't always turn out well. One time, White glanced at some new ad copy and headed to her spot on camera to tell viewers about a handy attachment for the kitchen sink. "You put the soap in here, then press this little button, and—and soapy water comes out of your—of your—" She could not remember the word for "faucet." She attempted to finish things off anyway: ". . . and soapy water comes out of your gizmo." Jarvis and cameraman Bill Niebling cried and shook with laughter—the shaking a much bigger problem for Niebling, who was holding the camera. Soon White convulsed with laughter as well.

Sometimes, as the show developed, hired pitchmen performed the ads. Many of the spots resembled a visit from a traveling salesman: the pitchman would toss dirt across the studio floor and demonstrate how well his vacuum cleaner sucked it up or tote in a sewing machine and offer it to the audience for the low price of $19.95. Lou Slicer came by to show off his kitchen gadget, which also, as the station learned from irritated letters, sliced many viewers' fingers. Charlie Stahl brought his sofas and jumped on them to demonstrate their resilience. White herself often couldn't resist the pitches delivered on the show: she purchased an O'Keefe & Merritt gas range as well as press-on manicured nails that took the top layer of her own nails off with them.

Animals emerged as another favored way to fill airtime. Betty loved animals, especially dogs, and had grown up in a pet-loving home. One episode of *Hollywood on Television* featured a Saint Bernard and her two-month-old puppy, who arrived on camera with a can of Dr. Ross Dog Food (sponsored!) tied under his chin with a red bow. White held the puppy up, did her signature look straight into the camera, and addressed one particular audience member who she knew for a fact was watching on her new ten-inch Hoffman set: "Mom?" Betty pleaded. Her mother kept the set on channel 13 for all five and a half hours every day. Stormy was the family pet for the next eleven years.

Almost anything could turn into a segment for the show, given the hours to fill. One time, White dressed as a young girl, sat on huge furniture, and sang "Young at Heart." Other times, she and Jarvis riffed on local news stories, even violent crimes, or discussed their ideas (mainly, Jarvis's ideas) about local politics. Those segments often elicited floods of viewer mail. One of Jarvis's particularly popular rants called for stricter penalties for sex offenders. Still other times, Jarvis opened a wooden gate on the set that led right out onto Cahuenga Boulevard. If someone passed by, he'd call them in to be interviewed on camera.

White and Jarvis added to their cast of regulars, which helped them to fill their allotted hours. Mary Sampley dressed in a kelly green uniform to deliver local car race results, sponsored by Kelly Kar Kompany. KLAC sports director Sam Balter offered updates from the world of athletics. Piano player Ronnie Kemper provided music. Station manager Don Fedderson's friend, a Unity Society minister named Dr. Ernest Wilson, closed out the show with a Thought for the Day. He told White he "loved doing the show because it was the only way he knew to be heard in every bar in town."

White realized that even the local fame she enjoyed could have gotten the better of her. But Jarvis was a good teacher, role model, and grounding force. He had rules to deal with audiences: "Never to talk down to them—nor, for that matter, over their heads. Without ever claiming such was the case, to give the viewers the comfortable feeling that you could have come to work on the bus."

Alas, the success White had so long hoped for took a toll on her marriage. A little more than two years after their wedding, during *Hollywood on Television*'s first year, Betty and Lane separated. He admitted that he didn't want a wife with a career as big as White's had become. She described him as "all the good things I thought I had seen," but she couldn't abandon her ambition. She resolved never to marry again. She realized she was a career girl at heart. "I love working," she later said in an interview with her friend Jane Ardmore, a journalist. "It's part of me. So . . . I love my freedom and this is how it's going to be. Forever." She remained friendly with Allan and attributed the marital breakdown to having made the wrong match at the wrong time.

At age twenty-eight, she had now divorced twice, but she was on her way to the kind of career she could love. Unlike Allan, White's parents supported her aspirations. She moved back in with them in their house in Brentwood. They celebrated with her any time she came home and announced a career victory.

Around this time, the average age of marriage for women was twenty-eight, and birth rates doubled in the postwar flush of economic stability. Middle-class white women such as Betty White were expected to get married, stay married, and remain happily at in their husbands' homes to raise children and tend to domestic duties. In fact, such a life was seen as idyllic: with so many new gadgets to make housework easier than ever, including washer-dryers and electric mixers, they had it good! Why wouldn't they want to give up working outside the home to enjoy the cozy satisfactions of unpaid home labor?

White, however, saw her life differently; she would devote herself to her work for the foreseeable future. Lucky for her, television's power was growing every day.

Local Los Angeles television had proven that power in 1949 with a real-life tragedy. A three-year-old girl named Kathy Fiscus fell into a well in the Los Angeles suburb of San Marino on the afternoon of April 8, and the rescue effort was broadcast live on KLAC's main competitor, KTLA. Crews with drills, bulldozers, and trucks from surrounding towns, aided by Hollywood studios' floodlights, convened to save her. By the time they got to her on the evening of April 10, she was dead. At that point, twenty-five thousand people, beckoned by the news coverage, had gathered on the site. Thousands more watched at home on television. Her headstone reads, "ONE LITTLE GIRL WHO UNITED THE WORLD FOR A MOMENT."

The reach of television on Hollywood's home turf was undeniable. But that didn't mean anyone knew how to make a cohesive, professional daily entertainment broadcast. White, Jarvis, and KLAC did their best to figure out what daytime television might look like, with no references to guide them. The same was happening at KTLA. Monty Margetts, an actress and radio announcer, became one of the station's biggest stars by hosting the city's first televised cooking show, Cook's Corner. The subversive twist: she didn't know how to cook. Viewers delighted in writing in to give her pointers.

As White, Jarvis, and Margetts bluffed their way through their first year on the air, television had come a long way since the first commercial TV networks began in 1941 in New York City, but it had a long way to go before it would overtake radio as the nation's main form of mass communication. At this point, it was a relative rarity that appeared mostly in the homes of the wealthy. The first

TV owners on any given block would find themselves suddenly very popular, their home a gathering spot for folks eager to catch a glimpse of Milton Berle or William Boyd, who played Hopalong Cassidy.

Critics differed as to what television might become. Around 1950, the media scholar Charles A. Siepmann predicted that TV would "conform rapidly to a few ... stereotyped conventions. It will be technically ingenious and inventive but artistically poor. Except on rare occasions, and for some time to come, its true scope as a medium of expression will not be fully realized." But the critic Gilbert Seldes, one of the first to take TV seriously, said, "The extraordinary sense of actuality given off by live television programs can show up the fictitious quality of the movies, the artifice which has become their art."

In any case, movies had no reason to fear television yet. Most of the TV schedule consisted of variety shows, which were easy to produce live because of their loose and unscripted structure, and daytime talk shows such as *Hollywood on Television*, which were equally uncomplicated. East Coast production was developing rapidly, but the West Coast had Betty White, Monty Margetts, and little else. Further hampering the medium's progress, the Federal Communications Commission in fall 1948 froze new station applications while the government agency figured out how to proceed with licensing. It had allowed several stations to cluster too close together, causing interference. Too much was happening too fast. That meant that the western half of the country, in particular, remained isolated from the East Coast stations, which were being connected by a growing cable network that allowed them to receive New York's live broadcasts. East Coast shows made it to White's side of the country only via inferior kinescope recordings, days or weeks after they had aired. And shows that originated on the West

Coast mostly stayed on the West Coast, forced to be content with only regional success.

Still, the TV industry was inching toward viability. As TV sets proliferated, broadcasters diversified their offerings, including children's programming such as *Howdy Doody* and dramas such as *The Lone Ranger*, sitcoms such as Gertrude Berg's *The Goldbergs*, and Irna Phillips's daytime soap *These Are My Children*. As of 1949, the TV business remained welcoming to such women. From the late 1940s on, women's trajectory in television would be one of revolution followed by retrenchment, several times over. Each of these women would experience inevitable setbacks but would move us farther forward than back.

The first revolution was just getting started, and one more true revolutionary was about to join: the glamorous jazz superstar Hazel Scott would soon become the first Black person to host a prime-time network television show.

4

A Holy Terror

Hazel Scott

Hazel Scott just wanted to stay home these days, but the world—and specifically television—needed her.

The jazz pianist played to sold-out crowds of thousands across the country and around the world, and, of course, she loved to play. She was a sensation for good reason: her virtuoso piano playing set her apart in the jazz world, which had its share of Black female superstar vocalists such as Billie Holiday and Ella Fitzgerald—but rarely anointed female instrumentalists. She was also a voluptuous beauty with milk chocolate–colored skin and a dazzling smile who favored strapless gowns and toggled effortlessly among moods as she played: sultry, dramatic, joyful, flirtatious. She was a delight to watch as well as hear.

She was in demand, and the only way she could slow her travel schedule down was by her own conscious choice. She wanted to find a way to keep playing regularly without constantly having to traipse across the country and around the world, often to and through places not hospitable to Black people, much less equal-treatment activists such as herself.

Her home life had become particularly cozy by 1949, making it that much harder for her to pack up and leave. On a Saturday afternoon in June 1949, for instance, her handsome husband, Congressman Adam Clayton Powell, Jr., threw a garden party for her twenty-ninth birthday. More than twenty family members and friends surrounded her as she opened Powell's gift, a necklace of graduated pearls. They gathered at the couple's two-story, five-bedroom Colonial-style home in Mount Vernon, a suburb just north of the Bronx. They sipped wine punch and ate sandwiches, cake, and ice cream served by the Powells' house staff, a Korean couple who filled the roles of driver, cook, maid, and nanny to their son, Skipper, who would soon turn three. From Mount Vernon, their driver could whisk Scott to appearances in the city.

No matter where Powell or Scott was during the week on business, both made it a rule to come home to be together on Saturday mornings. They went for walks with Skipper. Scott might play touch football with the neighbors, even though she was technically prohibited to do such activities: her hands were insured for a million dollars by Lloyds of London, which meant she wasn't supposed to do much with them besides play the piano. She was not allowed, as her son remembers her saying, "to cook or play sports or do anything interesting." Powell would preach on Sundays, fulfilling his other role as the pastor of Abyssinian Baptist Church in Harlem.

The couple was, by all accounts, deep in love at the time, and they were often held up as a model couple in Black media. A January 1949 *Ebony* cover story with Powell's byline celebrated "My Life with Hazel Scott." "After three years of seeing her first thing in the morning and the last thing at night," he wrote, "I'm still crazy about my girl."

He wrote admiringly of her principles: "Lady has 'filled out' re-markably since that memorable day in 1945 when I put the little gold band on her finger, and I don't mean physically. She has be-come a larger woman in many ways. She has become very militant in terms of her peculiar position as a Negro Artist and in relation to the struggle of her people for equality everywhere. She accepts no Jim Crow bookings nor will she play in a town where unsegregated hotel facilities are unobtainable."

This phrasing reads as condescending to modern eyes, and she was certainly principled before she met him, but the fact remains that she showed extraordinary strength, first in exerting control over her own image as a Black woman in the public eye and then in risking her career to make larger points about racism in the United States, all while trying to live up to the high standards of being a politician and preacher's wife. Her husband's emphasizing this in his public praise of her—right alongside her physical beauty and cooking skills—was significant. She thought all Black people, par-ticularly women, should always be presented in a dignified fashion, and she and her husband were in a unique position to spread that message.

Later in life, she joked about the period to her son. "You un-derstand," she said, "your mother was a holy terror." He recalls her saying, "There were just some things that I would insist on doing. And some people would say, 'Oh, you know, it hasn't been done.' Of course it hasn't been done. *Nothing* has been done." That was, of course, the whole problem: no one was doing enough, by any stretch of the imagination.

She loved her work and the opportunities it brought her for both music and activism. But she had tired of the travel that took her away from time at home with her young son and husband, time filled with warm pancakes, beer and crackers and cheese on the terrace, and evenings in front of the fireplace with Rachmaninoff's Second Piano Concerto on the record player. Being on the road took its toll on her.

Her salvation would come from the new medium beginning to infiltrate American homes in 1949—Sears, Roebuck had just started offering televisions for sale in its catalogs. And it would come, in particular, from the struggling new television network, DuMont.

Hazel Scott had possessed a strong will for all of her life. This determination may have resulted from being an immigrant with a racial pride some attributed to her beginnings in Trinidad, a place where she was in the majority as a Black person. Born in 1920 in the Caribbean island nation to scholar R. Thomas Scott and music student Alma Long Scott, Hazel emerged as the only surviving child of six. After her baby brother died of blood poisoning and her father left the family, her mother and grandmother emigrated with four-year-old Hazel to New York City's predominantly Black neighborhood of Harlem. They arrived in 1924 in the era of Jim Crow. But Hazel didn't know that then, and Harlem in its renaissance was full of cosmopolitan artists who looked like her.

If Gertrude Berg, Irna Phillips, and Betty White faced difficulties in show business as white women, Hazel Scott faced even more as a Black immigrant woman.

But as young Hazel became more cognizant of the racism that awaited her outside Harlem, she discovered that her extraordinary talent allowed her to slip past certain racial barriers. Sometimes that talent not only gained her entrée into the whitest halls of power, but also allowed her to challenge the systems that kept such power in place. Other times it lent her a confidence that got her into trouble.

She discovered the piano at the age of three and quickly demonstrated an ability to play by ear. She improvised on the instrument by five. By the time she was eight, a Juilliard professor had deemed Hazel a musical prodigy, and that would drive everything that happened to her for the rest of her life. Hazel got a scholarship to Juilliard to be privately tutored by the professor, who had confirmed her as a "genius." There she mastered classics by Bach, Chopin, and Rachmaninoff. By age fifteen, she was playing regularly with her mother's all-female touring jazz band, the American Creolians.

Soon she developed the idea of "swinging the classics"—adding modern jazz flourishes to classical piano pieces, a reliable crowd pleaser. She played gigs at night while attending Wadleigh High School for Girls, Gertrude Berg's alma mater, and graduated with honors. At sixteen she began to perform solo, watched over at adult clubs by the other entertainers, including Billie Holiday. During her teens, she hosted her own radio show on WOR.

At eighteen, she debuted at the establishment that would forge her fame: New York City's first integrated nightclub, Café Society. Her debut came on the 1938 opening night of the club itself, introducing the crowd to her talent for swinging classics. The same evening, Holiday brought the house down with the devastating protest song about lynching, "Strange Fruit." ("Southern trees bearing strange fruit/Blood on the leaves and blood at the roots.")

The club made Scott a top-billed star. *Time* magazine, with a headline calling her the "Hot Classicist," raved, "But where others murder the classics, Hazel Scott merely commits arson. Classicists who wince at the idea of jiving Tchaikovsky feel no pain whatever as they watch her do it. . . . Strange notes and rhythms creep in, the melody is tortured with hints of boogie-woogie, until finally, happily, Hazel Scott surrenders to her worse nature and beats the keyboard into a rack of bones."

She became known as the "darling of Café Society," and the club became famous as a lefty hangout that attracted progressive Jewish activist performers such as the comedian Zero Mostel and his best friend, the actor Philip Loeb, soon to play Gertrude Berg's husband on Broadway and then on the TV version of *The Goldbergs*. Black performers such as Scott played for mixed audiences, and Jewish comedians such as Mostel tried out new material. Between shows, civil rights activists mingled with labor organizers.

Scott developed new performance tricks, including sitting between two grand pianos and playing both at once. She expanded her act to venues around the country, some of them predominantly white. Her popularity across demographic lines led to more radio spots as well as Broadway and movie roles as jazz was peaking in mainstream popularity. Scott appeared in Broadway productions such as the 1938–39 revue *Sing Out the News*, which also featured Loeb. She toured clubs throughout the country and performed at the 1939 World's Fair, where Irna Phillips was among the crowds who also saw television introduced for the first time.

By the early 1940s, Scott was entertaining a number of movie offers. Many films at the time had a strong musical element, often with a flimsy plot that served as an excuse for a string of performances by popular artists. They functioned as proto–music videos, enabling moviegoers to see their favorite musicians in action in the days before television. The artists appeared in self-contained scenes that could be cut—Black performers' scenes were routinely excised for southern theaters. Scott made $4,000 a week for her efforts, or almost $60,000 in 2020 terms. She was even considered for the iconic role of Sam the piano player in *Casablanca*, which ultimately went to Dooley Wilson—who didn't actually know how to play the piano. There was almost a world in which Humphrey Bogart pleads with Hazel Scott to play "As Time Goes By" once more.

Scott performed in five films in the 1940s, including a showy number in the George Gershwin biopic *Rhapsody in Blue*—which also features blackface's biggest star, Al Jolson, playing himself. It was a problematic time, but she made her own point with her presence in a scene in which she plays "The Man I Love" in a Paris nightclub, singing in both English and French. The historian Donald Bogle wrote, "Scott was about as elegant and sophisticated as they come, a blazing symbol of the contemporary Black woman completely at home in the most continental of settings."

Those starkly racist times prompted Scott to draw certain hard boundaries. She turned down, for instance, a number of what she called "singing maid" roles. She had strict stipulations if she did take a part. She always appeared as herself, credited as such, and she demanded final review of her own scenes as well as wardrobe approval. Those restrictions were more than necessary at a time when minstrelsy was still a common trope in mainstream movies.

In so many ways, she was made for the pictures of the 1940s. Her wide eyes and sweet smile lit up the screen; she had a velvety coo of a speaking voice, a full and raspy singing voice. She was all curves—her hips, her hair, her eyes, her cheeks, her lips, her shoulders. Her overall effect on film was mesmerizing. She had become a marquee star in concert venues across the United States, and, eventually, in the music-driven movies of the 1940s.

Then she crossed one of the most powerful men in film.

The Heat's On put Scott's strict standards to the test. In the movie, she is among the performers involved in a war between two Broadway producers over a star played by Mae West. Scott's second musical number in the picture appears as part of the fictional play being produced, and it portrays Black women sending their husbands off to war while Scott plays and sings "The Caissons Go Rolling Along," her husky vibrato the epitome of 1940s pop.

In the scene, Scott wears a Women's Army Corps sergeant uniform of skirt suit and hat, but she objected to the original costumes offered the other Black actresses in the scene: "Am I to understand that these young women are to see their sweethearts off to war, *wearing dirty Hoover aprons?*" she asked, referencing the Depression-era president Herbert Hoover. Scott refused to come to the set as long as the dirty aprons were in the segment.

After three days of work stoppage, she won. No more aprons. Instead, the nine women who played the men's wives and dance partners wore a selection of clean, pressed floral and solid-color dresses.

But such a brazen act of defiance—which could cost tens of thousands of dollars on such a production—had its consequence. Columbia Pictures cofounder Harry Cohn swore she would never work in film again as long as he was alive. She boarded a train and left Hollywood to return to New York. That would become a pattern for the rest of her life, even a philosophy. "I've been brash all my life, and it's gotten me into a lot of trouble," she said. "But at the same time, speaking out has sustained me and given meaning to my life."

Scott's personal life became a national story when, in 1945, she married pastor and US representative Adam Clayton Powell, Jr., just weeks after his divorce from the actress Isabel Washington. Powell—a distinguished, light-skinned Black man—presented like a movie star himself, with a Clark Gable mustache and a rousing oratorical style. He and Scott had long moved in the same circles: he had admired her as her musical renown grew, and she had been impressed when she had seen him preach.

They felt a spark when they met one-on-one, even though he was still married to Washington. "We both were tired of leeches," Powell later wrote. "We knew neither of us wanted anything but each other." He liked to call her pet names such as "squirt" and "character," and he loved the musical lilt she gave to his first name. They were spotted at Café Society together and went on dinner dates to Reuben's and "21." Surrounded by a cloud of her floral perfume, they discussed "philosophy, politics, boogie woogie, and war."

Powell and Scott's courtship caused a scandal, but their wedding was commemorated by a *Life* magazine photo spread and attracted three thousand fans, constituents, and onlookers who hoped for a glimpse of the famous couple, as well as a contingent of uninvited photographers. The reception included a cake in the shape of the White House.

Scott had become a multitalented superstar and a national politician's wife. Adam Clayton Powell, Jr., loomed large in the Black community of Harlem, just as Scott did. In 1937, he succeeded his father as the head pastor of the prominent and powerful Abyssinian Baptist Church. He agitated for the 1939 New York World's Fair and Harlem Hospital to hire more Black workers. He published the Black publication *The People's Voice* from 1941 to 1945.

Powell would represent Harlem in the US House of Representatives from 1945 to 1971. When he was elected, he became one of only two Black congressmen, along with Chicago's William Levi Dawson, until 1955. Powell worked to challenge segregationists, champion civil rights, and fight poverty, though his tactics were sometimes questionable. (He later disagreed with civil rights leader Martin Luther King, Jr., over King's plan to demonstrate at the 1960 Democratic National Convention and even threatened to feed the press an erroneous story that King had had a sexual affair with his gay adviser, Bayard Rustin. The incident passed with little effect, and Powell and King appeared to move past the rift, working together again.)

Powell and Scott made a great political match. A few months after their wedding, they hatched their first antisegregationist action together: Scott would ask to play a concert at Constitution Hall in Washington, DC. They both knew it was owned and operated by the Daughters of the American Revolution, who allowed only white artists to play there. They understood that her request would be denied, which it was. Powell and Scott took the story public, and Powell sent a telegram of complaint to President Harry S. Truman.

The president wrote back and voiced his support for Powell's position, though he declined to intervene "in the management or policy of a private enterprise such as the one in question." The letter said, "One of the marks of a democracy is its willingness to respect and reward talent without regard to race or origin. We have just brought to a successful conclusion a war against totalitarian countries which made racial discrimination their state policy. One of the first steps taken by the Nazis when they came to power was to forbid the public appearance of artists and musicians whose religion or origin was unsatisfactory to the 'Master-race.'"

When Truman's wife, Bess, attended a DAR tea after the blowup, however, Powell called her the "last lady" of the United States, prompting the White House to freeze Powell out for the remainder of Truman's term. A subsequent debate on the House floor also led Representative John E. Rankin, a segregationist Democrat from Mississippi, to insinuate that Powell was a Communist.

But at least the Scott-Powells had made their point.

A year after they married, Powell and Scott welcomed a son, Adam Clayton Powell III, whom they called Skipper. Meanwhile, the couple worked to fit into their public roles in each other's contrasting worlds. They felt that they were doing pretty well thus far. Powell told a story about a time when he had been at home reading the *Congressional Record* and listening to the popular Aaron Copland orchestral suite *Appalachian Spring*. Scott had arrived home with her white musician friend Toots Camarata, who had written some arrangements for her. After she had introduced the two, Toots had listened to a few notes of the record and gestured toward Adam. "He *digs*, doesn't he?" Toots had said to Hazel. Powell cherished that as a great compliment.

Thanks to Scott, Powell also grew fond of newer strands of jazz such as bebop and "hep" artists such as Charlie Parker and Dizzy Gillespie. The couple attended Nat King Cole's wedding at the Abyssinian Baptist Church with Powell officiating, the ultimate joining of their two worlds.

They learned to appreciate each other's crafts, even if they didn't grasp every technicality. Powell was once so overcome while seeing her play a Brahms concerto during a San Francisco concert that he left the venue, bought a dozen roses, and rushed backstage to meet her with them when she finished. The smooth talker was suddenly awkward. "This is for being a wonderful musician," he said. "I think Brahms would love you, too."

In turn, she always let him know when she was bowled over by one of his sermons, or if another was a bit "off the beat," as she said. He wrote in his *Ebony* piece, "She is a great help to me in everything I do, even when her assistance consists of merely sitting in the audience and fixing me with those great big beautiful dark eyes of hers. That kind of moral encouragement is 'out of this world' to revert to the language of our show folk friends; it's impossible to assess it in material terms."

They loved to sail, fish, and swim together. They liked to dress for dinner when they were home together. She set the table with tall candles, flowers, and sterling. For dessert, she made her specialty, devil's food cake. She knitted, making socks and sweaters for Adam and clothes for Skipper. Powell quoted Proverbs when he described her as the "ideal wife": "She looketh well to the needs of her household . . . her husband hath no need for spoil."

Scott's career stabilized in the years after she fell out with the movie industry. In 1947–1948, she made $85,000 in one concert tour, the equivalent of nearly a million dollars in 2020. She got an offer of $60,000 to appear in London and Paris in the summer of 1948. She signed a new record deal with Columbia and released a warmly received album, *Great Scott*. The piano and vocal numbers included "Soon," "Brown Bee Boogie," "Love Me or Leave Me," and "Nightmare Blues."

She drew crowds of thousands on her tour across the North American continent, which sent her from New York City to Massachusetts, Vancouver, the West Coast, Virginia, and back home to New York again. Audiences ranged from 2,500 at St. Louis's Auditorium Opera House to more than 14,000 at New York City's Lewisohn Stadium at City College of New York. There, wearing a white strapless gown, she played Beethoven's First Piano Concerto in C major "with a freshness of approach and a sympathy for the melodies that occasioned bravos and applause from audience and musicians alike," the *New York Times* said. Walter Hendl conducted for the occasion, which marked her debut as a soloist with the New York Philharmonic-Symphony Orchestra.

The *New York Herald-Tribune* noted that the audience "seemed unintimidated by gloomy skies and . . . naturally enough, reached its highest enthusiasm at the end of the concert when the pianist presented her 'specialties' in a light musical vein"—that is, her jazz and contemporary pop numbers. The hometown crowd mobbed her backstage afterward for autographs.

But in the Jim Crow era, touring the country as a Black artist—even one as admired as Hazel Scott—had its share of difficulties. And Scott never knew when a racist roadblock might suddenly appear in front of her. Even in Canada, where she had anticipated a smooth trip, she boarded a train, holding her ticket, and was asked to leave. That particular train line, the staff explained, was designated whites only. She called her husband and told him about the incident. He later told Assistant Secretary of State Edward Miller, "If this happens again, I intend to air it with a full speech on the floor before the House."

In some even more egregious cases of racism, particularly where she had some clear leverage or legal recourse, she used the moments to make a public statement.

In November 1948, she refused to play a scheduled concert at the University of Texas in Austin when she saw that the sold-out 7,500-seat stadium was segregated, a red carpet down the middle as a line of demarcation between the races. Her lawyers told her that she'd be "financially liable" for pulling out of the contract, which would set her back $2,000. She walked out anyway. "Why would anyone come to hear me, a Negro, and refuse to sit beside someone just like me?" she later said to *Time* magazine.

When she got home, she was still livid. Her son overheard his parents talking about the incident. "Oh, don't tell the boy," he later recalled his father saying. Hazel's reply: "Well, he should know that his mother was escorted out of Austin, Texas, by the Texas Rangers last night."

A few months later, as she headed to Spokane, Washington, for another tour stop, her train got stuck in a snowdrift. Exhausted from touring, she had fallen ill with a fever. She was sleeping in her fur coat when she was awakened to find that she and her friend who was traveling with her, Eunice Wolf, had to get off the train with the rest of the passengers and board a bus that would take them to their destination. She and Wolf disembarked from the bus at its first stop in Pasco, Washington, to get something to eat. When they entered a nearby diner, the waitress told the women that the establishment didn't serve "colored."

Scott was aghast to encounter that kind of treatment so far north. She insisted on finding a police station to report the incident but found an unsympathetic desk sergeant. "Are you going to get out of here or am I going to have to run you in for disturbing the peace?" he asked.

The women did eventually make it to Spokane, where they were greeted by concert booking agent Roy Goodman and his wife at their hotel. Scott told him, "I want the following things in the following order: a hot bath, a hot drink, and a lawyer."

The next year, she filed a $50,000 lawsuit against the restaurant. The case made national headlines.

Such controversy might not seem attractive to television networks that were trying to appeal to as many viewers as possible. But to the upstart DuMont network, Scott's passionate fan base—and perhaps even her predilection for provocation—looked like a reasonable gamble as the 1940s came to a close. The network had its eye on her as she toured the country that year.

DuMont launched in 1942 and aimed to compete with the powerful radio networks that had transitioned to television, CBS and NBC. Yet another radio network, ABC, came to TV in 1948. In the late 1940s, all of the networks were still experiments, but the DuMont network faced particular challenges, with smaller budgets than the other networks and no radio talent pool to pull from. Its first experiment had been programming daytime and including in that lineup Amanda Randolph, the first Black woman to host her own regularly scheduled show.

But DuMont was looking to make more headlines. The network needed stars, and Hazel Scott was on its radar. She numbered among show business's biggest names, but she also had liabilities that could make her attainable for the smaller network.

Other market factors made her attractive to DuMont at the time. Television signals were concentrated in large cities on the coasts and primarily in the North, where racism wasn't as overt and many Black people had moved since the beginning of the Great Migration. That wave of relocation began in World War I as industrial jobs proliferated, offering better opportunities away from the segregated South. It also meant Black households' buying power was on the upswing, making them desirable targets for some advertisers.

As of January 1949, the coaxial cable that linked the East Coast hub of television production to the rest of the country reached as far west as St. Louis, which brought Chicago, Milwaukee, Detroit, and Cleveland into the New York–centric fold. A chasm remained between East and West Coast production. So Scott's main goal would be to appeal first to local New York audiences, and then, possibly, to northern cities in the East and Midwest with sizable Black populations of their own.

She tried out the new medium first as a guest on Ed Sullivan's variety show *Toast of the Town* and on comedian Jackie Gleason's *Cavalcade of Stars*, one of DuMont's biggest hits. The network carried a number of musical and variety shows, which tended to be simpler to shoot and have lower budgets than scripted comedies and dramas. It was looking to take chances in that format that would make a splash.

Scott got the call in 1950: Would she like to try a television show of her own on the DuMont Network? The offer felt like the perfect thing at the perfect time. First, it would provide a regular income without travel. Second, it would allow her to play herself, as she preferred, wearing what she wanted, portrayed the way she wanted, nothing but Hazel Scott and her music on camera.

She would appear for fifteen minutes every Friday night on DuMont's New York affiliate, WABD. It would make her the first

Black woman to host her own prime-time solo show. (The Black actress and singer Ethel Waters had hosted a very early NBC special in 1939, but it had been a onetime broadcast. It had featured both Powell's ex-sister-in-law Fredi Washington and *Goldbergs* actor Philip Loeb.)

Hazel Scott headed into 1950 at the top of her game, with a new television show to look forward to. But other societal storm clouds were gathering that had more to do with her than she could have imagined. TV was gaining traction in a time in which progress and paranoia wrestled for Americans' attention—a battle that would determine Scott's career. In 1949, the de Havilland Comet, the first commercial passenger jetliner, took its first flight; as world travel grew to be within reach for everyday citizens and a spirit of globalism surged in international politics, nationalism and tribalism rose in reaction. The Soviet Union's first nuclear weapons test jump-started an age of American fear. Rodgers and Hammerstein's progressive antiracist musical *South Pacific* opened on Broadway, while much of the South clung to segregation. Major record companies introduced the 45-rpm single, which enabled young people to buy the less expensive format en masse and revolutionized the way music was marketed. Combined with the spread of television, it enabled a national pop culture to take shape. It also made those in power quite anxious to control who was seen and heard through these powerful media.

Signs of this need to control entertainers were bubbling just under the surface as DuMont signed Scott to its lineup. One sign that hit close to home for Scott came when both New York City locations of Café Society—downtown, where she had made her name on opening night, and uptown, where she had become a mainstay act—were closed by 1949. The House Un-American Activities Committee (HUAC)—a congressional committee that had been terrorizing film actors with unsubstantiated, career-ruining accusations of Communist ties—went for the clubs, which were known for their left-leaning patrons and their free racial mixing.

Café Society's owner Barney Josephson's brother Leon, a lawyer, was called before HUAC, which wielded its government power to question the loyalties of leftists. Their mere implications could ruin a reputation or put someone out of business, and Leon openly identified as a Communist. His refusal to appear on one occasion, and his refusal to answer questions on another, incited bad publicity from the columnists Westbrook Pegler and Walter Winchell, and the clubs' patronage dropped to the point where both locations had to close.

At the time, it seemed that TV would be Scott's new Café Society—a dependable, regular, New York–based gig. But the year ahead would test both her and Gertrude Berg to their brink as anti-Communist panic swept through the nascent industry and ensnared them in the process just as their wildest television dreams were coming true.

5

One of Us

Gertrude Berg and Hazel Scott

From the outside of the Goldbergs' now-familiar apartment window, we see the closed shade. Then, with a bit of a fuss from inside, it flips open to reveal the entire family—Molly, Jake, Sammy, Rosie, and Uncle David—waving at us and buzzing with energy. Molly and Rosie both wear hats with flowers that stick up out of them, and Uncle David is in a fedora. They've just come in from some sort of occasion together. After the enthusiastic greeting, they disperse, with mutterings of "We better go unpack."

In the opening scene of this late-1949 episode of *The Goldbergs*, Molly stays at the window and fixes her gaze straight through the camera lens. She wears a blouse with a bow at the neck, her pearls laid beneath it. "Hello," she says in her trademark breathless delivery. This harried mother is always out of breath. Her words tumble out as if trying to beat each long exhale. "I don't know, 'hello' is such a little word for such a big feeling." We don't know where she's going with this, but we can't stop watching. That's *why* we can't stop watching—that and the feeling that the woman is talking to us specifically and that she will be devastated if we look away for even a second.

She's just getting warmed up. She continues, "I want to say hello to you with all the letters of the alphabet. Hello." We can see Rosie crisscrossing the room in the background as she unpacks. But we're focused on Molly, as usual. "Have I stories for you from Pincus Pines." (They've just returned from spending some time at their favorite fictional Catskills resort.) "You sit on a rocking chair for six weeks, you hear plenty and you talk plenty and everybody knows you and you know everybody."

Then her monologue takes a familiar turn. She explains that there can be a lot of restlessness, a lot of irritability, among the guests at Pincus Pines. The children get antsy. The older folks aren't sleeping well on these unfamiliar mattresses. The windup is complete, and it's time for the weekly pitch. There's a certain thrill now in knowing what's next: "That's why I didn't hesitate, the same as I tell you about Sanka, so I told them about Sanka coffee, that it's good for restlessness, it's good for irritability, and that's why I told them that. After all, those that didn't know, I told them that ninety-seven percent of the caffeine is removed."

Gertrude Berg had proven herself, and her show, a natural fit for television. Four years after her radio career had ended with an unceremonious cancellation to make way for newer, shinier shows in that medium's Golden Age, her shrewd move to TV had put her back on top of pop culture. TV certainly benefited from her starry presence as well; she lent it legitimacy and drew audiences with her brand name.

After *The Goldbergs* had been on for several months, viewers felt as if they were a part of this family. They knew Jake was always coming up with new ways to get ahead at the dress company where he worked. They knew that Uncle David would always be there for

Molly, helping with her schemes to matchmake or meddle. And they knew that Molly would entertain them, especially when she delivered those warm, rambling, never-the-same-twice Sanka ads.

The Goldbergs had settled into its live weekly broadcast from 9:30 to 10:00 p.m. Eastern Time on Monday nights on CBS. Radio had taught Berg that she could dominate media by playing America's favorite mother, Molly Goldberg, infused with her powerful charisma. Television now multiplied that effect.

The Goldbergs had, in fact, shot to the top of the Hooper ratings, the audience measurement of the time. It became the first old radio show to succeed so much on television that it returned to radio. (The same cast and stories were broadcast in audio form, simultaneously with the TV broadcast.) But for the lucky Americans who had television sets, seeing the Goldbergs on TV, rather than just hearing them on the radio, provided a unique kind of thrill. Critics and fans alike went wild for the new sensation of intense intimacy with the family. "Visuality has made the story of this Bronx family even more realistic than it was on radio," a *Chicago Daily Tribune* review raved.

Fan mail flooded Berg and CBS. It came from all parts of the country, from Jews and Gentiles, from high-powered media executives and workaday midwesterners. But many of the letters bore a similar message: the only thing more heartrending than listening to the Goldbergs' family travails was watching them. Viewers were mesmerized by the feeling that they were in their living rooms *with* Molly, Jake, and their children.

Fans sent Berg gifts, which she appreciated and acknowledged in the best possible way. "I can truthfully say that tears came to my old eyes when I saw before them, you wearing the apron I especially made for you," said one letter from a sixty-seven-year-old fan.

A Mrs. McInerney wrote from Chicago, "A shut-in who wants

to thank the Goldbergs for coming into our homes each Monday evening over WGNTV, surely the greatest thrill I have received was their friendly voices returning to us through television and seeing all of them was just so much more thrilling. . . . Little did we think we would get to see them on our television screen just one year after my husband got me the set to keep me company while he was away to work, and television has played a great part in my lonely life, for I have been a heart patient for the past six years."

Twentieth Century–Fox Film Corporation's director of television, Alfred H. Morton, couldn't contain his *Goldbergs* ardor, either. He wrote to Berg, "I have been resisting the writing of this first fan letter for two months but each Monday night a little more of my resistance crumbles and I can't resist pressing my face up against the window of the Goldbergs' flat. I feel almost indecently close at times to your warm unravelling of the assorted problems that beset the family. It is an intimate medium, and how very beautifully you have made the transition."

That intimacy—that *visual* intimacy—gave Berg a worry that had heretofore not crossed her mind. Fans had rarely recognized her on the street when she was a famous voice. Now she had a famous face. She didn't mind the attention. Not one bit. But she did mind that it hampered her ability to move anonymously among the crowds at the Lower East Side pushcart markets where she had always liked to roam to do research, as she said, to "pick up dialect and color."

Such culture-specific detail didn't sit well with everyone, rapturous fan letters notwithstanding. At least one early review worried that TV's vividness would allow it to heighten stereotypes to new levels (an accurate prediction) and that *The Goldbergs* was among the offenders. "For years radio has been properly accused of perpetuating unfavorable stereotypes—the blackface, illiterate Negro;

the English-mangling Jew; the shanty Irish; rumpot Italian," Jerry Franken wrote in *Billboard* in January 1949, taking aim at Molly Goldberg's penchant for malapropisms. "Now, via its television adaptation of the highly successful Goldbergs, CBS is adding the new, and final dimension to this lamentable stereotype."

But a fan letter from later that year provided powerful evidence to the contrary. Among the loving messages Berg kept in her archive was one from Mrs. Carrie Welch of Cleves, Ohio, who reached out to the network with a confession about *The Goldbergs*: "When I first heard that program I felt a strong distaste for it and had an urgent desire to dial another station (old Satan trying to inject his venom in my heart!), but knowing as I do that we come to understand that with which we become familiar, I forced myself to listen then and a number of times since. Now I am beginning to *like* the Goldbergs. Programs like this one . . . help to prove that folks of different nationalities and creeds are as human and lovable as people of our own kind. In my opinion they are stepping stones toward world peace."

Among the relatable family moments and the sweet comedy, Berg fleshed out mainstays of Jewish life, depicting seders and visits to synagogue for high holidays. Jewish fans, of course, loved to see themselves reflected on television. The Jewish Ukrainian immigrant M. Lincoln Schuster, a cofounder of the publishing powerhouse Simon & Schuster, sent a telegram to Berg: "MRS. SCHUSTER AND I DEEPLY STIRRED BY YOUR MAGNIFICENT YOM KIPPUR PROGRAM."

Berg took her contribution beyond the Jewish experience as well, displaying her progressive values through her scripts and casting. For one 1949 episode, she cast Fredi Washington, a Black woman and outspoken civil rights activist. In fact, in addition to acting, Washington wrote a politically tinged entertainment column in *The People's Voice*, Adam Clayton Powell, Jr.'s, publication. (She was the sister of Powell's ex-wife, Isabel.) Fredi Washington argued for more Black representation in media and urged action so that "the Motion Picture Industry and the radio shall become more conscious of the tremendous revenue paid by Negroes for their products and be made to handle, with regard and respect, all material dealing with and pertaining to Negroes."

In 1949, Washington appeared on *The Goldbergs* in what her ex-brother-in-law's new wife, Hazel Scott, would technically have to consider a maid role, for it was literally a maid. But it had a subversive twist, courtesy of Berg. In the episode, Washington plays a cook/maid named Louise—after Berg's own trusted in-house cook—whom Molly hires at Jake's insistence when he's doing well at work. Molly resists the idea, cleaning the house before Louise arrives so as not to embarrass herself. The two then spend their time together chatting and singing as Louise plays the piano. Molly finally concedes that Louise can make the family dinner. But the meal is so good that Molly is upset: she doesn't want anyone in her own home to cook better than she does. Molly gets Louise a new job with her neighbor Mrs. Dutton instead and returns to doing her own cooking and cleaning.

That humanized portrayal of a Black domestic worker compared favorably with the overly sweet, simple, superficially wise "singing maid" roles Scott fought so hard against. It was also astute and funny.

At the start of 1950, Hazel Scott's television series was coming together behind the scenes. The network's advertising sales representatives had secured the New York–based company Sitroux Tissues to sponsor *The Hazel Scott Show*, which would air on the local station, WABD, starting in February.

To Scott's great delight, she would have the opportunity to continue to play "herself," this time on television in her hometown. TV was in a unique position at the moment that served Scott well: it was still experimental enough to take its chances on an outspoken Black female star, but gaining enough traction to widen her audience and have a real effect on her career.

According to her son, Adam Clayton Powell III, who was then four-year-old Skipper, she seemed excited by the possibilities as she talked about the show at the dinner table on Saturday nights, when her husband was home, too. The three of them gathered to enjoy their carefully protected family time and eat peas grown in their backyard, broccoli from their neighbors' yard, and greens with fish or chicken. Adam Sr. would throw out his own suggestions for her TV show: "There's this wonderful song, and I've heard you do it in the clubs . . ."

She'd respond, "Well, we'll see if that works."

She loved that she worked with other Black people on her show: she had a band, the Hazel Scott Trio, which included bassist Charles Mingus and drummer Max Roach, both to become jazz legends. According to her son, they also served as her TV band. ("I became (re)acquainted with Max Roach 21 to 22 years ago," Powell III wrote to me in a 2020 email, "and he said he really liked working on the show.") Actual recordings of her show, like many on DuMont, have been lost, but Scott did collaborate with Mingus and Roach five years later on the revered record *Relaxed Piano Moves* and often performed publicly with one or both men.

This lack of recordings is exactly why the historic, founding work of Scott, as well as the other women who invented television, has been largely forgotten. TV, in its early days, was regarded as disposable, and its technology was experimental. That means that Scott's TV show is practically forgotten, despite its staggering historic nature: it featured the first Black person to host what would become a national prime-time series *and* two jazz greats backing her on it, but we can't see any of it. *The Goldbergs* is only slightly better remembered because some recordings exist; they are sporadic and low quality, which makes them hard to sell in reruns, but at least they are easier to study.

Most of all, Scott rejoiced at having regular work in New York that allowed her to stop traveling. No longer would she have to go to great pains to fly home for their family Saturdays; she would be home all week. She could spend every day with Skipper, who didn't know her as the famous Hazel Scott; he knew her only as Mommy. She could make his favorite chocolate cake whenever she wanted to. She could practice in the middle of the afternoon, playing the same phrases over and over, even if it disturbed Skipper's nap. She could commute to DuMont's Manhattan studios, just eighteen miles from their house, with the help of their driver.

Sometimes she would bring her son to the dark, quiet, cold TV studio from which her show aired. It was likely located in the DuMont studios that took up a portion of the Wanamaker Building downtown, at 770 Broadway, which spans the entire block between 8th and 9th Streets on the east side. The terra-cotta and stone building, with Renaissance Revival architecture and a palazzolike design, boasts arched windows that line the bottom two floors where Wanamaker's department store was at the time. Wanamaker's shoppers could sometimes look in on daytime rehearsals in progress in the adjoining DuMont studios.

Scott's son would sneak onto the neighboring set of *Captain Video and His Video Rangers*, a child-pleasing mishmash of live-broadcast story lines about the titular hero fighting vaguely for justice in a sci fi–tinged interplanetary future with robots, spaceships, and other futuristic contraptions. To save money on the production, each half-hour show contained about ten minutes of old cowboy film footage that was explained as a look at Captain Video's "undercover agents" on Earth. Little Skipper was disappointed to see the set without the magic of television cameras: Captain Video's rocket was just a cardboard box with no windows.

On show nights for Hazel, the only light in the studio shone on the piano, blasting heat like a small indoor sun. Circa-1950 cameras required intense lighting to capture a decent picture. Just outside the spotlight's center sat the bass and drums. The cameras and their operators skulked around in the dark filming Scott's performances.

On the fifteen-minute show, Scott created the atmosphere of an elegant, luxe, New York City apartment party where she was the high-class entertainment for the evening. The set looked like a living room off the terrace of a penthouse. She opened each show with her theme song, "Tea for Two," then announced herself to the camera with a sultry "Hello, I'm Hazel Scott." Like Gertrude Berg and Betty White, she had a special relationship with the TV camera; her show-opening greetings were her calling card, her equivalent of Berg's Sanka commercials and White's ability to deliver lines straight through the lens to viewers.

From there, Scott deployed her mainstays, singing and playing numbers such as "'S Wonderful," "I'll Remember April," and "Hungarian Dance Number 5." The performance required adjustment for Scott, who was used to playing for large crowds in concert or on a crowded set with multiple takes on film. Now she played to a silent TV studio with a few camera people and sometimes her director, Barry Shear. And she had only one take; no do-overs on live TV.

Shear, then twenty-seven, had gotten his start directing the network's *Newsweek Views the News*, a public affairs series that featured *Newsweek* magazine editors. A white man with thick, sandy hair, he would go on to become one of television's most prolific early directors, overseeing episodes of *The Eddie Fisher Show*, *The Donna Reed Show*, *The Mod Squad*, and many others. Shear displayed an eagerness to make his mark in the new medium with *The Hazel Scott Show.*

Shear often employed unusual camera angles—sideways, diagonal—and quick cuts that required gymnastics from the cameramen, given the limitations of their 1950 equipment. Cameras were usually mounted in their pedestals and not built for easy movement, but Shear would have the camera operators pick up the cameras and tilt them, a process that required strength and created lower-back strain.

Scott's classy operation shone like a small, polished gem among 1950 television's glut of variety shows (Milton Berle's *Texaco Star Theater, Your Show of Shows, The Colgate Comedy Hour*) and game shows (*What's My Line?, Beat the Clock, Truth or Consequences*). A *Billboard* review compared Scott favorably to the glamorous white actress Faye Emerson, another female TV pioneer who had transitioned from films with a late-night interview show on CBS: "Pianist Hazel Scott, she of the luscious looks and talented fingers, may be Harlem's answer to Faye Emerson. The lady's très-telegenic."

Scott's show delivered better-than-expected Hooper ratings, with minimal objections from white viewers. It expanded from once a week on DuMont's New York affiliate to three times a week—Mondays, Wednesdays, and Fridays at 7:45 p.m. More work in New York kept her from flying around the country for other appearances, but it wasn't five days a week, so she could still play the Latin Quarter or another New York club if the opportunity arose. She had found an ideal arrangement.

An episode of *The Hazel Scott Show* in April, as described in reviews, demonstrated that the production had hit its stride. At the beginning of the episode, the camera appeared to pan across a cityscape and into the penthouse set. Scott sat at a grand piano in an elegant gown, her large brown eyes and warm smile greeting the audience against the backdrop of Manhattan.

She lit up the screen, and Shear's unique directorial style was on display. *Variety* called it "a neat little show in this modest package" and praised Scott's ability to reach viewers through the television: "Most engaging element in the airer is the Scott personality, which is dignified, yet relaxed, and versatile enough to switch from a reverent spiritual (accompanying herself on the organ) to a sultry torch tune. Lighting is used effectively, closing down at times to a small spot which can give the singer's face an exotic quality to point up a torrid mood."

On that April 19 episode, Scott performed the breakup lament "I'll Remember April" and the Broadway musical tune "Buckle Down, Winsocki," among other numbers. At the end, the camera panned out of the window on the set and back across the skyline once again. There, a billboard was lit with the commercial message from her tissue company sponsor: "Sitroux—Stronger—Softer."

During her newfound time at home, she loved to watch television herself. She enjoyed her fellow DuMont Network star Jackie Gleason's *Cavalcade of Stars*, and one of her absolute favorites was Gertrude Berg's *The Goldbergs*. She would watch it with Skipper, who was delighted at every "Yoo-hoo!" Berg trilled.

Scott monitored the programs for other Black stars. When she spotted another Black person on her television set—perhaps a Black singer on *The Ed Sullivan Show*, for instance, or even her husband's ex-sister-in-law, Fredi Washington, on *The Goldbergs*—she called her friends to tell them: "Hey, turn the channel, one of us is on!"

Scott was at the forefront of a hopeful movement toward diversity on television. A 1950 article in the Black publication *Ebony* reported, "Negro performers win better roles in TV than in any other entertainment medium." As many as ten all-Black shows of various genres had aired in recent months, the magazine said, likely including regional shows from across the nation. Popular Black stars, it reported, "are cast in every conceivable type of TV act—musical, dramatic, comedy. Yet rarely have they had to stoop to the Uncle Tom pattern which is usually the Negro thespian's lot on radio shows and in Hollywood movies."

In May 1950, the Hollywood trade publication *Variety* proclaimed in a headline, "Negro Talent Coming into Own on TV, Without Use of Stereotypes." The article said that TV's "insatiable demand for talent" meant that Black performers had more opportunities than ever. "The thinking," it said in its trade magazine parlance, "is that by being accepted as artists in their own rights during these early days of video, the colored entertainers can escape the stereotyping which they feel handicapped them in AM [radio] and pix [movies]."

TV overall continued its takeover of the American cultural landscape. Five million sets were sold in 1950, compared with just 172,000 two years earlier. Television was in nearly one-fifth of American homes and would be in almost 90 percent by the end of the decade.

The Zenith Radio Corporation began to market what it called a Lazy Bones, the first TV remote. It connected to the set by a cable; buttons on the remote turned the tuner clockwise or counterclockwise with a motor. It could also turn the set on and off. "Complete automatic program selection in the palm of your hand ... from anywhere in the room," a print ad bragged. It did not become popular; owners kept tripping on the wire that ran from the set across the living room to the sofa and the remote.

TV was reaching still more of the nation, and thus heading toward becoming an influence unlike any American culture had seen—the visuals of the movies combined with the ubiquity of radio made its potential force incalculable. The critic Gilbert Seldes argued that TV would eventually rise to the level of film in terms of cultural importance: "Without prejudice one thing can be said of the harassed men and women who have tried to make television an entertainment while it was running away with them as an industry: Television has undermined the confidence of the movies, revolutionized the structure of broadcasting, and seriously affected half a dozen other types of mass diversion without creating a single significant entertainment of its own. The natural question is: what will television do when its capacities are fully exploited?"

Thus far, television had remained mostly in the realm of the improvised to loosely scripted variety and game show formats as well as drama anthologies that presented a different story and characters every episode. Top shows, aside from *The Goldbergs*, included the drama anthologies *Fireside Theatre* and *Philco TV Playhouse*; the vaudeville-like *Colgate Comedy Hour*; and the boxing-centric *Gillette Cavalcade of Sports*. Groucho Marx hosted the game show *You Bet Your Life*. Milton Berle became one of the medium's first superstars with his variety program *Texaco Star Theater*—which earned him the nickname "Mr. Television"—and Imogene Coca and Sid Caesar weren't far behind with their *Your Show of Shows*. They were all optimal for TV's live broadcasting, which was both a holdover from radio and a technological necessity; it was much cheaper and simpler than filming and editing a show like a movie, though some series would begin to use film in the coming years. Videotape wasn't widely available or affordable for TV budgets until 1956.

But television's rising profile in American life—especially its diverse, progressive programming from stars such as Berg and Scott—placed it on a collision course with domestic worries about traitors. As its popularity grew and its massive influence on culture came into focus, it moved into the political crosshairs of the group that had taken down Hazel's old employer, Café Society, a year earlier. In the late 1940s, that group of conservative politicians had been fixated on movies, determined to stomp out what they called communism—but was often simply liberal ideals. Soon they would turn their aim toward TV stars.

Peace remained tentative in the years that followed World War II. Tension lay just underneath even international cooperative efforts: the North American Treaty Organization, for instance, was formed by the United States, Canada, and ten Western European nations as a bulwark against the Soviet Union and the spread of communism to its surrounding countries. After the Soviets' successful atomic bomb tests in 1949, US president Harry S. Truman started 1950 by announcing his approval of the development of the hydrogen bomb, a weapon hundreds of times more powerful than the atomic bombs the United States had dropped on Japan during the war. Albert Einstein warned that nuclear war could lead to mutual destruction for superpowers like the United States and the Soviet Union. And by the late summer of 1950, the United States found itself fighting the Soviets in an armed conflict by proxy, entering the Korean War on the side of the democratic South Korea while the Soviets fought for the communist North.

The Cold War was upon us, and fear of Communists gripped Americans. While TV occupied ever more Americans' living rooms, eyeballs, and imaginations, the powerful new medium became a target for this fear, which would turn to paranoia.

Hazel Scott found out from a fellow musician that her name was listed as a suspected Communist in the June 1950 special edition of a publication called *Counterattack: The Newsletter of Facts to Combat Communism* titled *Red Channels: The Report of Communist Influence in Radio and Television*. Many major advertisers subscribed to *Counterattack* to learn right away if controversy was coming for them. The cover of *Red Channels*, the size of a small paperback novel, pictured a red hand about to grab a black microphone. It cost $1 per copy on the newsstand ($10 in 2020 terms). It named 151 actors, writers, musicians, and broadcast journalists as possible Communist sympathizers. The group behind both the magazine and the book, American Business Consultants, consisted of former FBI agents who had created a company that purported to help radio and TV networks remain Communist free. They would vet talent and weigh in on new hires' possible Communist ties.

They were essentially running a government-aided protection racket: they promised to safeguard networks and advertisers from a threat they themselves had invented. They perpetuated a whisper network among film, and now television, executives, suggesting that certain performers might cause "controversy" and should thus be run out of show business. *Red Channels* took that whisper network a step further, and it was a powerful step: committing those "suspicious" names to print.

The introduction laid out the group's beliefs: "Several commercially sponsored dramatic series are used as sounding boards, particularly with reference to current issues in which the Party is critically interested: 'academic freedom,' 'civil rights,' 'peace,' the H-Bomb, etc. . . . With radios in most American homes and with approximately 5 million TV sets in use the Cominform and the Communist Party USA now rely more on radio and TV than on the press and motion pictures as 'belts' to transmit pro-Sovietism to the American public." That was bound to strike fear into sponsors, whose entire motivation for financing shows was to reach the greatest number of people in the most pleasant way possible—not to have their products suddenly associated with the United States' new Cold War enemy, the Soviet Union.

Those listed were accused of such crimes as attending meetings on civil rights, protesting censorship, and union organizing. Scott's listing included such possible Communist associations as the Artists' Front to Win the War, the Musicians Congress Committee, and the Civil Rights Congress. It also mentioned a performance she'd given, with several other Black musicians who regularly played Café Society, at an electioneering event for Benjamin J. Davis, Jr. Davis, who had declared himself a member of the Communist Party, was Scott's husband's choice to succeed him on the New York City Council; Davis did, in fact, win the seat. Scott also stood accused of supporting Soviet troops, which she had indeed done: in 1943, when the Soviet Union was allied with the United States in World War II, she and several other Café Society mainstays put on a benefit concert at Carnegie Hall to raise money for watches to be used by Soviet troops.

Wisconsin senator Joseph McCarthy, a Republican with prominent eyebrows, a constant glower, and thinning hair, had recently become the face of the anti-Communist movement, giving it a renewed boost in the public eye. A February 1950 speech in which he alleged that the US State Department was overrun with Communists and Soviet spies attracted national attention, which fueled his fanaticism. The practice of lobbing wild accusations and blacklisting those accused without evidence became known as "McCarthyism."

McCarthy and *Red Channels* perpetuated a new wave of the Red scares that had been rolling through the United States since 1919, when the Russian Revolution that eventually established the Soviet Union had coincided with the rise of the US labor movement, which shared some goals with the Russian Bolsheviks. The most recent iteration of the Red scare had come three years before *Red Channels*, when a new fear of communism had swept the

United States during the rise of the Cold War in the years following World War II. That Red scare had given rise to the House Un-American Activities Committee (HUAC), which was meant to investigate Communist influence in the United States. One of its most famous targets was the film industry, whose struggling actors and crew members had forged leftist ties with the labor movement during the Great Depression. Film was, essentially, an easy target for the paranoid grandstanding of the committee, though there is little evidence of a Communist agenda expressing itself in the movies of the time; and it's important to note that even if those accused were Communists, holding such beliefs was not illegal.

This previous Red scare wave had culminated in 1947, when dozens of people with Hollywood connections had been subpoenaed to testify before HUAC. Many did. But ten film writers, producers, and directors had resisted the committee, either refusing to appear or denouncing its tactics publicly during their testimony. The group, who had become known as the Hollywood Ten, had maintained their innocence but had been convicted of contempt of Congress and sentenced to serve a year in prison and pay a $1,000 fine. They had subsequently been blacklisted from official work in Hollywood, but many were writers who continued to produce work under assumed names after the ordeal. Blacklisting worked in a nebulous, unofficial capacity: Hollywood producers and executives simply wouldn't hire those understood to be blacklisted, without further explanation. Despite government officials' involvement, it was not legal. But it was difficult to fight, as a mere accusation could tar a writer or performer with being "controversial," which studios and later advertisers saw as sufficient grounds for dismissal.

The patriotism of Black Americans was particularly questioned, and they were therefore ripe for blacklisting. This was prevalent enough that in 1949, the baseball pioneer Jackie Robinson had appeared before HUAC to defend Blacks' loyalty, in general, to the United States. Thus Hazel Scott was all but assured a place on the 1950 list: she was a prominent entertainer, she was an outspoken progressive, she was Black, she was married to a rabble-rousing congressman, and now she had a television show.

Ironically, it was Scott who had first brought herself to the FBI's attention. In an attempt to do the right thing, she had reported a telegram she received in 1944 from someone who claimed to be FBI director J. Edgar Hoover. The message had asked her to work on behalf of the US government to root out Communists. The FBI never determined who had sent the telegram. But the report earned her a file at the FBI and eventually made her a target; the file noted her association with Café Society, which had been recognized as a leftist establishment and shut down.

The question now was how she would respond to her listing. She wondered whether there was any path toward clearing her name and keeping her television show, the best job she ever had, as conservative forces amassed to wipe out her burgeoning career, along with those of other progressive women and minorities who had so far enjoyed such freedom in the television industry.

Powell and Scott talked of little else after *Red Channels* was released. They wondered if Powell's place in Congress had anything to do with it. And she, in particular, wondered what she should do about it. She wanted to fight, just as she had when faced with so many other injustices: segregation, discrimination. She was considering appearing before HUAC voluntarily, but Powell thought that was a terrible idea. It would likely make the situation worse unless she groveled, which Powell knew Scott was not about to do.

Scott was joined on the list by her husband's ex-sister-in-law, Fredi Washington, and a number of others who knew one another from

the radio or TV version of *The Goldbergs*. That included Papa Goldberg himself, Philip Loeb.

Loeb was born in 1891 in Philadelphia. He broke into Broadway in a 1916 play called *If I Were King* at the Shubert Theatre
and went on to act in thirty-six Broadway productions and direct
seven. He also cowrote the screenplay for the 1938 Marx Brothers
comedy *Room Service*, based on a play by Allen Boretz and John
Murray that Loeb had appeared in onstage. By the time of *The
Goldbergs*, he had been divorced from his wife, the actress Jeanne
La Gue, for ten years; she had died in 1942, two years after their
split. He had one adult son who suffered from mental illness. Loeb
was paying for his son's ongoing care at an institution called Chestnut Lodge.

Loeb loved the theater but found something he loved even more:
fighting for performers' labor rights. He became involved with the
Theatre Guild and Actors' Equity Association, helping to forge support for an idea that was novel at the time: that actors deserved fair
treatment and fair pay for their work. That activism led to actors
being able to make a reasonable living at the craft. It also ultimately
landed him in *Red Channels*.

But at first there was little worry behind the scenes of *The Goldbergs* when Loeb was listed. Rehearsals and broadcasts proceeded as
usual over the next few weeks.

In fact, in late June, a *Newsday* reporter visited the set for a standard rehearsal, observing as the cast, crew, and visitors chatted and
rushed around to get the job done. "The set looks like nothing so
much as the lobby of a Bronx apartment," the paper reported. About
thirty-five people milled about *The Goldbergs'* soundstage inside
Liederkranz Hall, a four-story brownstone, German Renaissance–
style building on East 58th Street in Manhattan. It had been built
in the mid-1800s for a German music club but was now used as

studios for CBS television. The cavernous, acoustically well tuned space provided a perfect setting for television production.

The mood read as familial: people on set often addressed the actors by their characters' names, and the actors amicably responded to being called, for instance, Jake instead of Philip. A cameraman gave young Rosalie—that is, the actress Arlene McQuade—some "fatherly advice," while Berg told the reporter, "I raised my children along the same principles I use with 'Rosalie' and 'Sammy.'" There seemed to be no tension between Loeb and Berg or concern about the show's future.

Soon after that rehearsal day, *The Goldbergs* broadcast its final episode for the season on CBS. Then the entire cast headed west for two and a half months of making *The Goldbergs* into a movie—and assuming that nothing more would come of Loeb's listing.

After all, Berg and *The Goldbergs* dominated television and pop culture at that moment. The Boys Club of America had just voted Loeb "television's father of the year" for his portrayal of the harried, hardworking Jake Goldberg. M. Lincoln Schuster of Simon & Schuster continued to write admiringly to Berg, telling her in February 1950 that he and Mrs. Schuster "have marked down Saturday nights . . . as a special engagement deep in our affectionate regard for you and *The Goldbergs*."

CBS, looking to duplicate that success, approached another of its radio stars, Lucille Ball of *My Favorite Husband*, and asked if she would bring her show to television. She said yes, but only if her real-life husband, the actor and musician Desi Arnaz, could play her spouse. Network executives balked at the idea of their white star being shown onscreen married to a Cuban-born man—with an accent, no less, and sometimes even breaking into Spanish. Ball offered to do a test run: she would tour the vaudeville circuit with Arnaz that summer to prove that audiences across the country would love them together. After their successful run, CBS agreed to shoot a pilot episode with the two as the central couple. The show was set to run back to back with *The Goldbergs*. CBS was building one of TV's first sitcom lineups around *The Goldbergs*.

Berg's show was also about to become the first TV series adapted for film. It was one of the biggest TV success stories of 1950.

In March 1950, Paramount Pictures had purchased the screen rights for a *Goldbergs* movie. Berg was signed to a contract that would give her $3,000 per week as an actress on the film for ten weeks of filming, $7,500 for writing and supervising the film, and 25 percent of the gross box office receipts. She got first-class train travel and living expenses to film in Los Angeles. Her initial take would be more than $400,000 in 2020 dollars, plus a quarter of the film's profits.

The film's title, *Molly*, indicated Berg's star power nationwide. The script, credited to Berg and screenwriter/director N. Richard Nash, has son Sammy applying for college while Jake and Molly decide whether daughter Rosalie can go to camp. Work has taken a downturn for Jake. His misery is exacerbated when they get news that an old beau from Molly's teenage years, Alexander (played by Eduard Franz), is coming to town for a visit—and is unmarried. Worse still, Alexander has become a wealthy department store magnate known as "the Marshall Field of South Carolina."

Jake gets a reprieve when Alex arrives with his inappropriately young fiancée, Debby Sherman (played by Barbara Rush). Things get going from there: Debby stays with the Goldbergs in the city while she amasses her trousseau and happens to meet Molly's music appreciation teacher, Ted Gordon (played by Peter Hansen), who is handsome and closer to her age. Ted and Debby share an illicit kiss after a group concert outing. Molly's meddlesome instincts perk up:

she manipulates a breakup between Alex and Debby, a coupling between Debby and Ted, and, not to worry, another coupling between Alex and an age-appropriate widowed mother in the Goldbergs' building, Mrs. Morris.

The film itself appears to be lost, like so many of these influential women's artifacts, but the script, available in Paramount's archive, is sensitive, with lines like this from Molly: "The trouble with our language is it only has one word, *love*, for so many different feelings." It's funny, too. One of Molly's friends is chagrined at the advent of "show and tell" as a regular practice at their children's school: "Since show and tell, all the skeletons are out of our cupboards." Another woman replies, "You should hear what my Mercedes got up and said in class. I'm embarrassed even to repeat it."

The original draft of the script has a climactic Passover scene, with the Goldbergs sharing fish and matzos with their neighbors. The final film, however, takes great pains to orient audience members watching from other parts of the country and from other cultures and religions. After the Paramount symbol, the opening shot dissolves to an aerial view of New York City, with a narrator explaining patiently, "The great metropolitan city of New York is composed of five boroughs—Manhattan, Brooklyn, Richmond, Queens, and the Bronx." (Staten Island was known then as the Borough of Richmond.) We next learn that the family in question lives in the Bronx.

The studio required certain changes in the script before it proceeded, to further placate audiences far beyond the five boroughs: Alex's department store chain moved from South Carolina to Indiana. Debby's character was more clearly specified as "a young Gentile." And, most significantly, Passover became a regular dinner party that just happened to be on Shabbat. There's no record of Berg's reaction to those changes.

Berg and her entourage arrived in early summer on Paramount's Los Angeles lot to shoot the movie. To Berg's young costar, Barbara Rush, it looked as if Berg's entire extended family were arriving, every one of them with a part to play. In reality, it's possible that Berg's then twenty-seven-year-old son, Cherney, came along to help; he would later play a key role in production of the TV series. In addition, she brought her secretary, Fannie Merrill, with whom she was so close that they were like family; and her TV family, with whom she had enough chemistry to seem like a real family. It felt like a clan on a trip who happened to be making a movie together.

According to Rush, Berg graciously welcomed her costars and others who were not yet part of the Goldberg family. Rush was twenty-three at the time, performing in her first movie, and she was awed by the famous woman. Rush had spent most of her time onstage at the Pasadena Playhouse and she didn't have a television set, but she still knew who Gertrude Berg was. "Anybody in the world knew who she was," Rush told me. Because of the studio system, Rush hadn't chosen the role for herself, but she was happy to have been assigned to it by Paramount. Aside from her Paramount screen test, Rush had never seen herself on film. She had gone through the Paramount-mandated class on screen acting, and now here she was.

Filming went as planned over the quick, nineteen-day shoot, so the Goldbergs could get back to New York and resume their television show. Berg threw a wrap party at the Paramount lot to celebrate before they left Hollywood, complete with chicken soup and kreplach, blintzes, latkes, gefilte fish, and a six-foot-long loaf of pumpernickel.

At first, Hazel Scott's *Red Channels* listing had no effect on her television career. At the end of June, while *The Goldbergs* filmed in Los Angeles, *The Hazel Scott Show* expanded again, this time to five nights a week. *Variety* wrote, "Miss Scott is a lively performer. This Negro pianist has many showmanly attributes that help keep a viewer interested. She's no static performer. She gives the illusion of movement even in the headshots, having an expressive face which she uses to advantage." The publication even approved of the experimental camera work: "There are some interesting angle shots that help the overall of the show."

In July, *The Hazel Scott Show* got yet another promotion, this time from local to national. With that expansion, Scott became the first Black person to host a prime-time network television series. Though credit for "firsts" can be murky, the National Museum of African American History and Culture acknowledges her for the feat. And according to Carol Stabile's study *The Broadcast 41: Women and the Anti-Communist Blacklist*, even the museum initially forgot Scott's achievement, at one time listing 1970's *The Flip Wilson Show* as the first variety show to star a Black person.

Ethel Waters was the first Black person, male or female, to host a TV special way back in 1939, when very few people had televisions, on NBC. The cast of the onetime, one-hour show included Fredi Washington and Philip Loeb. Scott's achievement went much further, with a larger audience and a regular schedule.

It was astounding that Scott achieved this at a time when much of the American South was still segregated, given that she was an outspoken Black female civil rights activist. Her face beamed into white families' living rooms, even as the races maintained separate schools, restrooms, and water fountains in some regions. Though Scott was focused on the minutiae of producing a weekly, and then daily, TV show, her mere presence on the screen was extraordinary. Not only was she among the first Black people to host a variety show and the first to do so in a national prime-time spot, but she also brought her carefully calibrated image, under her own control, to television audiences. The show provided her steady work at a critical time in raising her young son, but it also continued her tireless activism on behalf of Black Americans.

That influence expanded as she went national. "Hazel Scott had carried her off-screen image—that of a political/social firebrand—to the little screen," the Black media historian Donald Bogle later wrote. "African American viewers watching her were aware of her past and what she might represent for the future, especially during the rise of the civil rights era. The modern Black woman—appearing regularly in American homes—had unexpectedly surfaced." She emerged as a forerunner not only to future Black talk show hosts such as Oprah Winfrey but also to icons of modern Black womanhood such as Phylicia Rashad's Clair Huxtable on *The Cosby Show*. Both came to TV thirty years after Scott and were still revolutionary in their own time. "There sat the shimmering Scott at her piano," Bogle wrote, "like an empress on her throne, presenting at every turn a vision of a woman of experience and sophistication."

In August 1950, *The Hazel Scott Show* was going strong. *Billboard* declared, "Here is a gal who deserves to become one of TV's leading personalities. . . . She should get longer and more frequent outings."

Just a month later, in September 1950, the forecast for both *The Goldbergs* and *The Hazel Scott Show* darkened. The *Red Channels* list claimed its first casualty: Jean Muir, who played the matriarch on the sitcom *The Aldrich Family*, was removed from the show, at sponsor General Foods' request, after being listed. Though General Foods and the network, NBC, claimed that a handful of audience complaints had prompted the firing, her listing—and *Red Channels* in general—didn't get mainstream press coverage until *after* Muir was dismissed. In fact, the complaints had come from activists who had already been preoccupied with anticommunism, as well as from groups with similar ongoing concerns, including the American Legion, Catholic War Veterans, and the American Jewish League Against Communism. The *New York Times* made its first mention ever of *Red Channels* after that small group's protests got Muir ousted on August 28, 1950.

The National Association for the Advancement of Colored People (NAACP) publicly supported Muir, a white actress who had worked with the group to fight against racism and advocate for better roles for Black performers. The organization also appealed to the FBI on her behalf and considered leading a boycott of General Foods, which she asked the group not to do. *The Aldrich Family* continued on without Muir.

The incident was enough to scare any performer listed in *Red Channels* but contained particular seeds of concern for *The Hazel Scott Show* and *The Goldbergs*. Scott had been involved with the NAACP through her activism and was likely paying close attention to Muir's situation. And *The Goldbergs* was sponsored by General Foods, which had demanded Muir's ouster. The September 9 issue of *Billboard* magazine, largely dedicated to the "hysteria" that had bubbled to the surface of the industry with Muir's firing, contained a small, foreboding item headlined "TV Character Actor Next, Say Rumors." It's impossible to know who the unnamed actor "on a top rated network show" was, but there's a good chance it was Philip Loeb of *The Goldbergs*.

The morning of September 16, two weeks after Muir's firing and a week after the *Billboard* item, General Foods' representatives, emboldened by their successful interference in *The Aldrich Family*, told Berg she had two days to take Loeb out of her cast or the company would end its sponsorship of the series.

Later that day, Loeb headed to Berg's Park Avenue home accompanied by a lawyer from Actors' Equity, Rebecca Brownstein. There, they met with Berg; her husband, Lewis; her lawyer; and her agent, Ted Ashley. Berg told Loeb about General Foods' threat, and according to a later account of the day by Loeb, she offered him $85,000 to buy out the remaining portion of his five-year contract.

"I don't want to take the money," he recalled telling Berg. "I want to fight it."

Berg understood and backed down. "I will not fire you," she said, hugging him. "I will stick by you." She agreed to sign him to a "run-of-the-play" contract, which meant he would be employed by her as long as *The Goldbergs* remained on television.

Afterward, she met with her children to tell them the news, an indication that she knew things could get ugly for her publicly. "I will not fire him," she reiterated to them. His political affiliation, she added, "has nothing to do with what he's doing for me."

Around the same time, Scott, her nerves wracked by the Muir case, decided to act. She asked to go before the House Un-American Activities Committee, using her leverage as a congressman's wife. She would clear her name and speak truth to power. The plan made sense: She was uniquely situated to make a difference for herself and others. She had political connections. She had spent her life speaking out about injustice. She knew she was not a Communist. She could save her own career and maybe help stop this McCarthy nonsense from taking down other innocent television stars. Though she had lost a few jobs by speaking out, she had also won many of her battles. Success didn't seem impossible.

Scott's young son, Skipper, knew she was determined to testify when he heard her talk about herself in the third person that fall, a telltale sign that she was fired up. "Your mother cannot just let these things happen without saying something," he recalls her telling him.

She continued, "I have to do this, it's just not fair. It's not right what they're doing."

Scott's husband, Representative Adam Clayton Powell, Jr., did not think she should testify. According to their son, "he thought it was the craziest idea in the world." But he also knew there was no stopping her.

The decisions Hazel Scott and Gertrude Berg would make over the next year, both of them trying their best to respond to the historic blow of the blacklist, would determine the fate of both women's promising and historic television careers and legacies.

6

What Are You Going to Do About Your Girl?

Hazel Scott and Gertrude Berg

The frustrated Hazel Scott called a press conference in New York City on September 15, 1950. She was certain that the world should be listening to her.

She told the assembled reporters that her DuMont television show had been growing at the time her name had appeared in *Red Channels* as a suspected Communist sympathizer three months earlier. About a half-dozen companies had expressed interest in sponsoring *The Hazel Scott Show*, she said, and it had now gone national. Then, she said, *Red Channels* had come out, and an advertising agency executive had asked her manager, Michael Vallon, "What are you going to do about your girl? She's in the book, you know?"

At that point she had realized her career was in danger,

she explained to the assembled reporters, and so she had asked the House Un-American Activities Committee for a chance to state her case before them and clear her name. The day before the press conference, September 14, she had traveled to Washington, DC, hoping to "go on." But the committee had told her they had previous commitments and couldn't fit her in.

So she'd taken another path: on this day, she was releasing her prepared statement, which denounced communism and excoriated *Red Channels*.

"This is the day for the professional gossip, the organized rumor-monger, the smear artist with the spray-gun," her statement said, referring to American Business Consultants and *Red Channels*. "The game of attacking and defaming your neighbor is not only practiced by the overzealous, the misguided and the super-patriot, but also by the Communists themselves to spread confusion, hysteria and ultimate panic."

Her lengthy statement, published in full the following week in an issue of *Billboard* dedicated to the blacklist crisis, also suggested that entertainment unions stand up for performers' rights: "I call upon my colleagues to present a solid front against the bigots—and against those networks, sponsors and agencies which seem willing to tuck their tails between their legs and knuckle under to the bigots. If an entertainer is dropped from a job because of a mere private accusation, the unions should forbid any other member from filling that job."

Scott's ordeal with the committee also highlighted suspicious connections between HUAC and *Red Channels*, which presented itself as an independent, quasi-journalistic enterprise. The *Chicago Defender* newspaper noted, "House Un-American Activities Committee's pussyfooting on Hazel Scott's request to voluntarily appear and clear herself of that '*Red Channels*' smear label strengthens rumors going the rounds that the four former FBI agents editing the sheet are working in collusion with the Committee. Or maybe Chairman Wood, a Georgia red-necker, can explain how the quartet quotes verbatim out of confidential committee files listing line and verse."

After the press conference, HUAC chairman John Wood—the "Georgia red-necker"—said the committee didn't have time in its schedule to host Scott for her full testimony. But Scott refused to accept his dismissal. She still believed she could make a difference in the battle against the blacklist, and for good reason: it felt, at the time, as though the industry had some fighting spirit. The issue of *Billboard* dedicated largely to the blacklist included a strongly worded editorial. "A method must be found to prevent innocent performers and other show business personnel from losing their means of livelihood," it said. "Showfolk must have the opportunity to defend themselves against charges that they are disloyal to their nation."

The continued public pressure worked. Wood changed his stance, suddenly finding some open time in his committee's schedule to hear Scott's testimony before the end of the congressional session.

On September 22, a week after Scott's press conference, HUAC granted her hearing. That rainy morning in Washington, DC, she arrived at the Old House Office Building, a white marble structure with huge colonnades like those of a courthouse.

She headed to room 226 to appear before the committee and Chairman Wood, a segregationist with connections to the Ku Klux Klan. At 10:40 a.m., the committee swore her in under her married name, Hazel Scott Powell.

Wearing a dark jacket and skirt with a white, lacy blouse and minimal makeup, she held her speech notes as she appeared before the committee. Wood made it a point to say that her appearance had been granted as a favor out of respect for their colleague Congressman Powell.

She countered each of the charges raised against her in *Red Channels*. She argued that the committee should stop requiring those listed to clear their names or face unemployment. She denounced the idea of "guilt-by-listing." She called her inclusion "a lie" and the list overall "vile and un-American." When asked if she was now or had ever been a member of the Communist Party, she replied, "I am not now, never have been, have never entertained the idea, and I never will become a member."

The prepared remarks stuck to the statement she had released the previous week, including calling McCarthyites "headline-seeking superpatriots." She concluded, "The actors, musicians, artists, composers, and all of the men and women of the arts are eager and anxious to help to serve. Our country needs us more today than ever before. We should not be written off by the vicious slanders of little and petty men. We are one of your most effective and irreplaceable instruments in the grim struggle ahead. We will be much more useful to America if we do not enter this battle covered with the mud of slander and the filth of scandal."

She explained that her appearance at a campaign function for Benjamin J. Davis, a known Communist, had been arranged "by direction of my employer"—Barney Josephson, the owner of Café Society, who had also managed her career at the time.

A committee member asked, "Did the publishers of this pamphlet ever contact you in order to verify any of these statements?"

She answered, "In no way. It was brought to my attention I was in the book. I never heard from them by wire, phone call, or anything."

She sparred at length with a white congressman, Burr Harrison, who asked, "What I am getting at is whether the listing is false or the information is false?"

"The information is false and the listing is unjustified," she replied.

"I don't agree with you it is a false listing," he later said.

Her response: "If you were in danger of losing your job because of this you would agree with me." She later said, "May I ask you a question? If any committee, an official committee, lists me as having two heads, does that make me have two heads, and does that give Red Channels a right to publish I have two heads?"

"They make no bones of the fact that they do not evaluate the listings," he later persisted.

Her answer: "They simply prepare a blacklist."

She had done what she could, what she always had done: she had spoken out when she saw people—including herself—treated unfairly. To her, that treatment wasn't just objectionable; it was offensive. The *Amsterdam News* celebrated: "As often and expertly as she has played Bach-with-a-boogie-beat, Mrs. Hazel Scott Powell has never struck a truer note than she did in her recent reply to *CounterAttack*."

The mainstream white press remained impartial, with headlines that matter-of-factly stated, "Hazel Scott Assails Listings of Artists as Red Supporters" and "Scott Denies Knowing Any Links with Communists."

HUAC appeared to regret having allowed Scott's appearance. A week later, Wood announced that there would be no more hearings by request. Only those named in other testimony before HUAC and/or called by HUAC could testify from now on.

The afterglow of her triumph did not last.

One can imagine Hazel Scott in her once idyllic Mount Vernon home, now assaulted by telephone calls full of bad news. Her testimony may have done some good in the long run, and it certainly allowed her to feel that she had personally done what she could to stand up for herself and others named in *Red Channels*. But the only immediate effects were evidence that her plan had backfired.

First, a week after her appearance before HUAC, she got word that the DuMont Network was canceling *The Hazel Scott Show* seven months after it had premiered. By her account, the ratings had been rising, but DuMont killed her show in mere anticipation of a protest. A network executive told an ACLU investigator later, "It was just that we felt we could more easily sell the time if somebody else was in that spot." Conservatives had effectively weaponized sexism, racism, and anti-Semitism through Americans' fear of communism and targeted it at Hollywood, with Hazel Scott's elimination as a prime example.

Then she had to hear about folks on what she thought of as her side of the whole ordeal, activists like herself, thinking she had "named names," the worst of sins on the left. This was apparently because she referred to Josephson in her testimony when explaining her appearance at the Davis campaign event.

Though he was never called before the committee as a result, her career-long relationship with Josephson, which dated back to her teens, ended instantly and painfully. Decades later, Josephson asked the jazz pianist Mary Lou Williams, "Why did Hazel do that to me Mary? . . . Why did Hazel do that to me after all I did for her?"

Finally, in the aftermath of the hearing and her show's cancellation, Scott realized she had little choice: to make a living, she would have to go back on the road. Once again, she had to post the carbon copies of her typed travel schedule on the kitchen bulletin board, so her son, Skipper, could at least know where his mother was at any given moment, since she would no longer be at home.

She booked an engagement at the Los Angeles nightclub Ciro's that started well enough, with her husband joining her for the first part in early November. But at the end of the month, she suddenly fell ill and had to cancel the rest of the engagement on doctor's orders, even though she was playing nightly to sold-out audiences. Her son recalls her returning home around this time, irritated by a doctor who had told her to drink "a couple malted milks" to build up her energy. For a woman who had to stay in show business shape, malted milks did not figure into any menu, no matter how grave her illness.

She had grown wary of her adopted country. Of the United States, she said, "It's so wonderful, they're ruining it."

Still she soldiered on. Accompanied by her son, Skipper, she headed down to Washington, DC, yet again, this time to attend her husband's swearing in the following January, the start of the 82nd session of the US Congress. It would be a much colder January than the previous year's.

Gertrude Berg was fighting the blacklist on another front, trying to keep her television family intact and the blacklisted Philip Loeb as her Jake Goldberg. *The Goldbergs* had pulled in an impressive one-quarter to one-third of all TV viewers during its run on CBS, which gave her significant leverage. She began meeting regularly with CBS president Frank Stanton and General Foods representative Clarence Francis in the hope of negotiating a compromise.

The discussions began with great hope but quickly took a turn for the worse. Stanton wanted Loeb to officially "clear his name" in public, perhaps appearing on Voice of America—a radio broadcast channel run by the US government—to defend himself. Loeb, however, continued to take a hard stance against any form of clearing his name, which he felt would lend credence to both the charges against him and, worse, those leveling the charges. He felt that such a procedure would be "humiliating." Animosity built between Loeb and

General Foods, which saw him as obstinate. Francis asked Loeb, during one meeting, when he might "remove the cloud" hanging over him.

Finally, Berg had had enough.

During a September 25 meeting, she threatened to launch a public campaign against General Foods' products if it insisted on sticking to its blacklisting policy. That was unheard-of and likely unprecedented. In a time when sponsors determined which shows lived or died and what went into their scripts every week, she was attempting to reverse the power dynamic.

She said she would "appear on every available platform from coast to coast," telling consumers not to buy General Foods' products.

That private pressure, no doubt helped along by Scott's public excoriation of blacklisting and the urging of the Actors' Equity Association, won them a reprieve: General Foods announced that it would lift its ban on entertainers listed in *Red Channels* and would support Loeb's continuing on *The Goldbergs*.

That should have been a historic moment, one that would have made a true hero out of Gertrude Berg. It should have been the moment when one woman wielded her power to stop the practice of blacklisting in the television industry by using its weakness—its reliance on outside sponsorship—to her advantage.

"Discussions are now taking place in the industry to find a constructive solution to the broad problems growing out of such disloyalty charges," the corporation's statement said. "In view of this development and in consideration of any who are associated with our radio and television programs, General Foods will temporarily suspend application of the company's long standing policy covering use of controversial material and personalities."

But the respite was short lived, as the statement made clear in its skillful use of the word *temporarily*.

Gertrude Berg tried to enjoy the relief of the *Red Channels* unpleasantness having passed, at least for the moment. She continued to meet with CBS and General Foods every thirteen weeks, when the show's contract was up for cancellation or renewal. The meetings were meant to find that "lasting solution."

Meanwhile, she tried to focus on what she loved: being Molly Goldberg. The show, after all, was still airing on CBS with Loeb as Jake, as if nothing the least bit unusual were going on behind the scenes.

Berg had played America's favorite Jewish mother for twenty-two years now. While she was very much Gertrude Berg–ing off camera in those meetings with CBS and General Foods, fans could hardly recall that she was *not* Molly Goldberg. Berg herself did not seem to mind this one bit. A typical headline on a profile of her read, confoundingly, "Gertrude Berg More like Her Amiable Molly Than She Is Herself." Even Procter & Gamble rep Bill Ramsey, a pro who'd dealt with her since her radio days, addressed a December 1950 letter to her "Dear Molly." He went on, "It shames me to realize how long it's been since we've held reunion. One of my relatively few vows for the New Year is to correct this situation by giving you a call at the earliest possible opportunity. . . . P.S. Olivia and I positively dote on the TV version of *The Goldbergs*." Often fans asked her to sign autographs as "Molly Goldberg," not "Gertrude Berg." She signed both names.

Another typical article on Berg promised, "Molly Goldberg Tells How to Make Blintzes." That was extraordinary for two reasons: One, Molly Goldberg was a fictional character. And two, Gertrude Berg did not cook. She rarely graced her own kitchen. But she knew how to find a recipe for blintzes and how to tell others about it for a pleasant media hit during what had been an unpleasant time for her and her show.

Her grandchildren insist that Berg never thought of herself, in the privacy of her own mind, as Molly. Frumpy Molly loved to cook, spoke with a Yiddish accent, and mangled English expressions. Gertrude Berg did none of those things. "She was always the very elegant, extremely well-dressed, well-spoken, accent-less Mrs. Berg," Adam Berg told me. "We were taught to speak like newscasters. Conversation, command of syntax, language, vocabulary, the ability to create complex sentences on the fly. . . . That was how we were measured."

Gertrude Berg did not mind being treated like a celebrity. She frequented Luchow's, an old favorite of entertainers on 14th Street, and Sardi's, a celebrity scene in the Theater District known for its walls adorned with caricatures of its famous customers.

She liked to go to Schrafft's restaurant at 58th Street and Madison Avenue, she and her husband, Lewis, elegantly turned out as always. They would pass through the revolving door, and everyone inside would clear a path for them. Then she would order her favorite, a soft-boiled egg, which came on its own tiny throne. She would whack the egg to pop its top off, ready to eat its warm, gooey contents. Once Adam remembers seeing her go through the ritual, take a bite, and declare, "This egg is cold."

"Well," he continued, "eight waiters descended from the ceiling on ropes like ninjas." The offensive egg and its plate were replaced with a new egg, throne, and plate in a blink. The new one proved satisfactory, and everyone breathed again.

Her grandchildren were far too young to understand who Gertrude Berg was in the entertainment ecosystem. But they quickly learned that she was *someone*.

Gertrude Berg, in reality, lived a life somewhere in between what viewers might assume about her as Gertrude Berg and what she portrayed as Molly Goldberg. Her nice, but not palatial, apartment sat at 829 Park Avenue. The two-bedroom duplex, which encompassed the building's second and third floors, contained living and dining rooms, as well as a kitchen and study. It faced north, with no particular view and not much natural light. It was next to Lenox Hill Hospital, so siren noise was standard.

Berg also maintained a twelve-room house in Bedford Hills in the suburbs north of the city in Westchester County. Her country home happened to be next to that of actress Tallulah Bankhead. If Berg had any parties, they tended to be there. Famous people did not frequent Berg's Manhattan apartment, which functioned at least as much as her corporate office as it did her home.

In Manhattan, the upstairs bathroom housed stacks of books such as Henry James's *The Bostonians*. The study, of course, boasted still more books. Berg employed a cook and a butler. A print of Raphael's *Madonna and Child* hung over her bed, a fact that, when reported in a profile of her, caused some consternation among her Jewish fans. She met their consternation with irritation. She had no interest in being told how to decorate her own home. The office included photos of Gertrude with various presidents and keys to cities, including St. Louis and Cincinnati.

When her show was in production, Berg spent twelve hours a day, six days a week writing scripts, auditioning and hiring guest stars, rehearsing, and performing. To unwind she'd have a sherry and a cigarette. She needed a fair amount of help around the house from her quiet, good-humored husband, Lewis; her cook, Louise Capers; and her dedicated assistant, Fannie Merrill. Her son, Cherney, was now grown and worked on her show, but while still a child, he had once written this telling poem for his mother: "Committee on Molly/Headed by same/Whose work shall consist/Of repeating her name."

Now that her children were adults and out of the house, they chose different ways to deal with their famous, workaholic mother.

While her daughter, Harriet, spent some of her adult years estranged from Gertrude over her feelings of neglect, they later reconciled and spoke frequently on the phone. Cherney took another approach: he worked as a writer and producer on his mother's television show, which meant she spent much of those twelve-hour days with or near her son as he served her creative vision and image.

Gertrude Berg had built her entire life—the apartment and the country home, the sacrificed family time—around and on top of her identity as Molly Goldberg. As 1951 progressed, Molly's life would face challenges like never before.

In 1951, television began to evolve even more toward the conventions we would come to think of as standard for the medium. Daytime soap operas began to gain traction with viewers, including *Search for Tomorrow*, created by the radio writer Roy Winsor. It was written by Irna Phillips's onetime radio protégée Agnes Eckhardt (now credited with her married name, Agnes Nixon). Phillips herself had yet to find success on television, but she was still atop the radio charts with *The Guiding Light* and dreaming up some new ideas for the screen.

Also that year, the Emmys recognized actors and actresses with awards for the first time—and both Gertrude Berg and Betty White were up for the first-ever Best Actress trophy.

At the third annual Emmy Awards ceremony in Los Angeles in January, the two were nominated along with Judith Anderson, Imogene Coca, and Helen Hayes. It's unclear why White was considered for the "actress" category instead of as a "personality," a more typical category for a host like White. It was a confusing time for TV, and especially for the Emmys, which were little more than a fancy dinner with some trophies.

This was the first year the ceremony bore even a little resemblance to the Emmys of today. Categories now distinguished dramatic, variety, game and audience participation, and news programs, rather than simply the one category of the first year (Most Popular Television Program) and the two of the second year (Best Live Show and Best Kinescope Show). And this ceremony recognized a Best Actor and a Best Actress for the first time. Previous years had honored only hosts in two categories, Most Outstanding Kinescoped Personality (stars of recorded shows) and Most Outstanding Live Personality.

On a humid January evening, about eight hundred people filed into LA's Ambassador Hotel, known best as the location of the glitzy Cocoanut Grove nightclub. The sprawling, Mediterranean-style complex had hosted six of the film industry's Academy Awards ceremonies between 1930 and 1943. Television was still picking up the film industry's hand-me-downs. Thousands of fans watched the ceremony live on White's home station, KLAC, sponsored by Dr. Ross's Dog Food.

California governor Earl Warren, an honored guest at the ceremony, predicted in a speech that TV would soon take over American life in ways that were still inconceivable and affirmed the importance of the nascent TV industry to the state. With his wire-rimmed glasses and slicked-back, white hair, Warren looked as though he could be a TV newscaster himself. The governor's presence—and his grand prognostications—gave the gathering of the Academy of Television Arts and Sciences a sense of gravitas, a feeling something important was happening. His speech concluded that television would have a greater effect on humanity than the atomic bomb: "Just like one book, the Bible, affected more lives than all the gunpowder ever invented," he said, "so will it be with television."

Pulitzer Prize Playhouse won Best Dramatic Show, Alan Young won Best Actor for his sketch comedy series, *The Alan Young Show*, and *You Bet Your Life* host Groucho Marx won Most Outstanding Personality, beating out Faye Emerson, the only woman nominated in that category. If there were any doubt that patriarchy was firmly in place, Marx swept that notion away when he grabbed the presenter for his category, former Miss America Rosemary LaPlanche, and carried her off the stage. He later explained that he'd thought she was the Emmy. The ceremony did not include official acceptance speeches, but he cracked, as he received his trophy, "I've been a good father to all my children and a good husband to all my wives."

The academy had added the actor and actress categories that year in response to complaints from film actors who wanted some reward for slumming it on TV and from industry executives who wanted TV to have its own Oscars. When the winners were announced as Berg and Young, however, the awards took further criticism. It seemed that the film-trained side of the industry would have preferred a separate category for comedic types to prevent the likes of Helen Hayes and Judith Anderson from having to compete with mere comedians in the future. In subsequent years, the acting categories would indeed be divided into comedy and drama.

Berg's win recognized her power and fame in the industry. The Emmys had begun two years earlier as a regional celebration for Los Angeles television, and even this ceremony had remained West Coast–centric, with KTLA winning five of the fifteen awards and the broadcast of the event appearing on KLAC. The new Best Actor and Best Actress categories ended up rewarding two East Coast nominees whose programs aired via kinescope over California stations, a testament to Berg's nationwide appeal.

Molly Goldberg remained as strong as ever with American viewers. The film version of *The Goldbergs*, titled *Molly*, opened to pleasant reviews and decent box office returns. *Variety* called it "heartwarming," noting that it had been "produced with excellent taste." Berg, it said, "hasn't allowed control of the film to escape her, and thus the flavor of the CBS-TV show is maintained." *Boxoffice* magazine called it "great fun": "This offers delightful entertainment to a ready-made audience of the many thousands who have followed the fortunes of the amusing Goldberg family for years on the radio and now also see and hear its members on television. It is a warm, human comedy jam-packed with real laughs, and a sure-fire attraction." *The Goldbergs* had become the first property to succeed in radio, television, and film.

But just a few months after Berg's Emmy win, Loeb received a summons to appear before HUAC. Though *The Goldbergs* continued to pull in impressive ratings—it was TV's number nine show in April, reaching 2.2 million viewers—that may have pushed the show's sponsor too far.

Around that time, Berg's agent, Ted Ashley, and her husband, Lewis, had a sit-down conversation with her at the Park Avenue apartment. They begged her to fire Loeb and salvage her career. Her daughter, Harriet, was there at the time, but not invited into the inner circle. She overheard the fight from the stairs, as she later recounted.

"No, I will not fire him," Berg reiterated. The men both told her they were sure she would be out at CBS as a result. The network and General Foods' reprieve had been truly temporary, and it had come to an end, with no mea culpa forthcoming from Loeb.

The Goldbergs signed off CBS for the end of the season on June 18, replaced on the summer schedule by the quiz show *Who's Whose*. A week later, the show was canceled by CBS. No one in the industry was fooled by General Foods' or CBS's insistence that the show had been ousted for "economy reasons," to be replaced with less expensive shows. (It cost about $11,000 per episode, putting it into the middle of the pack for top-twenty shows. Other, lower-rated CBS series cost more; April's number eleven show, the drama anthology *Ford Television Theatre*, for instance, cost twice as much.) "The Columbia Broadcasting System may deny it, but won't most of their 'Red Channels' listees find it necessary to earn their crackers and caviar on other networks next fall?" asked Jack O'Brian of the *New York Journal-American*. "Including Philip Loeb of The Goldbergs?"

Later, CBS president Frank Stanton would admit that the network had had to blacklist "to survive," though he blamed the US government and sponsors for pressuring him and other TV executives into the practice.

Stymied like never before in her career, Berg made an uncharacteristic move. Instead of using her hiatus to do a promotional tour or write or film a movie or stage a play or expand her brand with a new book or product line, she went on a trip. Some might even call it a vacation. It was her first in twenty-two years, though it's unlikely that she felt very relaxed. She had no intention of ending *The Goldbergs*. She was determined to find it a new network and sponsor.

Gertrude and Lewis Berg numbered among the excited travelers who bustled onto the *Queen Mary* in June. Gertrude told a reporter, "I'm going to find a nice quiet resort over there and sit back and rest for a month." Though she would be thousands of miles away touring Paris, Rome, Austria, and Switzerland, she wouldn't be able to leave work completely behind; she would use at least part of the time away to ruminate on the biggest questions yet of her two-decade career: how to save Philip Loeb and how much more to sacrifice for him.

Hazel Scott may have resisted touring, but since her health had recovered, she was back in Los Angeles proving that fans still loved her. Her tour broke ticket sales records, a fact, ironically, attributed to her television fame. Her show was likely still being shown via kinescope recordings on the West Coast at the time, and fans were ready to see her in person.

On television, representation of women and people of color waxed and waned in her absence.

The Chinese American movie star Anna May Wong got a show on the DuMont Network, *The Gallery of Madame Liu-Tsong*, the first US TV series to star an Asian American. Once again, DuMont had produced a historic first for a woman. She even played a detective. But it lasted for only ten episodes.

In June 1951, Amanda Randolph, DuMont's early daytime star and forerunner of Hazel Scott, returned to television. But this time, she appeared on the popular and widely criticized TV version of the radio show *Amos 'n' Andy*. Randolph's decision to accept a role on the infamous program was a testament to the complexity of navigating a television career as a Black woman at the time.

For television, the show would at least feature Black actors playing the Black title characters, instead of the white minstrelsy of the original radio program. But that development represented infinitesimal progress. The TV production of *Amos 'n' Andy* had been in the works for at least two years before making it on the air, facing obvious difficulties in the changing, but not yet changed, times. The TV series kept the radio theme, "The Perfect Song," originally written to score the white supremacist, pro–Ku Klux Klan silent film *The Birth of a Nation* in 1915. The white radio leads, Freeman Gosden and Charles Correll, who had been hired as the producers of the TV version, understood that they could no longer play the Black characters Amos and Andy on television but, astonishingly, considered hiring Black actors who would lip-sync to the white men's voices. Godsen and Correll eventually scrapped that idea, too, instead choosing the Black actors Alvin Childress and Spencer Williams as the leads and allowing them to use their own voices. Randolph played the prominent role of Ramona Smith, the mother-in-law of the sidekick character Kingfish.

Representative Adam Clayton Powell, Jr., was among the many critics of the show and its racial stereotypes. The Black newspaper the *Pittsburgh Courier* had encouraged protests of the radio version; now it organized a similar campaign against the TV show. The NAACP issued a clear bulletin about the show after its first two months on the air, titled "Why the Amos 'n' Andy TV Show Should Be Taken Off the Air":

1. It tends to strengthen the conclusion among uninformed and prejudiced people that Negroes are inferior, lazy, dumb, and dishonest.
2. Every character in this one and only TV show with an all Negro cast is either a clown or a crook.
3. Negro doctors are shown as quacks and thieves.
4. Negro lawyers are shown as slippery cowards, ignorant of their profession and without ethics.
5. Negro women are shown as cackling, screaming shrews, in big mouthed close-ups, using street slang, just short of vulgarity.
6. All Negroes are shown as dodging work of any kind.
7. Millions of white Americans see this Amos 'n' Andy picture of Negroes and think the entire race is the same.

The call for a boycott gained support from college students; the YMCA; the League of Women Voters; the Congress of Industrial Organizations; the American Federation of Labor; the United Hatters, Cap and Millinery Workers International Union; and the Improved Benevolent Protective Order of Elks of the World. The series lasted for two seasons but was canceled in 1953 despite strong ratings.

Hazel Scott, meanwhile, took her act from Los Angeles to London, where she played with another blacklisted performer, burlesque artist Gypsy Rose Lee (whose memoir was later adapted into the 1959 Steven Sondheim musical *Gypsy*). The two proved their continued power with audiences, playing to a sold-out crowd for their two-week engagement at the London Palladium. Scott proceeded from there on a tour of Europe that was expected to gross about $100,000.

Her husband and son joined her for some of the tour. On such trips the Scott-Powells learned to shift their weighty public roles, as Scott's fame outshone Powell's abroad. "We share each other's glory and find it great fun to be identified in terms of the other," Powell explained in an interview. "I'm as frequently referred to as 'Hazel Scott's husband' as she is as 'Congressman Powell's wife.'"

Powell often didn't fit in with the bohemian musicians, however. Backstage at a Paris nightclub, Powell, in a buttoned-up tailored tuxedo, waited with Scott. One of the musicians asked, "Hey, man, you gonna MC?"

Her transformation back to "Congressman Powell's wife" required an even more taxing kind of performance. The strain occasionally showed in their relationship. She sometimes missed her Café Society days, when she had known all of her fellow performers, had no reputation to uphold, and had gone back to her own home every night. "A person needs to go off somewhere and be alone so that his body can catch up with his soul," she said. "Before I got married, I did have some private life. But I find being a public figure and being married to a public figure makes privacy a luxury."

That feeling, plus the emotional impact of her blacklisting and its aftermath, began to take its toll.

But for the moment, she tried to forge ahead with work. While in Paris, she recorded a new album that included her TV show's "theme," "Tea for Two"; the jazz standard "Body and Soul"; and the original "How Blue Can You Get?" She played a week's worth of shows at Salle Gaveau, where she sang George Gershwin and Cole Porter songs in French. The audiences loved her, and she loved it there. She enjoyed the laid-back vibe and felt less restrained than she did in the States.

She also inadvertently made a different kind of recording there. The Scott-Powells stayed in a hotel run by the US armed forces, but they soon felt they were being watched. They suspected that the FBI had them bugged. She would shout out, "All right, we're going to bed now. You can turn off the tape recorder!"

One night Skipper wandered down the hotel hallway to an open door next to their room. When he looked inside, he saw microphones that appeared to be directed toward their room. "In case you're wondering, we'll be out until ten tonight!" Scott would call as they left for the evening.

Powell later inquired as to why he and his family were under surveillance. The FBI told him it was for their protection. But Powell knew that many of his colleagues in Congress didn't like the way he flashed his political power overseas. Even more, they didn't care for his military base investigations, which were meant to gather evidence for his efforts to help desegregate the US armed forces in accordance with the law. And FBI director J. Edgar Hoover was notoriously racist, fixating especially on the private lives of Black leaders; he later wired the hotel rooms of civil rights organizer Martin Luther King, Jr., in the hope of uncovering unsavory information to use against him.

By the fall, even Paris could not soothe Scott's weary body and mind. Offstage, her moods swung between sobbing outbursts and stony silence. The worried and desperate Powell took her to the American Hospital of Paris, where she was diagnosed with a nervous breakdown. Adam, Hazel, and Skipper flew back to the United States on a US Air Force jet, and her remaining tour dates were canceled. A short news item in *Jet* magazine reported her condition as "serious."

Once home, Scott went in for a psychiatric evaluation. She received no clearer diagnosis than that of "nervous breakdown," according to her biographer, Karen Chilton. A doctor prescribed Scott sedatives and electroconvulsive therapy, a standard treatment for major depressive disorders that had become popular in the 1940s. She showed little improvement, though. Powell arranged for staff to care for her and Skipper while he went back to Washington for the congressional session.

Scott preferred to keep her difficulties private and reached out to few friends. In her diary, she mentioned Judy Garland, Yul Brynner, and Errol Flynn as friends who had been empathetic during her struggle but offered no further details. She may have been referring to those celebrities' own legendarily addictive behaviors: she had begun to drink excessively and smoked two packs of Chesterfields a day. She gained weight and felt worse all the time.

Serious illness, in fact, was becoming all too common among the women of early television, a physical manifestation of the racism and sexism that menaced their careers as they tried to progress. Irna Phillips, in fact, was facing her own medical crisis as she tried, yet again, to bring her soap operas to television.

7

Aren't You Ashamed?

Irna Phillips and Betty White

Here Irna Phillips was, needing doctors again.

Phillips had checked into the hospital, an echo of the last crisis point in her life when everything had fallen apart before she had had the chance to escape Los Angeles. It couldn't have been a good sign to find herself surrounded by doctors and nurses once again, though this time she was in Chicago. Before, her guts had been twisting and cramping; now her heart raced and ached.

She had been biding her time with her successful radio soap opera *The Guiding Light*, waiting for her moment to try television again. And now, in making another run at TV, she had gotten herself so worked up that she'd gotten sick.

It had always been doctors, since the beginning, or at least the beginning of her adulthood. That charming doctor in Ohio had wooed her and charmed her and made her feel special. She couldn't help giving him her first time, like a young character on one of her soaps, and then she had found herself impregnated, abandoned, so far away from her home in Chicago and her trusted mother. But she didn't back down. She sued him and won with the help of Ralph Skilken, the boy who'd truly loved her.

Her life had gotten back on track afterward, thanks to her ingenious radio soap operas, most of all *The Guiding Light*. She learned that she couldn't bear children, but she realized she could raise them on her own, so she adopted a boy and a girl. Still, over and over, life had told her she couldn't do it all, couldn't have it all. Whenever her career prospects dipped, she panicked: If she couldn't provide for her children, what would happen to them?

Here she was again, in the hospital again, her career in question again. The last time she'd been in a hospital like this, the doctor had told her—nicely, benevolently—that it was all in her head. He had simply pointed to his head, not said the word out loud. Somehow that had made a difference.

What was it about hospitals? She knew hospitals; she liked the drama they provided. She liked to put them in her shows. She just didn't like to be in them. She always preferred that the drama stay on her shows, not in her life.

At a routine appointment in Chicago recently, her doctor had noted a concerning change in her cardiogram and admitted her to the hospital. After ten days there, the diagnosis was the same as it had been back when she had been hospitalized in Los Angeles for intestinal problems: she was too tense and needed to relax. Like Hazel Scott, she had landed in the hospital due to extreme anxiety caused by balancing too many conflicting roles and trying to accomplish too many things in a world that wanted to stop her.

She went home and tried to relax as directed. Really, she did.

But her brain wouldn't turn off. She couldn't go to sleep at night, she was so sure she would never wake up. How could they be certain her heart was fine? It didn't feel fine. Her brain churned in the night: if something happened to her, what would become of her children?

Tom was now eleven years old and Kathy nine. Phillips obsessed over who would care for her adopted children if she were suddenly gone. This was what happened when you raised children on your own, with no father: you worried about being their only source of care and love and sustenance.

Churning and churning: her will had named her brother Arno and his wife, Myra, as guardians. That wouldn't do. Arno had tried, but he didn't connect with the kids. After all the years of having a working mother who couldn't give them her full attention, after all the years of being without a father, now they would be stuck with the *wrong* man?

Phillips changed their designated guardian instead to her friend Bernice Yanacek, a single woman who was younger than Phillips. The children loved her and called her Aunt Neecie. Neecie loved the kids, too. After that, Phillips felt better. It turned out that in the end, after all her worrying about the children's lack of a father, she preferred another single woman to raise her children, rather than a man or a couple. She didn't think too deeply about that.

Phillips's latest bout with anxiety likely stemmed, in reality, from trying her damnedest to get *The Guiding Light*—her signature radio triumph, which had now been airing for fourteen years—to make the jump from radio to television. She had written and produced her own pilot episode, using her radio cast, footing the $5,000 bill herself—just to show the guys at Procter & Gamble, or any other sponsor who might want it, that her show belonged on television.

Now she had been waiting for months and months to hear back from P&G executives after she had sent them the tapes. No word had come.

The idea had struck her in 1951, after *The Guiding Light's* fictional

Meta Bauer had stood trial for murder—a sensational moment in the radio soap's life.

A former model, Meta had endured a lot, which was what made her such a good radio soap character: She had been romantically involved with Ted White, the head of the advertising agency that handled her modeling career. She had gotten pregnant with Ted's child, a boy named Chuckie, whom she gave up for adoption. But then she reunited with Ted and married him, suing Chuckie's adopted parents for custody. Ted and Meta won. But it turned out that Ted was abusive, and Meta divorced him. After another dramatic court battle over custody of Chuckie, this time Meta versus Ted, Meta emerged victorious—but Ted still had some visitation rights. During one visit with Ted, their five-year-old son died in a freak accident. Overcome with rage and grief, Meta went to Ted's house and shot him dead.

All that had happened during a few years of *The Guiding Light*. The show had returned to the top of the ratings after the drastic dip when it had been pulled off the air during the legal battle over its authorship years earlier amid Phillips's difficult sojourn in Los Angeles. Its comeback had been largely due to Meta's tribulations.

Meta's murder trial couldn't have come at a better time for Phillips and her television aspirations. In the fall of 1951, Phillips looked over scenes from those recent scripts and picked out the most melodramatic of all of them. It's not clear which she chose, but Meta's trial and insanity defense were prime candidates. Phillips reworked two fifteen-minute scripts to get them ready for television, even though, it should be noted, no one in television had asked for them.

By that time, Phillips believed she could succeed at bringing one of her radio serials to daytime television. She had watched as a new daytime TV serial called *Search for Tomorrow* had landed with audiences on CBS that September. The show had been created and written by three people Phillips knew well: William Craig, Procter & Gamble's head of television; The radio writer Roy Winsor; and Agnes Nixon. Phillips saw their success as proof that one of her creations would work on television.

She also used it as a chance to poach Nixon, whose talent Phillips felt was underrated and underused. Nixon had worked for Phillips in radio until Phillips's move to Los Angeles in the mid-1940s. Then Nixon had moved to New York to write for television, most notably adapting successful Hollywood films into hour-long dramatic scripts for the series *Robert Montgomery Presents*. She and Phillips had kept in touch, and Phillips had even talked Nixon through the early stages of writing *Search for Tomorrow* during one of her New York trips. "In my opinion she knew more about writing a serial than either Bill Craig or Roy Winsor," Phillips wrote of Nixon. "Unfortunately Bill Craig, who represented the program's sponsor, had a different opinion of Aggie's talent." Nixon was fired by Craig after just seven weeks. Phillips hired her to write for *The Guiding Light* instead.

Even so, Procter & Gamble approached Phillips, whose *Guiding Light* was now once again the number one daytime radio show, and asked her to take Nixon's place as the head writer for *Search for Tomorrow*. Phillips said she'd do it for $1,000 a week. They balked at her price.

No matter, Phillips told Craig. She was more interested in getting *The Guiding Light* onto television than she was in writing someone else's creation. "No one seemed overly enthusiastic," she wrote. Even her old friend at Procter & Gamble, Bill Ramsey, didn't rush to argue in her favor. He remained too focused on running the company's radio department, and unconvinced this was the right idea for Phillips's transition to television.

But Phillips believed in her project. Her two scripts for radio episodes adapted for television in hand, she traveled to New York to meet with the "unusually talented and photogenic" cast, producer David Lesan, and director Ted Corday. They agreed to work together to make a pilot tape.

While in New York for the taping, Phillips ran into Craig in front of the Waldorf-Astoria hotel. He had heard about her rogue operation and told her not to bother. *The Guiding Light* would never be on television.

Phillips sent her tapes to Ramsey anyway. And thus began the long wait for news that landed her in the hospital.

Los Angeles daytime star Betty White had an entirely different problem: she couldn't stop the jobs from coming in. By 1951, seven channels were broadcasting in Los Angeles. One of them, KLAC, might as well have called itself the Betty White Network. She was stepping out of the shadow of her cohost, Al Jarvis, to become a television personality in her own right, and she was consumed with work. In fact, daytime simply couldn't contain her anymore.

Luckily, she loved her work and wanted little else in life but to do more. But the next several months would buffet her about in a maelstrom of opportunities, endings, and new beginnings as TV itself began to find its footing—and figure out the right place for the talented jewel named Betty White.

She still cohosted *Hollywood on Television* for more than five hours a day, six days a week. KLAC gave the hosts a slight break when it added an afternoon movie to the schedule, alleviating a few hours of nonstop live broadcasting; however, Betty and Al still had to break in frequently to deliver commercials, so they weren't off duty. Then White added *The Betty White Show* to her schedule, on which she read viewer letters aloud and doled out romantic advice on Sunday evenings. (She bit her tongue and did not tell them all to stay happily unmarried as she was.) She sang, accompanied by the pianist George Tibbles. For the first episode, she brought her dog, Bandit, along "just for luck," she later said. He stayed at her feet the whole episode, enjoying every minute of camera time, so he became a permanent cast member.

Permanent was a relative term in TV at the time, however. After just a few weeks of *The Betty White Show*, White and Jarvis decided to do an hour-long evening show together instead, on Saturday nights, on which Tibbles also accompanied them. Jarvis pitched the idea of an amateur talent show, and White agreed: it would beat her reading letters and giving out suspect romantic advice. They even figured out how to tie the series to their daytime show: the winner of each week's talent contest would be featured as a paid performer for a week on *Hollywood on Television*. (One of their winners, the singer Gogi Grant, went on to have a number one hit with "The Wayward Wind" in 1956.) The name of the show is lost in time, though White has guessed that it was something like *The Al Jarvis Hour.* "Had we overextended our energies?" she later wrote. "Did we find ourselves exhausted after yet another hour on the tube? Not in the least. I can't speak for the audience, but we were fine."

To introduce her musical numbers and distinguish them from the contestants', she and Jarvis would do comedic sketches to lead into them. Tibbles, who had toured with the musician Eddie Cantor and written the popular "Woody Woodpecker Song" for the cartoon bird, turned out to have a knack for writing sketches as well. He became the show's main writer, replaced on the piano by Cliff Whitcomb.

Their comedy method landed somewhere between unconventional and nonexistent, but it marked one of the first times White was essentially writing and producing her own segments deliberately—even if she didn't quite see it that formally. Tibbles and White would visit Western Costume Company in Hollywood and look for something White liked. Once she chose her outfit, they'd come up with a song to go with it. Then Tibbles would write a sketch to lead into the song. "Oh, you like that gypsy thing?" White recalled Tibbles saying. "Okay—say we have a campfire—we get a funny fiddler—you tell a funny fortune, then go into 'Golden Earrings.'" Today we wince at the stereotype. But it worked okay for the audiences at the time, at least enough to get White through another show with a few laughs.

The second sketch of the evening always featured a fictional married couple Al and Betty had invented named Alvin (Al) and Elizabeth (Betty), though Elizabeth was the more distinctive of the pair; Betty was by far the more engaging performer. Impish and a bit manipulative, Elizabeth telegraphed her intelligence and humor as she traded witticisms with Alvin and then burst into song to end the skit and get back to the show. This sketch would eventually prove to be the key to White catapulting to even greater regional, and then national, fame—something this workaholic who loved being in television certainly had her eyes on by now.

But that was far from clear. That show, too, was to have a short life. Worse, White's partnership with Al—the guiding force in her fortuitous career thus far—was about to dissolve without notice.

Jarvis had often mentioned how much his wife, Marilyn, *really* wanted to be on TV. Marilyn had visited *H.O.T.* once in a while to sing a song or participate in a comedy sketch. "On a few occasions, however, Al had indicated that inviting his wife to guest on the show was the best way—and sometimes the only way—to keep the peace at home," White wrote. Though Marilyn had always been sweet to her, Betty wondered, mostly jokingly, whether Marilyn had herself a Betty voodoo doll at home as she plotted a takeover.

Instead, in 1951, White got a different, equally upsetting surprise: Jarvis resigned from their show to cohost a dance program with Marilyn on rival station KABC. "Whether Al was using Marilyn's ambition as a cop-out for jumping ship I will never know, but the dismal fact remained—he was leaving," White wrote. "I couldn't begin to imagine what would happen to our little show without Al." The evening show ended, too, with his move to a rival network. Everything suddenly seemed unsure after two solid years of certainty.

The ubiquitous film star Eddie Albert signed on as Betty's new Al on *H.O.T.* Albert had starred in *The Fuller Brush Girl* alongside Lucille Ball and with Cary Grant and Jimmy Stewart in several romantic comedies. Albert was also among the suspected Communists listed in *Red Channels* along with Philip Loeb and Hazel Scott, a fact the *H.O.T.* producers and White gladly looked past.

White loved her new cohost, singing duets with him, sharing commercial delivery duties with him, and becoming great friends with his Mexican American actress wife, Margo, who was also blacklisted. White spent late evenings with the couple, listening to them harmonize on Mexican folk songs and learning from them how to drink wine straight from a goatskin. White would fondly remember that the couple kept their Christmas tree up until April, brown needles and all, and that they called their newborn son "The Counselor" because he looked so serious in his crib.

Albert brought only a few major changes to *H.O.T.* He added his own regular vocal performance, singing a song called "Just Around the Corner" at the beginning and end of each episode. Singing, in fact, became a larger portion of the show now with the addition of

Albert and a small band led by Roc Hillman, the bandleader White had met on her first Dick Haynes special.

Albert had to adjust from luxurious film shoots to hours of daily live television. Among other skills, he had to learn to deliver advertisements, sometimes at breakneck pace. But his lack of experience with ads served him well on at least one occasion: under urgent direction from the stage manager to deliver the Laura Scudder's potato chips commercial very very fast, Albert brought that panic to the message. He rushed through a desperate, extemporaneous account of Scudder's trucks as they sped through LA to deliver chips that were as fresh as possible. The Scudder reps loved it so much that it became their standard ad message.

After six months on *H.O.T.*, however, Albert got an offer to play a major supporting role in the film *Roman Holiday* with Gregory Peck and Audrey Hepburn, about a romance between a rakish news reporter and a princess trying to escape her stifling life. (Albert would play Peck's beatnik photographer friend, Irving Radovich, in the film cowritten by the blacklisted Dalton Trumbo, fronted by Ian McLellan Hunter.) Suddenly shooting a film in Italy looked much better than delivering ads at dangerous speeds on live television for hours daily. Albert's time with *H.O.T.* and White came to a close.

After he shot his memorable part in *Roman Holiday*, Albert would return to TV to star in a sitcom called *Leave It to Larry* in 1952 and appeared in more than a hundred television roles afterward, including the 1960s sitcom *Green Acres*. He may have bounced back from his blacklisting, at least somewhat, because of his extraordinary record in World War II: as the pilot of a Coast Guard landing craft, he had rescued forty-seven US marines stranded after the November 1943 Battle of Tarawa, a confrontation between US and Japanese forces in the Pacific. His time on *H.O.T.* had certainly provided a useful transitional time for his career. His wife's acting career, on the other hand, never recovered after she was listed.

After Albert left *Hollywood on Television*, KLAC station manager Don Fedderson told White, "You've attracted a large following, and I think you're a good enough risk. From now on, you get top billing." In other words, she was getting a promotion: she became the show's sole host. And why not? Her schedule had become so much lighter with Jarvis gone and only the one daytime show to do. And she had certainly put in the work to become a dazzling solo host.

But the reshuffling of White's duties wasn't quite over. Not long after Albert's departure, Fedderson called another meeting with White—this time with George Tibbles, too.

White and Tibbles got a message one morning that Fedderson wanted to have lunch with them at noon at the Wilshire Country Club. White was dressed for the air. But the meeting came as such a surprise, Tibbles had to borrow a jacket from someone to throw on over his rehearsal clothes so he could honor the club dress code.

The two sat down across from Fedderson, a man with thick, dark hair and thick, dark-framed glasses. He was going into the production business for himself, and he wanted to take them with him. He was already producing shows that starred the pianist Liberace, the comedian Johnny Carson, and the violinist Florian ZaBach.

His offer: a half-hour evening sitcom based on the popular Alvin-and-Elizabeth bits from Al and Betty's nighttime show. Tibbles had often participated in their banter and had written most of it. White would be star and cocreator of this new show. Tibbles would be the head writer. They would have to hire an actor to play Alvin now that Jarvis had gone off to another show and station with his wife.

White was skeptical that they could make that five-minute sketch into a half-hour weekly series, but she was willing to try. *Always say yes.*

The three formed a production partnership, with the rest of the details to be determined. Betty White was about to cross over from daytime to sitcom star.

White didn't know it, but she was holding the line, in her own way, against the incursion of total patriarchy onto the television business. This wasn't something she thought much about, though. She was simply enjoying her idyllic life without considering its historic import.

She happily lived back at her parents' home in the Brentwood neighborhood of Los Angeles, amid their shared menagerie of three dogs and perfectly contemporary decor: Around that time, she liked to sit on the sparkly, rose-colored sofa in the living room surrounded by their dogs Bandy, Stormy, and Danny. Or she would cuddle with one of them while she read a script on a cushioned lounge bench trimmed in bamboo. Or she would sit at a lacquered desk and take business calls on the white rotary telephone.

After two marriages that turned out to be far less important to her than her career, her home life with her parents provided a respite. Her parents proved to be the perfect support system for her, cheering her on in her work and even contributing ideas sometimes; her parents, she said, "had delicious senses of humor." This was more than she'd gotten from her husbands, and now, she didn't even have to do the housework and cook the meals.

That all worked out just swell. White was more interested in playing a housewife on television than in being one in real life: she was starting her own company, Bandy Productions (named after her dog), with Tibbles and Fedderson to make her new show, to be called *Life with Elizabeth*. That placed her in a rare—and disappearing—class of female creator-producer-stars such as Gertrude Berg and Lucille Ball, who both appeared in front of the camera and maintained control behind the scenes.

White, Tibbles, and Fedderson hired the actor Del Moore, whom Tibbles knew from a revue called *Going Around,* to star as her husband, Alvin. "Both Alvin and Elizabeth had a tendency to be a little flaky and they may have had almost one good brain between them, but they suited each other just fine," White wrote. "Maybe the reason I felt so comfortable with Delsy right off the bat was that both he and I *were* a little flaky."

To address White's concern about stretching a five-minute sketch into a full show, each episode would feature three separate vignettes in the couple's life, lasting seven to ten minutes apiece. Jack Narz would serve as the announcer, who would help audiences track the "situation" of the comedy with messages such as "Incident number one in life with Elizabeth took place one summer evening when Elizabeth was trying to keep Alvin from noticing her black eye." In a fourth wall–breaking gambit, Narz would sometimes interact directly with Elizabeth, with Narz directing questions to her and White shrugging or nodding in response. (Alvin didn't seem to notice.) Both men ably supported White's star turn as Elizabeth.

As White described it, each vignette felt like "a little anecdote that you would tell somebody." That allowed them total freedom; sometimes they might even skip around in time, flashing back to Alvin and Elizabeth's first kiss or first date, for instance.

The first of the three situations would always end similarly: the frustrated Alvin would huff off, then Narz's voice would come in: "Elizabeth! Aren't you ashamed?" She would look right into the camera, eyes gleaming with mischief, and shake her head: nope.

One of the few female directors working at the time, Betty Turbiville, oversaw the production. White later insisted that that had nothing to do with fighting for women's equality; she was just trying to keep up with the work as it came. She understood that any of the roles—her own and others'—were precious opportunities that could disappear at any time. She hired other women when they were right for the job, and that was that.

Her schedule grew still more hectic. She continued to appear on the air during the day on *Hollywood on Television* for five and a half hours. She now logged more than thirty-three hours onscreen per week between the sitcom and the talk show. For the sitcom, she would squeeze in a Friday-night rehearsal, a Saturday run-through, and then a Saturday broadcast, in addition to her daytime work. The closest *Elizabeth* got to a writing process was when White and Tibbles carpooled to rehearsal and talked through the next week's episode in the car along the way. He'd take those ideas home and make them into a script by the following Friday morning, for broadcast the next day.

Life with Elizabeth aired on KLAC at 8:30 p.m. on Saturdays, live and in front of an audience from the Music Hall theater in Beverly Hills. White loved doing the show that way; she got an energetic thrill from the audience in the room and the viewers watching that very moment. The marquee out front read, "KLAC TV LUCKY CHANNEL 13 TELEVISION THEATRE." Crowds streamed in as showtime approached. The room always crackled with excitement, and as the show got going, White could see when jokes landed.

Once in a while, given both her workload and the live nature of the show, she'd realize that she had no idea what her next line was—while she stood there, dumbstruck, up onstage in front of the audience, the cameras rolling while thousands more watched at home. Often her costar would make up the difference, going to his next line or rephrasing hers for himself to get her going again. But every once in a while, they would lock eyes and both knew: neither one of them had any idea what they were supposed to say next.

One time it happened in a restaurant scene, that blank, panicked, I-got-nothing look as they met each other's gaze. Moore excused himself from the booth on the set and walked offstage, leaving White alone with no lines. But the table housed some prop salt and pepper shakers, which she made dance. The sugar cubes on the table became bricks for little houses. "I started having so much fun that I was almost sorry to see him come back," she later said. He did, however, return, lines refreshed in his head, and got the show back on track.

Other times, Moore jabbed at White in the hope of getting her to break up on camera. He would leave silly messages inside anything she had to use as a prop: a box, a compact, a pot lid. It became so common that she once picked up a hand mirror, sure she'd see something there—and then she cracked up when she saw it was just a plain hand mirror. "That monster knew me so well, he got the exact reaction he had counted on," she wrote.

At the end of a broadcast, Moore and White would return to the stage to interact with the audience and sing a few songs. Then, finally, it would be time for White to go home.

White headed to the local Emmy Awards ceremony in early 1952 a true Los Angeles star. She had recently won an honorary "mayor of Hollywood" title, voted on by the public at large, who could cast their ballots for ten cents each, with the proceeds going to charity. She also got a star on the Hollywood Walk of Fame.

The Emmys at the time were still more like a business awards dinner than the glitzy spectacle they were to become, but she still felt glamorous going as a nominee. As her date, she took a man named Rudy Behlmer.

She had met him on the lot at KLAC, where he directed several shows. He asked to take her to dinner some evening after she signed off for the day. She agreed, though she apologized that she would have to go in her on-camera makeup. The next day, he sent her roses with a card that read, "For a lovely girl—with or without makeup." Even if the relationship didn't last, it was a nice little diversion, and he made a fine Emmys date.

Now that it was a year after she had lost an Emmy to Gertrude Berg, she had no more confidence in her chances this time around, mainly because she was competing with Zsa Zsa Gabor. Born in Budapest, the Hungarian American bombshell hosted a quiz show called *Bachelor's Haven* that apparently put her into the same loose category as White. Gabor occupied a unique niche in Hollywood; she was a socialite turned performer who was known for her flirtatious persona, referring to everyone as "dah-link." She made her film debut that same year in *Lovely to Look At*. It seemed obvious to White that "Zsaz," as White called her, was the favorite.

After the dinner portion ended, the awards ceremony began.

Gabor perhaps thought she was a sure thing, too. As White told the story, the announcer called, "And now, outstanding actress." Gabor powdered her face, refreshed her lipstick, and put down her napkin in anticipation as White watched her, in awe of Gabor's beauty and self-confidence. When White's name was called as the winner instead, White later said, "I don't know which one of us was the most surprised." (White's biography says that this awards ceremony took place in 1953, though published accounts have placed it in 1952.)

A Los Angeles success, White's *Life with Elizabeth* soon caught the attention of a national syndicator, Guild Films. Guild president Reuben Kaufman told White, "You're wasting your talent on the California climate. You belong to the nation. I'll put you on film as I did Liberace." The musician had gone from a local Fedderson production to a national show with Guild, which filmed series that were then sold to whichever stations wanted them across the country. Liberace had become a friend of White and served as her occasional date to official, insufferable Hollywood functions. She called him "Lee." It made sense to follow him to Guild.

Tibbles and White had dreamed of that moment. They had been dying to go national. Fedderson negotiated a deal with "Reub," as White called Kaufman.

Alas, this meant no more live, intimate shows with Los Angeles audiences. They would shift to a studio setting to film their episodes with the director Duke Goldstone; they had to replace Turbiville with someone who had experience shooting film.

White would soon become a national sitcom star like Gertrude Berg. Berg herself, however, was struggling to retain her crown.

A Note of Sadness

Gertrude Berg and Hazel Scott

Gertrude Berg was once again trying to save her show, *The Goldbergs*, from a premature death by McCarthyism. You can imagine her as Molly, in a rumpled apron, wiping her sweaty brow, out of breath as always, but this time running out of cheery aphorisms to share at the apartment window.

With General Foods out as a sponsor—no more Sanka to ward off that irritability—CBS was out of *The Goldbergs* business. So while Berg was on vacation in Europe, her agent, Ted Ashley, was talking with the network's main rival, NBC.

NBC executives had done their homework. A summer 1951 internal memo concluded that *The Goldbergs* "has had, and does have, a high level of public acceptance even though there is a nucleus of confirmed non-viewers to the show. . . . In general, ratings have been strong and the extent to which they have fallen off in the past year appears almost entirely due to stronger competition."

The cost-benefit analysis looked promising. Audiences

across education and income levels loved the show, though the typical viewer was an older woman who lived in a large city. The only real concern, the report concluded, was standard anti-Semitism, which caused about 15 percent of potential viewers to avoid the program: "Because of the nature of the characters there are probably many advertisers who would not consider this as a buy," executive Robert W. McFadyen concluded dispassionately in a memo. "To me, that is probably the most serious drawback this show has." There was no mention of Philip Loeb's listing in *Red Channels*.

NBC took the risk and offered *The Goldbergs* a ten-year contract starting on October 1, 1951, paying Berg a minimum of $120,000 per year, with cancellation options at the third, sixth, and eighth years. Step one in Berg's recovery plan had come to pass: she had a new network on the hook for *The Goldbergs*.

But Loeb continued to wait and wonder whether that meant he still had a job. She had sacrificed her show once to save him. Perhaps that meant she would insist on keeping him as her television husband for good. But he wasn't part of the discussions between Berg and NBC, so he couldn't know for sure. And how much longer could Berg stand to be separated from Molly Goldberg while those decisions dragged on?

The stakes only seemed to be getting higher when it came to Loeb's place in *The Goldbergs'* future. He wrote to his friend the comedian Zero Mostel in early fall 1951, "Molly Goldberg, a well-known European traveler, returns from Europe next Wednesday. Curtain going up?"

After her arrival, she and Loeb met in person, likely at her Park Avenue home office, and she leveled with Loeb: she might have to sacrifice him to save the show and the jobs of the dozens of people it employed. If NBC couldn't sell the show to advertisers because of the blacklisting, she was going to have to choose the show. She still had a few long-odds ideas for saving him, but the outlook was dimming. "Mrs. Berg is getting ready to unload me," Loeb wrote to Mostel. "My visit with her was pleasant and discouraging. I'm girding my loins for the battle."

A few weeks later, Loeb was fraying. "Would more analysis help me?" he asked in a letter to Mostel. "I'd like to write affectionately to you but the truth WILL tumble from my fingers. A basic question! Will our lives go on much longer?" That could look like an overreaction to the prospect of losing a job he'd had for only a few years, especially given that he'd known for some time that he might lose it. But several factors were piling on top of one another by that point: He was an idealist who had been treated appallingly and persecuted for no good reason. He had tax debt and bills for his son's psychiatric care to pay. He was about to lose a dependable source of income, and he likely (and reasonably) also feared that he would never get another job after that one.

Berg's almost literal "Hail Mary" came in the form of an appeal to Cardinal Francis Spellman, the Catholic archbishop of New York. Spellman, an outspoken anti-Communist, had built a reputation for having sway with the House Un-American Activities Committee in getting blacklisted performers "cleared." A strong rumor suggested that Spellman had exonerated the Black activists and singers Harry Belafonte and Lena Horne at the request of Ed Sullivan, who wanted to have them as guests on his variety show.

But Spellman rebuffed Berg's request. She secured a meeting with him, according to her biographer, Glenn D. Smith, but it did not go well. "She said she never saw such a closed face like Cardinal Spellman's," Berg's daughter, Harriet, later said.

Of course, Sullivan was Catholic and Berg was Jewish. The blacklisted dancer Paul Draper said in a later interview that Sullivan had told him he could get Draper cleared to appear on his show, but only if he converted. "He said he could fix everything up if I joined the Church. I have never done any television since."

If Spellman had asked the same of Berg, that likely would have proven too large a request for her as well. In any case, Cardinal Spellman's name was forevermore detested in the households of Berg and her descendants.

Geopolitics weren't helping matters, either: the Korean War raged on, with the Soviet Union–backed North Korea still fighting the South, which was aided by US troops. The Cold War continued to intensify, reinforcing Americans' fears of Communist infiltration. For instance, teachers with Communist ties were banned from working in US schools at this time. Meanwhile, the US economy continued to prosper, which only increased the tension between "controversial" figures such as Loeb, and the money advertisers were now willing to pour into feeding audiences' consumerism. It was the dawning of the age of fast food, fast cars (the first Corvette prototype was unveiled), and rock 'n' roll—a term the disc jockey Alan Freed had recently coined. It was a good time to make money from advertisers eager to buy time on television and a bad time to be a suspected Communist.

On October 18, 1951, Loeb wrote to Mostel, "Things coming to a head in L'Affaire Berg."

While Berg and NBC scrambled behind the scenes to secure sponsorship for *The Goldbergs*—possibly with Loeb, possibly without—television's future came to erase its past.

Back when *The Goldbergs* was still on CBS, the network had planned to run a new show as a companion to it, which would have made perhaps the first powerhouse network sitcom night, on Mondays in the fall of 1951. Instead, with *The Goldbergs* off CBS, *I Love Lucy* would make Mondays its own.

Lucille Ball would costar with her real-life husband, Desi Arnaz, on *I Love Lucy* at 9:00 p.m. Eastern Time on Monday nights. The half-hour sitcom featured Ball, a forty-year-old B-movie and radio star, as the restless wife of a nightclub singer played by Arnaz. Within six months of its October 15, 1951, premiere, it was the nation's number one show, with 11 million households tuning in every week at a time when there were only 15 million television sets total across the United States.

Under Arnaz and Ball's Desilu Productions, the two stars retained crucial control over their show at a time when it was becoming increasingly difficult to stand up to the white, male, corporate forces controlling the medium. In retrospect, they serve as a model for the right way to launch a sitcom in 1951 and make it last, even with a woman and an immigrant man at the center of it all.

Arnaz and Ball's strategy, prioritizing their autonomy above all else, allowed them to not only resist conformist pressure but also to control and prolong their legacy. Ball hired a woman, Madelyn Pugh, who had worked on Ball's radio hit *My Favorite Husband*, as one of the show's main two writers. Arnaz and Ball insisted on shooting their show in Los Angeles, where they were settled and starting a family, instead of in New York City, where their sponsors wanted them to be based. In fact, they filmed a few blocks west of KLAC, where Betty White broadcast for more than five hours every day.

Because the couple wanted to remain in Los Angeles, they had to come up with a new way to shoot the show. Live broadcast wouldn't work for a national show produced on the West Coast, at least not when *I Love Lucy* was in the planning stages; the East and Midwest were joined by a cable network that would reach the West Coast just around the same time *I Love Lucy* was debuting, and no one would immediately be equipped to use it for regular weekly national broadcasts.

Lucy built upon *The Goldbergs'* shooting methods to come up with the first major innovation in the sitcom on television: the multi-camera setup, live in front of a studio audience, on film. That came about via Karl Freund, the German Expressionist cinematographer, whom Arnaz challenged to figure out how to light a set to allow for both a live audience—which the couple felt enhanced Ball's performance—and the multiple angles that would be cut together later as the final product. Whereas a live show like *The Goldbergs* switched from camera to camera at the director's prompts, *Lucy* had three or four cameras capturing a scene the entire time.

The multiple cameras allowed shots from several angles throughout one scene, while the live audience captured the laughter and energy of watching with a crowd. It was all recorded on film to be edited later, which was significantly more expensive than broadcasting live. Arnaz and Ball agreed to a pay cut to help offset the costs, a deal that in exchange gave them ownership of the film of the show itself. For decades their method would be the industry standard for half-hour comedies. Though other shows, including *Amos 'n' Andy*, used some variation of the method as well, the reason some shows continue to use it until this day is *I Love Lucy*'s success.

A significant unforeseen benefit of shooting on film emerged later: it preserved the show in pristine recordings, which allowed it to be shown in syndicated reruns for decades to come and now even to be shown via streaming services. *I Love Lucy*'s influence reverberates today because of this decision, whereas so many of its contemporaries are as lost to us as a Shakespeare stage debut, the low-quality recordings having long since disintegrated or disappeared. The bargain Arnaz and Ball made to shoot on film so they could remain in Los Angeles also paid dividends for the rest of their lives; they owned the films, so they reaped the syndication profits.

Arnaz, who served as executive producer of the show, received due credit for those innovations. But Ball's physical comedy differentiated *I Love Lucy* from any of the other TV shows translated from radio. For instance, her memorable candy factory scene, in which she shovels bonbons into her mouth and blouse as they speed by on a conveyor belt, would never have worked on the radio. Her undeniable influence as a creator, producer, and visual comedy genius would grow larger over the decade as many of TV's early female pioneers faded from view. She was the explosion that came at the end of a long line of women before her, and she would shine so brightly that those women's contributions would be forgotten.

As the Red scare raged on, several other women led the defense from the television industry.

Martha Rountree had created *Meet the Press* for radio after she had first conceived and produced a women's issues show called *Leave It to the Girls* ("a roundtable of romance featuring glamorous career girls") in 1945. She also worked as a magazine journalist for *The American Mercury*, and she created a radio spin-off called *The American Mercury Presents: Meet the Press* with its publisher, Lawrence E. Spivak. It debuted on radio in 1945 and came to television in 1947; it would eventually become the longest-running show in TV history. (It's still on in syndication as of 2020.)

Though men such as Edward R. Murrow won acclaim for defending the fourth estate during the McCarthy Era, Rountree was also pivotal, and she subjected Senator Joseph McCarthy to tough questioning on her show several times. In one of his appearances, she and her fellow panelists calmly asked him about his claims that there were Communists in the State Department, with Rountree leading the discussion and calling on her colleagues in her South Carolina accent. One of the journalists asked about rumors that he had gotten a gun permit. "The only weapon I am using, the only weapon I intend to use, is the truth and the facts," McCarthy answered, "and that is a much more powerful weapon than any gun."

Rountree went in for the kill with this question: "A lot of people say, senator, that they hope you win out and they are at your side but that they are against your tactics," she said. "This has been said by a lot of Republicans too. If you had to do it all again would you have changed any of your tactics?"

His answer: "Miss Rountree, if by tactics, I assume you mean telling the public what's going on in the State Department, I assume you mean that, and I'm not equipped to use laced-handkerchief-type of tactics. We may have to use lumberjack tactics, bare-knuckle tactics, if those are the only kinds of tactics that Communists understand ... then those are the tactics that we will use!"

On August 7, 1951, McCarthy appeared again on *Meet the Press*, this time toting a gun. He explained that he had received threats that a member of the audience would shoot him if he went through with plans to reveal the names of those State Department employees he believed were Communists. He arrived at the studio with his gun in a briefcase. He took the weapon out and kept it on his lap throughout as he sat next to Rountree. She kept her journalist's cool and calmly asked him questions. The episode ended without incident.

Meanwhile, the Screen Writers Guild responded to the continuing Red scare by bringing back its first female president, Mary McCall, Jr., who had originally served from 1942 to 1944. She had helped negotiate the first standard contract between writers and producers and set the rules for how to credit writers with work.

McCall had started her career as a fiction writer in the early 1930s and risen to the top tier of MGM writers with her working-woman hit *Maisie* before she made her mark as a tough negotiator on behalf of her fellow creatives. When she had negotiated that first contract, the film executives Harry Warner of Warner Bros. and

Paramount's Y. Frank Freeman, who feared a loss of control and a rise in script prices, had tried to intimidate her in meetings. Unfazed, she had asked the Paramount head, who sat across from her at the table, "Is Y. Frank Freeman a rhetorical question?"

Her return to the guild's leadership in 1951 signaled a new desire to assert writers' rights in difficult times.

The situation had spun well beyond Gertrude Berg's control, and that would not do, not one bit. Sponsors still weren't biting on *The Goldbergs* after its move to NBC, just as she had feared. And she was indignant at trade papers' stories about her failure.

A fall 1951 *Variety* story declared, "Sponsor Standoff Bewilders NBC in 'Goldbergs' Bid." It quoted unnamed sources who said there was a "'silent conspiracy' against the program as an aftermath to the 'Red Channels' Phil Loeb listing."

Berg dispatched her lawyer to have words with the network: their messy portrayal of the situation did none of them any good. The article indicated the sponsors had been offered the show without Loeb in the cast, even though he was still publicly, officially with the show. It's hard to tell from the article itself or NBC's, Berg's, or Loeb's records what precisely was going on at this moment, but there are several possible explanations. Perhaps the network offered sponsors a Loeb-free version of *The Goldbergs* without Berg's knowledge to gauge interest. Perhaps they did it with Berg's knowledge, and she was angry that word got out before she could speak to Loeb. Regardless, she did not see any value in displaying the mess to the rest of the industry.

Berg was in a bind that was tightening beyond what she'd thought possible. She wanted to fight for what she believed. But she also needed to make sure her show survived. Who was she if she wasn't Molly Goldberg?

Evidence indicates Berg and Loeb were still seeking a way to keep him on *The Goldbergs*—or, as she had originally offered, to support his income if he was dismissed. "I am hopeful I won't emerge from this mess altogether sunk," Loeb wrote to Mostel in December 1951. "Since I occupy the livelong day with discussion and maneuvers on this matter and return home with my head spinning, not knowing just what is taking place inside and outside my poor overloaded ex-brain, please excuse me from dwelling any further on this subject." He concluded with the kind of morbid joke that was becoming common for him: "You will find all details in my will. I am leaving you the green carpet."

Berg's agent, Ted Ashley, assured Loeb that Berg was "sticking to" him. "Will Gertrude really stick to me?" Loeb asked in the same letter. "Time will tell. Meanwhile you can say you believe I have a contract and that she's true blue. If she proves otherwise, can you help it if colors run in a strong rinse."

As it turned out, you cannot.

Berg called Loeb the morning of January 8, 1952. The time had come. The colors had run. "Philip, I have some bad news," she said, as Loeb later told the story. "I have sold the show without you."

Loeb was not surprised, but it was a major disappointment at a dark time. She continued, "I would rather cut off my right arm than do this. Maybe when the situation clears up, I will take you back. I would like to have you back, but I can't sell it with you; therefore I am going to let you go. My lawyer will call on your lawyer today."

The *Variety* story had been correct, if premature. As 1952 began, the program had a new network home, NBC, but no advertisers to pay the bills. Releasing Loeb was the only clear way to secure advertisers and keep the show alive.

Berg was tortured, but she had reached the end of her options. She had not only herself and Molly and the rest of the Goldbergs to worry about; she also had her crew, as she told reporters, "twenty people depending on the show for a living and their savings are dwindling." She continued, "It's unfortunate that after doing what I did, waiting for the situation to clear, that I had to go on without him."

NBC hoped that banishing Loeb would turn *The Goldbergs* back into a hot property. The network touted Berg's abilities as a pitchwoman above all. "At no extra cost," one memo reminded the NBC sales force, "Gertrude Berg (Molly) will write and deliver some of the commercials in her inimitable, effective style." A network advertising brochure mimicked her Yiddish-inflected English with this come-on: "So recently, Molly sold a beverage (you should sleep)—and 57% more customers were gained among those who watched her than among those who didn't. And that's meaning an increase five times over as big as the average for all other TV programs advertising, you should excuse it, coffee."

It worked.

Finally, there were some takers: NBC was now trying a modified approach to advertising, moving away from the single-sponsor vestige of the radio business to allow multiple sponsors to split the costs of a show, closer to the modern model we're used to for network television. *The Goldbergs* would be paid for by Vitamin Corporation of America, the manufacturers of Rybutol supplements; the Ekco Products Company, which made kitchen tools; and Necchi sewing machines. Company representatives said they had been offered *The Goldbergs* without Loeb. The new sponsors had not demanded his ouster, they said, but had come on board only afterward. That shifting of responsibility did not go unnoticed: on January 22, 1952, the American Civil Liberties Union responded with a letter to Berg that asked who exactly had been responsible for his dismissal. But no answer is recorded.

Loeb released a statement that absolved Berg of blame:

> Despite the fact that I believe a grave injustice is being done to myself and others in the entertainment industry by this "blacklisting," I appreciate Mrs. Gertrude Berg's position throughout this situation. I see nothing gained in this particular case by creating a situation which will interfere with the return of *The Goldbergs* or which would deprive other actors of employment on this show or disappoint millions of viewers who have been looking forward eagerly to its return.

George Heller, the national secretary of the Television Authority, one of the unions backing Loeb, did the same, saying the organization wanted to "commend Gertrude Berg for her courageous stand during the past one and a half years against blacklisting in broadcasting. We appreciate that her discontinuance of Philip Loeb's services was necessitated by broad pressure beyond her control and does not constitute a reflection on Mr. Loeb."

After Loeb's departure was announced, he received several letters of support as well as donations to help with the loss of his job. The cast and crew of the Broadway play *I Am a Camera* sent him a donation, with a letter that said they were "most appreciative of the fight you are making against the blacklist," and they wrote "with gratitude and thanks for what you are doing indirectly for us." (The amount of the donation is not specified in the letter preserved in Loeb's archives.)

George R. Stryker from Bayport, New York, wrote, "It is hard to find words to convey the feeling one has when he sees a fellow human being crucified, because he believes in and has fought valiantly for the rights of his fellow men. You are a man of great courage."

A fiery 1952 editorial in the deceptively bland-sounding publication *Who's Who in TV & Radio* excoriated the TV industry for the hasty firing of Jean Muir back in 1950—and perhaps shed some light on Loeb's firing as well:

> It developed that she had been listed in *Red Channels*, that a few zealous, self-appointed policemen of the airwaves had found this out, and that a handful of protesting telegrams and 20 telephone calls had frightened Young & Rubicam, the advertising agency, and/or General Foods, the sponsor, into firing Miss Muir. Amid the resulting hue and cry, one of the men back of *Red Channels* entered the lame defense that "we've never said the facts in *Red Channels* were correct or incorrect." (So if a reputation was ruined, they felt sorry but blameless.) And the people back of the Jean Muir firing said they didn't necessarily believe those correct or incorrect facts; it was just that she had become "controversial" and if there was anything a sponsor couldn't stand it was that.

By the end of January, the final loose end of Loeb's time on *The Goldbergs* was tied up: the Television Authority negotiated a settlement that would give Loeb 90 percent of his pay for the remaining two years of his contract, about $76,500 total, from Berg, who owned and produced the show. He would receive weekly payments. But they would run only as long as the show did; the theory was that he would be paid almost as if he were still on the show, as long as it was on the air. As a result of the deal, TVA would not list *The Goldbergs* on its own counterlist to *Red Channels*, which labeled certain productions as "unfair."

Though that period is not as thoroughly documented in Berg's archives as some others, Loeb's archives contain one letter of complaint sent to her and copied to him. (NBC also received at least a few letters of complaint, according to copies kept in his archive.) For example, Luba Aronoff of New York City wrote to Berg, "I have been pained to find that the author and editor of one of my favorite programs has so yielded to mass hysteria as to fire and keep fired one of the more capable of the staff of the Goldbergs. Certainly Mrs. Berg, you must have known Mr. Loeb personally and certainly also you must have found him a good person to do business with, an artist and an American, a man whose beliefs perhaps being centered upon bettering the conditions of the people around him might have seemed peculiar or subversive to that neo-fascist clique which seeks to rule or ruin our economy with character assassination. As an admirer of your program which strikes so aptly into the hearts and problems of so many of us and which gives us from time to time such hope and encouragement in the solution of our own problems, I was disappointed in you."

There's no record of Berg's feelings about such complaints, which were tellingly preserved in Loeb's archives, not her own. When it came to Gertrude Berg, what she left out of her public statements— her interviews, her archives—was her comment on her personal reckoning with these issues.

What she seemed to be saying with her silence in this case was *This was not how it was supposed to go.* She had become one of television's first unlikely conquerors! At the age of fifty, she had won herself an entire second life in show business by bringing her successful radio show to television at just the right time. By that point in 1952, she and Loeb should have been celebrating their triumph as America's favorite TV mom and dad on the cover of *TV Guide.* They should have been right up there with Lucy and Desi.

And even with the blacklisting debacle, there was a way she could have seen them making it. Even more triumphant! In some alternate timeline, Gertrude Berg bravely stood up to General Foods, company executives saw the error in their ways, and her show was back on the air before long, fans all the more cheered by Berg *and* General Foods having done the right thing. In that timeline, maybe her victory would have even stopped blacklisting tactics from proliferating in television. Maybe it would have helped to turn public opinion against McCarthyism overall. Maybe Gertrude Berg's and Hazel Scott's stands against the blacklist both would have added up to something better together. Maybe Hazel Scott would have guest-starred in an episode of *The Goldbergs* as a knowing wink to their shared bravery. *Maybe, maybe, maybe.*

Instead, here was Berg, choosing between her life's work and her obviously ineffective stand against the blacklist. How much longer could she be expected to allow that life's work to slip away toward irrelevance while she kept losing the same fight? Her stand began to lose meaning as the months passed. What good would it do to allow her show to die a quiet death behind the scenes?

But surely Berg was at least a little disappointed in herself, too, for failing to find a way to save her coworker's job. And she was likely even more disappointed in the industry she had shown so much faith in when she had entrusted it with the crowning achievement of her life, Molly and her Goldbergs. General Foods' successful ouster of Loeb, and of Jean Muir on *The Aldrich Family* before him, signaled how much power advertisers would have over television as it came into its own—and how scared TV executives were of any suggestion of controversy. TV would grow into a notoriously safe and bland medium for the next several decades—a "vast wasteland," as Federal Communications Commission chairman Newton N. Minow would describe it in 1961. Loeb's blacklisting was one of the first, and most ominous, signs of the conformity that television would demand.

Now Berg faced a more practical problem: whether to write out the character of Jake—by killing the character or sending him away, for instance—or to recast him—swapping a new actor in for Loeb, as if he'd never existed. She settled on recasting. A death, after all, would weigh quite heavily upon her light family comedy; a divorce perhaps even more heavily, wrecking the memory of the Goldbergs' warm marriage and breaching a major taboo of the time.

Recasting Jake was painful, and Berg had no examples to follow. It was one of television's first recasts of a major character. *The Lone Ranger* swapped John Hart in for Clayton Moore as its title character at around the same time, to much viewer backlash. Though the practice was common in radio, where actors couldn't be seen— Berg had had two other Jakes during the show's radio run—no one was sure how it would go over on a prime-time television hit. Later, recasting would become a frequent maneuver, from Darren on *Bewitched* in the 1960s to Becky on *Roseanne* in the 1990s and on many, many daytime dramas in between. Even so, it was always risky to mess with cast chemistry.

Likely as a result of this pressure and her grief over letting Loeb go, Berg couldn't find the right man. Some actors refused to consider the role, acting in solidarity with Loeb. Plenty of others did want the job, though, and Berg sat through audition after audition. She saw thirty-five actors who hoped to replace Loeb. None quite got the idea. Just days before the show's scheduled return on February 4, 1952, she still had no Jake.

She called the actor George Tobias, a Broadway veteran who had fled to Hollywood. She flew him in from Los Angeles to try out for the part but in vain. She didn't see anyone but Loeb as Jake.

According to Arthur Sainer's *Zero Dances: A Biography of Zero Mostel*, at that point Berg offered the role to Robert H. Harris, who had carved himself an early niche on television playing bad-guy characters on drama series such as *Suspense* and *The Adventures of Ellery Queen*. But Harris turned it down. So just forty-eight hours before *The Goldbergs* went live again, Berg asked Harold J. Stone, a Broadway and movie actor who at least bore a resemblance to Loeb, with a full head of wavy gray hair. He agreed to take the job.

Stone was concurrently appearing on Broadway in the World War II play *Stalag 17*. He would pull double duty, filming the live fifteen-minute broadcast that started at 7:15 p.m. on Mondays, Wednesdays, and Fridays and then dashing to his Broadway role nearby. That worked out just fine, as Berg was still mourning Loeb's absence, and her scripts gave the new Jake little to do anyway. To make matters worse, the show was also transitioning from weekly, thirty-minute episodes to thrice-weekly, fifteen-minute vignettes. It did not go particularly well.

The critic John Crosby wrote, "The New Jake Goldberg—Mr. Stone—was made up to look like the old one as closely as possible and had nothing much to say as if he didn't quite know his own family very well yet. . . . 'The Goldbergs,' once one of the most highly rated shows on television and one of the early successes, limped back on the air again last week, mighty subdued, its earning power diminished, its chief male actor missing, its format extensively re-arranged."

A mid-February episode demonstrates how the move to NBC, the compression from thirty minutes to fifteen, and the loss of Loeb sapped the series of its luster. Halving the running time changed the show from a character-driven sitcom to a sketch. The February 13, 1952, episode, for instance, centers on a bit in which Molly's extended family members visit to haggle over who will get to use

Cousin Simon's Florida vacation home for each of five weeks in the summer. That forces Molly to choose between her midterms—she's working toward a college degree—and the trip. It's essentially a one-joke, one-room setup with one punch line.

Molly has only an extra minute or so to make a detour to the kitchen, where the show has banished Jake for expediency, away from the family discussion, and he is sitting with son Sammy. As Sammy scarfs down a leftover chicken leg before going back to college, Molly notes her husband's lack of lines. "Jake, why is it when it's my family assembled, you become a man of very few words?" she scolds.

"And if I had something to say," he replies, "who would hear me?"

The *New Republic* may have said it best when it surmised that viewers "may detect a note of sadness in the popular program of Jewish humor—Philip Loeb, who so aptly played the part of soft-spoken Pa (Jake) Goldberg, has left the family." The transition felt to some viewers, according to Berg's family members, as though Molly was cheating on her husband.

Loeb still wondered if he could get his old job back. "Have I given up all right or claim to be reinstated?" he wrote in his personal notes two days after the show's return. "What shall I do?" He continued the next day, "Summary I am an innocent victim of blacklisting, which TVA condemns and promises aid on. I ask the union to aid me to demonstrate my innocence and assist me in clearing my name before the public and reinstate my employability."

Through a contact, Loeb received advice from US assistant attorney general H. Graham Morison in an unofficial capacity. Morison thought Loeb should sue the sponsors of *The Goldbergs* (General Foods), the network (CBS), and *Red Channels*. He told their mutual friend in a letter passed on to Loeb, "It does not make much difference whether he wins the suit, the publicity and the opportunity for him to speak to the American public through the lawsuit will afford him the only forum I know of by which he can call to the attention of the American people the great injustice that has been done to him behind closed doors." Morison did not mention Berg as a possible defendant in such a lawsuit.

Some newspaper clippings from the era mention Loeb's intention to pursue a lawsuit, but there's no evidence that he took the intention far enough to make it to court. (The radio talk show host John Henry Faulk, who also lost work after being named in *Red Channels*, did win a $3.5 million lawsuit against the publication in 1962. He ended up collecting $175,000.)

The new version of *The Goldbergs* soldiered through the season, delivering solid ratings and a well-received Passover episode that featured thirty-four seder guests and more than 597 special items gathered by the show's crew. In fact, the series returned to high enough demand that an internal NBC memo in May reminded ad reps that *The Goldbergs* was spoken for by Vitamin Corporation of America, would continue to be sponsored in the fall by Vitamin Corporation of America, and no further rumors should circulate down at everyone's favorite watering hole, Hurley's, that any other company could even have a chance with *The Goldbergs*. The rumors were upsetting Vitamin Corporation of America.

Loeb continued to visit the set on occasion to see his former TV family, "as a friend, a genial spirit," Arthur Sanier wrote in *Zero Dances*. Otherwise, Loeb and Berg rarely saw each other or talked after his dismissal.

Later that spring, Loeb was compelled to testify, along with fellow performers Judy Holliday, Burl Ives, and Sam Levenson, before the Senate Internal Security Subcommittee—roughly the Senate's equivalent of the House Un-American Activities Committee. Loeb did not name names in his testimony and was left in a kind of black-list purgatory, not proven guilty but without his name cleared.

As 1952 unfurled, television was becoming big business. The cost of a black-and-white television set had dropped to less than $300 (nearly $3,000 in 2020 terms); it was a significant expenditure at the time but about half the price of a similar-sized set four years earlier. And those who didn't have big living room sets bought smaller sets or watched at neighbors' homes. With 15.3 million TVs in use across the United States, a third of the country's homes could now tune in, up from less than 1 percent in 1948. And the first transcontinental coaxial cable was now up and running, which meant that nationwide live simultaneous broadcasting was possible. Television could now originate anywhere—most importantly, on the West Coast—and be seen almost anywhere.

The American Federation of Radio Artists, the main union for radio actors, merged with the Television Authority and became the American Federation of Television and Radio Artists. The new union set fair minimum rates based on ten-, fifteen-, thirty-, and sixty-minute shows, only to run into one problem: Betty White's *Hollywood on Television*, which aired thirty-three hours per week. If the show had to pay union rates, her paycheck would bankrupt the production. The union decided to place the show in a special category, though she still got a $400-per-week raise, with a seven-year contract that called for raises of $50 per year. She could make $750 per week by her seventh year if the show went on that long. Meanwhile, a new national morning show debuted on NBC that combined the entertainment elements of White's local show with more serious news reporting to make the *Today* show, hosted by the radio and TV personality Dave Garroway. It was the start of a new genre that would become a mainstay and cash cow for networks, the morning show. Long gone were the days when networks couldn't figure out how to program daytime hours.

The television industry still worried about how to make its advertising-based profit model sustainable while improving production values and expanding programming. But television was coming into its own. TV allowed corporations to sell products directly to consumers more compellingly than radio. It helped to put new brands on Americans' radar: sales of Hazel Bishop lipstick, for instance, increased from $50,000 a year in 1950 to $4.5 million in 1952 thanks to TV ads. (Founded by Bishop, the company made smear-proof lipstick—"Stays on YOU . . . Not on HIM!"—that used a formula she'd concocted as a chemist.) The same year, General Dwight D. Eisenhower's presidential campaign placed television's first political ad. TV commercials had already become iconic enough to spoof: *I Love Lucy* ran a 1952 episode called "Lucy Does a TV Commercial," in which Lucy gets progressively more drunk as she tries to tape a spot for a brew, Vitameatavegamin, that could have been made by *Goldbergs* sponsor Vitamin Corporation of America.

There were now 108 stations in sixty-five cities across the country, and that number was about to balloon. A Federal Communications Commission freeze on station licenses for the previous four years, enacted to give the agency time to come up with a plan to allocate stations, was lifted in April 1952, the commission's plan finally in place; that allowed for 1,875 new commercial stations across the country.

CBS invested heavily, opening its Television City production studios on a twenty-five-acre lot at Fairfax Avenue and Beverly

Boulevard, which began to shift the network's center of gravity from New York to Los Angeles. The entire industry would shortly follow to consolidate movie and TV production in one region, with the national cable network now reaching the West Coast. The sprawling CBS complex consisted of several squat, modernist buildings, none of them rising more than a few floors high, all of them combining stark black-and-white surfaces with lots of glass. It would become an icon of television production for decades to come.

The exponential growth unnerved the movie industry. Television was on its way to achieving the historic level of influence Governor Earl Warren had predicted at the 1951 Emmy Awards. Movie ticket sales dropped by 40 percent as more Americans stayed home with their new television sets. The tension between the TV and movie industries was so great that the Motion Picture Association of America prohibited its contract players from appearing in television roles. Desperate movie theaters tried to compete by using what they called "theater television," showing select TV programming on their big screens, particularly sports events and political news coverage, in the hope of recapturing audiences.

There was money to be made in television. TV had gone mainstream, and the progressive vibe of its 1940s era was disappearing, a victim of McCarthy's crusade and the big business invading the airwaves. The women who invented television were now fighting an influx of powerful men into a booming industry.

Among the many Gershwin tunes Hazel Scott was apt to play was "A Foggy Day (in London Town)," which she would start plaintively, with a spare piano line, as she sang of being alone on the streets of the city on a particularly gray day. "What to do, what to do, what to do?" her voice pleaded melodically.

The song, as she performed it, would eventually shift to a boppy beat as she signaled the change in mood—"The age of miracles hadn't passed," the lyrics cheered—with her smiling, flirtatious delivery. But at that time in her life, she felt as though she were stuck in that dark opening verse.

At one time not so long before, she had loved to boast about being a "holy terror," giving the racists she encountered a kind of hell they likely had never expected from a young, Black woman like herself. She hadn't just shot them a look or told them they were wrong, either; she always used the most explosive weapons in her political arsenal. She had led a work stoppage on a major movie set. She had caused a national uproar over a segregated concert venue in Washington, DC, and forced the president of the United States to take notice. She had sued a restaurant that wouldn't serve her and made headlines. She had walked out of a segregated Texas concert and made still more headlines. And it had worked, on some level, every time. She had drawn attention to her cause and sometimes, as in the case of the movie, effected clear change.

Her blacklisting had been different. This time, every decision she'd made—though morally right—had gone terribly wrong. She had lost her show, she had lost friends, and she hadn't made any discernable dent in McCarthyism. Her testimony had come and gone, and the boycott she had suggested had never come to pass. Actors were still losing TV jobs because of *Red Channels*, and no one seemed to be doing a damn thing about it.

The Hazel Scott Show had been special. It had been the perfect job at the perfect time, a way for Scott to be near her young son as well as a landmark achievement with the potential to make a difference for women and Black people in television. But it was becoming clear that no matter how talented she was, and no matter how firm her place on the moral high ground, that job was not coming back, and no similar jobs were forthcoming.

Now she was having morbid thoughts.

She tried to soothe herself with alcohol and cigarettes. That, along with prescription medication, sent her still further into a downward spiral. She does not appear to have reached out to anyone for help at that time, likely to guard her precarious public image. (Perhaps she was following the advice of her mentor Billie Holiday, who had told her, "No matter what the motherf***ers do to you, never let 'em see you cry.") Scott's biographer, Karen Chilton, reported that at that low point in late 1951, "she is believed to have taken a handful of pills in an attempt to take her own life."

Scott's congressman husband, Adam Clayton Powell, Jr., was traveling for his reelection campaign. He received word of Scott's attempted overdose and returned home. Scott remained in the hospital for several weeks, and Powell worked to keep her crisis out of the press. The cancellation of her concert dates was explained as due to illness in general or influenza specifically.

Scott returned to the family's Mount Vernon home to recover. She did her favorite things: cooking, knitting, decorating, gardening, and spending time with her five-year-old son.

She took great pride in Skipper, calling him "very self-sufficient." He now attended Riverdale Country School in the Bronx, a private college preparatory primary school for boys, and he embodied the worldliness he had acquired on their family's trips abroad. Scott took him to Sardi's on West 44th Street in midtown Manhattan's Theater District, a place known for its Broadway star clientele—with signed celebrity caricatures on its walls to prove it. Scott went there early one evening to show off her five-year-old date. Afterward, she recalled proudly that the other patrons "were delighted by the way Skipper pulled out my chair for me and in general acted like a gentleman."

Scott began to feel like herself again, at least privately.

By May 1952, she was back in top performance shape. She returned to Carnegie Hall to play a full program of Gershwin music with the New York Philharmonic-Symphony Orchestra. A few months later, she headed to Los Angeles to record her first album for Capitol Records. The result, *Hazel Scott's Late Show*, is an instrumental tribute to the American composers Richard Rodgers and Lorenz Hart, Jerome Kern and Harold Arlen, George Gershwin, and Cole Porter. She added some swing to new American classics such as "The Way You Look Tonight," "I Get a Kick Out of You," and "That Old Black Magic." Powell was reelected to Congress.

Her blacklisting's aftermath continued, mostly without her participation. The American Civil Liberties Union filed a complaint in April 1952 with the Federal Communications Commission against TV stations WPIX and KOWL, as well as the national networks NBC, ABC, DuMont, and CBS, accusing them of wrongfully terminating artists "on the basis of alleged past and/or present beliefs," including Scott. The ACLU asked the commission not to renew the networks' licenses unless they added a no-blacklist clause to advertising contracts.

The ACLU accused DuMont of canceling *The Hazel Scott Show* "probably because of alleged pro-Communist affiliations, when she is in fact violently anti-Communist." DuMont's lawyers denied the blacklisting accusation. The network responded (apparently without irony) that such charges were "both unfounded and lacking in responsibility." Scott's contract, DuMont said, had simply expired, and her sponsor had not renewed. "With a relatively low popularity rating (next to the lowest in the four networks), the show became a liability, financially and program-wise, to the DuMont Network," its statement said. Never mind that it was a common occurrence for DuMont shows to rank as "next to the lowest in the four networks"— that phrase could have been DuMont's unofficial tagline. Beating ABC was often all it could hope for. The network cited the show's "high cost," $400 to $600 per fifteen-minute installment, and called the show "discarded merchandise." As further evidence of its inno- cence, DuMont pointed out that it had allowed Scott to appear on the network in the time since her firing, most likely a reference to her appearances on *Cavalcade of Stars*.

Even as the networks and government agencies debated the consequences of Scott's blacklisting, there was no doubt that to many, Scott had risen to the occasion and become a hero. The fa- mous bandleader Duke Ellington praised Scott in the pages of *Eb- ony* magazine for her talent, intelligence, and political awareness—as well as her "exciting man," Adam Clayton Powell, Jr. "Remember how she went straight to the Congress and told her story," he wrote. "She didn't apologize for wanting and contending for justice for American Negroes. She didn't deny that there were insidious propagandists who had tried to use her. She wasn't defending herself. She was de- fending America and what it ought to be. . . . It demonstrated that we still have the kind of country where reason, intelligence and skill can live and breathe."

Scott had been a beacon of hope, even though the television in- dustry had not. Gertrude Berg, Irna Phillips, and Betty White were not done fighting that industry, now dominated by white men, from their own corners. And they were about to pull off some surprising victories, big and small, despite the forces arraying against them.

9

Dramatic Pause

Irna Phillips, Gertrude Berg, and Betty White

A blond woman in a dark dress named Trudy can't believe what she's hearing: her older sister Meta, an elegant brunette, is about to go out at 10:30 at night. Even more shocking: Meta is going to say good-bye to some friends. She's leaving town. Trudy asks, "Don't you want to discuss what happened between you and Bruce?"

Meta looks down, bemused. "Nothing happened, Trudy," she says. "It's just that I've finally decided to do what I've been wanting to do ever since I came to New York: go back to California."

The organ music plays, and the scene cuts to black. Then a man appears onscreen, eating a chicken drumstick. "Believe me, Tom didn't always look so happy when he was eating my fried chicken," a woman's voice tells us. The camera switches scenes to follow her in the nearby kitchen. "He used to say my fried foods tasted greasy. And they did! I used to be fine with those ordinary fats then. And you know, they often have a taste and smell of their own that can drown out natural flavor. But then I changed to Crisco. And what a difference!" She hoists a tub of vegetable shortening toward the camera.

The Guiding Light had at last made it to television. After months of silence, Procter & Gamble executives had traveled to Chicago to take Irna Phillips and her secretary, Rose Cooperman, out for dinner and announce the good news: Phillips had proven herself with her tapes.

And now she finally seemed to have a TV winner on her hands. At the age of fifty-one, she had created her first hit television soap, the screen version of her radio juggernaut *The Guiding Light*. In 1952, while Gertrude Berg was struggling to recast her television husband after firing Philip Loeb and Hazel Scott was recovering from her emotional breakdown after being blacklisted, Irna Phillips premiered her first successful television project at last. *The Guiding Light* was the first soap opera to transfer from radio to TV.

The Guiding Light's story line picked up on TV right where it had left off on radio: Meta had moved on from her murder trial by dating the newspaper reporter who had championed her innocence, Joe Roberts. But she declined to marry him because his teenage daughter, Kathy, didn't like her. Instead, Meta had run off to New York, where her sister, Trudy, lived with her husband, Clyde. There, Meta dated Clyde's friend Dr. Bruce Banning.

Unlike the clumsy, experimental rollout of *These Are My Children*, Phillips and her crew now knew how to put her scripts onto the screen. They had developed a signature style similar to her radio soaps, with most of the melodrama unfolding during hushed dialogues between characters in living rooms, punctuated, of course, by organ cues. By that time, Phillips regretted the organ music that had been her signature from almost the beginning of her career, but it was an inescapable part of the formula. "I know for a certainty that organ music is the one element most people immediately associate with the serial," she wrote. "Why did I turn to the organ for background music? *The Guiding Light* was the first program to use this music, and the explanation, in this instance, is logical. Mary, the daughter of Doctor Rutledge, was the organist in his church." Phillips now realized that the organ music had "come to annoy me and has probably annoyed many listeners and viewers." But they were all stuck with it now.

Phillips wrote succinct scripts that were perfect for live television. It was essential to cut down on the dialogue the actors had to memorize to put on a daily show, where they couldn't be seen on camera reading off paper (or visibly gaze at a blackboard off camera that contained their lines). Phillips and other soap writers had learned to balance the amount actors had to do in a given week, often giving a cast member more lines on Tuesday, for instance, if he didn't have as many on Monday. If a director complained that a script was too short, Phillips would ask that the actors take more dramatic pauses. She loved pauses and made no apologies for them. She complained to one writer in a script critique, "Please let me repeat, as I have in the past, make better use of pauses." The actors learned to fill their pauses with long, pensive looks onscreen, per Phillips's direction. This remains a central, defining trope of classic daytime soaps, still lampooned, for instance, in *Saturday Night Live*'s recurring soap opera sketch, *The Californians*.

By that point, the sponsors most interested in soap operas had also cracked the code for bringing them to television. They knew to run them in blocks of similar programming, rather than stranding a fifteen-minute soap alone in a lineup, surrounded by other types of shows. "You've got to have at least two strips in a row, and it's better to have four," explained Roy Winsor, the soap opera producer-director who had recently switched sides and taken a job as an executive at the Biow Company ad agency. He was referring to the soaps by the technical term "strips," called that because they ran at the same time across the entire week's schedule. "Then [the shows] have a magnificent corrosive effect on the audience." TV soaps must, Winsor said, also favor emotional arcs rather than physical ailments, which were common tropes in radio soaps: "There's not so much amnesia and creeping diseases of the foot as on radio," he said.

In contrast with prime-time sitcoms such as *The Goldbergs*, daytime soaps had gotten used to swapping out actors in the same part when a cast member got a different job—a more common occurrence in daytime, which required the drudgery and commitment of daily broadcasts. "In a few weeks everyone accepts the new man as Martha's husband, Peter, or whoever he was," Winsor explained.

The Guiding Light was the first soap to successfully transition from radio to television and run on both simultaneously—just as *The Goldbergs* had been the first sitcom to do so. Cast members Jone Allison, Herb Nelson, Susan Douglas, Lyle Sudrow, and Charita Bauer played their roles both for the cameras and for the audio engineers who broadcast the series to the radio audience live from the New York studio. Phillips was paid for both the TV and radio versions, although they were the same. Director Ted Corday made sure his actors played to both media. Phillips's trusty sponsor Procter & Gamble underwrote the entire endeavor on CBS. It advertised its Ivory soap, which made *The Guiding Light* literally a soap opera, along with another of its products, the Crisco that made Tom's wife's fried chicken so good.

The show premiered at 2:30 p.m. Eastern Time on June 30, 1952. It would run every weekday at that time. The *Variety* review complimented the production, if with great restraint: "While it's difficult to judge the production credits on the basis of a single installment, the two sets used on the initialer, plus camera work and other mountings, reflected careful planning on the part of producer Dave Lesan and director Ted Corday."

Though Phillips believed in herself as a businesswoman and believed that her audience full of housewives was valuable and worth taking seriously, she had not completely resisted the country's overall lean toward the right. She wrote, "I had also come to believe that I had made a serious mistake in writing stories of strong women and weak men for too long. The climbing divorce rate of the 1950s alarmed me. I had begun to question just how much influence daytime serials had on this rate."

These thoughts aligned with the times, as army general Dwight D. Eisenhower, a Republican, swept into office on a landslide victory. The 1952–53 season showed that television was finding its place in the American Dream vision of the time, full of sock hops and white middle-class teens slurping up milk shakes alongside idealized versions of law and order. *The Adventures of Ozzie and Harriet* starred the real-life Nelsons—a white, suburban, middle-class, perfect family. And *The Lone Ranger* and *Dragnet* brought us white, authoritative men who neutralized the dangers of the world. *The Lone Ranger* featured a title character who was a white former Texas Ranger who seeks out vigilante justice in the American Old West with a Native American sidekick named Tonto; *Dragnet* set the tone for all future police dramas, depicting LA police detective Joe Friday as a soothingly competent, no-nonsense cop who always gets his man.

The white men of the Eisenhower era would take over and erase women's legacies in television. The women would have to fight for their basic career survival, and to defend any life choices that deviated from the nuclear family norm: remaining single and child free, like Betty White, for instance, or raising children without a father, like Irna Phillips.

The battle between HUAC and Hollywood revived once again, emboldened by the conservative climate to churn out yet another round of inquisitions. The actor Lionel Stander, called to testify, spoke to the committee with a cigarette hanging from his lips in a sign of deliberate disrespect. He offered an ironic pledge to fight "subversive" elements: "I know of a group of fanatics who are desperately trying to undermine the Constitution of the United States by depriving artists and others of life, liberty, and pursuit of happiness without due process of law. . . . I can tell names, and I can cite instances, and I am one of the first victims of it. . . . [This is] a group of ex-Bundists, America Firsters, and anti-Semites, people who hate everybody, including Negroes, minority groups, and most likely themselves. . . . And these people are engaged in the conspiracy, outside all the legal processes, to undermine our very fundamental American concepts upon which our entire system of jurisprudence exists."

The Red scare infiltrated the stage and screen. Anti-Communist films flourished: *Walk East on Beacon, Big Jim McLain*. Plenty of other works came down on the side of free expression, most notably the 1952 Arthur Miller play *The Crucible*, which used the Salem witch trials as a metaphor for McCarthyism. The screenwriter Carl Foreman, who had been called to testify before HUAC, wrote a Western that was a clear allegory of the blacklist: in the gripping 1952 film *High Noon*, a town marshal played by Gary Cooper is abandoned by the previously good people of Hadleyville (i.e., fellow Hollywooders) when outlaws who had once terrorized his town (i.e., McCarthyites) return to wreak more havoc.

Hazel Scott was recovering from her struggles with her mental and physical health in the wake of her blacklisting. Some signs of hope had buoyed her: The lawsuit she had won against the restaurant that had denied her service inspired civil rights organizations to pressure the Washington State legislature to pass a Public Accommodations Act in 1953. She had a new record deal and continued to tour Europe. She had moved past the television job she had loved and on to other things.

Like Phillips, Betty White was thriving in television for the moment, hosting *Hollywood on Television* on her own and starting production on her sitcom *Life with Elizabeth*.

But Gertrude Berg, now twenty-four years into her reign as a sitcom queen, was not done fighting to maintain her television career.

By summer 1952, Berg had emerged from the loss of Loeb with some version of her power intact—but without the force of moral certitude or the sheer dominance she had enjoyed just a year earlier. The tired Berg, now fifty-two, told the network she needed one thing: an eight-week summer hiatus so she could rest. She boarded the *Queen Mary* with her husband in July 1952, this time sailing for Cherbourg and Southampton. Those sailing trips had become her respite from her increasingly tense work life.

The Goldbergs was set to return to NBC after her trip, in the fall of 1952, but not enough stations across the country had cleared time for it on their schedules, a problem because individual stations had final say as to what played over their airwaves and when. The upshot: *The Goldbergs* was yet again in a holding pattern. And once again, when she returned to US shores, Berg figured out how to keep Molly Goldberg alive in the public eye, no matter the circumstances.

Mr. Television himself, Milton Berle, had wanted to book Berg on his variety show for years, but back in 1950 NBC wouldn't approve her appearance. "I realize now at the time that I wanted her, she was fighting the witch-hunters, who demanded she get rid of Philip Loeb, who played Jake to her Molly," he later wrote in his autobiography. "Those 'super patriots' had enough juice to hurt Mrs. Berg in every way to force her to do what they wanted."

In February 1953, however, Berg was officially an NBC star and, apparently, forgiven for having been blacklist adjacent. She did a guest appearance on Berle's *Texaco Star Theater* in character as Molly Goldberg, and viewers loved it. She and Berle planned more such appearances as she waited for NBC and its stations to find a time slot for her show.

When Molly Goldberg showed up, even on the show that belonged to the man known as Mr. Television, she took over. It wasn't a choice; it was just her magic. The live audience roared when she appeared, and she basked in the reaction, something she didn't get on her show—which was live, but not in front of a studio audience. The May 26, 1953, episode of Berle's show became what was ostensibly a full-length *Goldbergs* episode, with Molly and Rosalie, along with Berle, as main characters. In the episode, Rosalie asks Milton to accompany her to her prom when she's stood up by her date. Much of the action takes place in a re-creation of the Goldbergs' living room set.

TV's prevalence now made jokes about the medium common, including this exchange when Rosalie develops a crush on Berle: "I'll never let you go," she says. He replies, "I wish you were my sponsor."

Molly hit so big on *Texaco Star Theater* that she was back just two weeks later. This episode was a frenetic, star-filled send-up as Berle turned in his final show to be sponsored by Texaco. The singers Margaret Truman (the daughter of President Harry S. Truman, who'd just left office) and Ezio Pinza performed numbers and played themselves alongside Berg as Molly, who showed up to give Berle a farewell basket of what she described as "American food," with a wink: blintzes, chopped chicken liver, borscht, and gefilte fish.

Berg, of course, wanted one thing: to keep up her image as America's mother, Molly Goldberg, by any means necessary. She had not come this far to sit around waiting for local affiliates to clear her show. She continued to entertain options—she was in talks to do a music-based show, for instance—but her Berle gambit worked. Her appearances drew "'best yet' accolades from the network brass," *Variety* reported, which "sparked the revival of interest in taking Mrs. Berg off the sidelines and getting her before the cameras pronto."

As a result, in the summer, *The Goldbergs* was back on the air with yet another shot at returning to its former glory. The series would revert to its half-hour format on NBC and had what was considered a great time slot, 8:00 p.m. on Fridays. Though it would conflict with the sabbath for many of her viewers, Berg said she had turned down an even more problematic time slot on Monday nights—opposite *I Love Lucy*. She was being particularly strategic: the show's contract with NBC ran until September 30, 1961, but there were cancellation provisions at the end of the third, sixth, and eighth years. At that point, the third-year cancellation date loomed about four months away. Her future hinged on the current season.

The network set the return for June. The cast would convene on set at noon the day of the broadcast, block the scenes until 5:00 p.m., have a dress rehearsal from 6:00 to 6:30 p.m., deliver a promotional spot from 6:30 to 6:45 p.m., have another dress rehearsal from 7:00 to 7:30 p.m., and air live from 8:00 to 8:30 p.m. That would be their new norm, hopefully for years to come.

Changes abounded. The television manufacturer RCA, the parent company of NBC, was now sponsoring *The Goldbergs*. Goldberg son Sammy shipped off to the army for the season, as actor Larry Robinson wanted to leave the show to pursue other roles, for fear of being typecast. (The radio Sammy had also joined the army back in 1942 to fight World War II, and though the Korean War was still in progress at the time, it would end in the summer during *The Goldbergs*' run.) The "new" Jake was replaced with an even newer one, the film actor Robert H. Harris. Berg had reportedly offered Harris the job once before she hired Stone, and she reached out to him again after the first NBC season concluded. This time he accepted. Harris looked quite different from Loeb and Stone, with a receding hairline and a smirky demeanor to Loeb's harried one. But the second choice for the second Jake stuck, whether because Harris was better at the role or because everyone had resigned themselves to the new circumstances.

Critics thought Harris was . . . fine. "The new Jake Goldberg, Robert Harris, displays qualities in the part that perhaps were not shown before, but, accepted on his own terms, does a satisfactory job of acting," one *Billboard* review said. "Moreover, his acting personality, being less warm than Molly, offers a good contrast." *Variety* declared, "Robert H. Harris segued into his new role of Jake quite ably, being properly tractable, gruff, and capable."

Harris hewed closer to a Silent Generation stereotype of a WASP man, no matter what the script designated him as. He was withdrawn, dismissive, and casually misogynist, especially as the show progressed. He tended to shrug from behind his newspaper at Molly's foolish emotionalism. It feels as if Berg wrote the new version of the character to work out her resentment at having a stranger in Philip Loeb's place. Loeb's Jake had loved Molly, fought with her, gotten caught up in her schemes, and confided in her. Losing Loeb and replacing him with Harris transported *The Goldbergs* several miles closer to the 1950s WASP family that was coming to dominate television.

In general, however, the Goldbergs' return cheered critics. The *Billboard* review went out of its way to laud Berg, as if to make clear that television needed her and should, perhaps, stop torturing the woman with its business machinations. The critic Leon Morse praised her "open-faced warmth" and "the rare and wonderful virtues of the program that features her. They are a humanity, a life-like humor, a naturalness that seems uncanny for its lack of theatricality and artificiality—all achieved by an understatement that has the potency of life." The *Philadelphia Bulletin* quipped, "After the dose of witless situation comedies we've seen all winter, Molly Goldberg and friends are particularly welcome."

Even after that warm reception, the same old problem reared up in the fall as *The Goldbergs* concluded its summer season: NBC had too many shows and not enough time slots. The network once again didn't know if it would be able to find a place for *The Goldbergs* even after, as *Variety* said, the show had "re-established itself as a major hit this summer, as did Gertrude Berg on the Milton Berle show last season."

With that, television had finally pushed Gertrude Berg to her limit.

In late 1953, she suffered the only illness violent enough to side-line her for three months from her beloved work. As she was carried from her Park Avenue home on a stretcher, she later told the talk show host Faye Emerson, she asked to pass by the living room to catch a glimpse of her new drapes. "I didn't know when I would see them again, and I wanted to make sure they were alright," she said. She was hospitalized for several weeks, into early 1954, with gastric hemorrhages, at one point being listed in critical condition.

After reports of her illness circulated in newspapers, more than 10,000 fan letters poured into New York City's Lenox Hill Hospital, just around the corner from her home, urging her to get well. Berg's assistant, Fannie Merrill, was by her side and read some of the notes aloud to Berg. Many industry associates reached out as well, including Joseph Moran of Young & Rubicam, who wrote, "I can only do two things for you . . . pray, which I'm doing, and offer you my blood, which I eagerly do. Just have someone call me and I'll be there, whenever they say." (She had hemorrhaged and had been given at least thirteen quarts of blood by the time he wrote.)

Berg barely spoke of the failed battle she had fought to save Loeb or her eventual capitulation, although it radically altered her career and, family members say, was among the worst of her life's personal trials. The illness was the closest she got to expressing her grief and frustration—a common theme for many of the exhausted women forging their way through the TV industry at the time. This woman, who kept herself buttoned up and private, whose role subsumed her actual self, fell ill in her darkest moment, her body speaking when she couldn't.

In her personal archives, she kept one separate file of the scores of newspaper clippings that documented Loeb's blacklisting and her battle to save him from it. This file is more pristine and neatly arranged than her other scrapbooks full of press clippings, which were often bulging and haphazard. There is little other mention of him in her records from the moment of his firing and afterward. She was, it seems, forever protecting Molly Goldberg from the unpleasantness of the world that Gertrude Berg knew all too well. Looking back on her with contemporary eyes, we might have seen another hero like Hazel Scott, except that Gertrude Berg is still hidden behind her character's malapropisms and aprons, her folksy wisdom and her character's endlessly feigned kitchen wisdom. And she had yet to find a surefire way forward for her career in the aftermath.

In fact, she could be forgiven, even celebrated, if she had chosen to quit at this point. Taking it easy was the more reasonable option. But Gertrude Berg did not take things easy for longer than the duration of a *Queen Mary* trip. She was not done fighting.

By 1952, Irna Phillips knew she had competition from other daytime serials, such as *Search for Tomorrow* and *Love of Life*. But she knew how to make soap operas better than anyone. She would survive and thrive.

A young man named William J. Bell believed Phillips was the best, and his experience with Phillips demonstrates what it was like to work for the queen of soaps. At age twenty-one, he was a comedy writer at WBBM-TV in Chicago, and he overheard someone in the office mention that Phillips lived nearby. He couldn't believe it. "I just figured a lady of her enormous talent and with her shows lived in either California or New York," he later said. "And there she was, just a mile away from where I was standing at that moment."

Working through some shared connections, he eventually got her number and called her office. He secured a meeting with her and was summoned to her home for the nerve-wracking occasion.

Phillips's secretary, Rose Cooperman, answered the door and led him to an office with a card table in it. "It was a very luxurious card table, but it was a card table, with four chairs," Bell later recalled. That served as Phillips's version of a writers' room. An ashtray sat on top of the card table, awaiting Phillips's cigarette butts throughout the day. (I saw occasional cigarette burns throughout her script pages, notes, and letters in her archive.) Rose instructed him to sit there and wait.

Finally, he heard footsteps echo in the corridor as Phillips approached.

When she appeared, he was struck by how small she was, given her huge stature in his mind. He relaxed a bit. She asked him questions about his life and his career, and chatted about her work. She wasn't at all as harsh as some people made her out to be. She suggested that Bell take an outline for one of her upcoming episodes and write it up as a sample script.

At the time, Phillips had recently filled her last opening for a writer, so Bell didn't get a job with her immediately. But Bell eventually did get himself hired for *The Guiding Light*. He understood her in a way few others did at the time: "Irna was tough," he said. "Know why she was tough? Because she was a little lady, ninety pounds, in a man's world. If she didn't eat guys alive, she wasn't going to survive." After he was hired, he went to her home each morning to listen and observe as she dictated scripts for *The Guiding Light* to Rose. He learned how Phillips outlined long-term story lines, how she developed characters, and other techniques.

He accompanied her on story conferences with Procter & Gamble, when the company would send representatives out from Cincinnati to Chicago to talk about upcoming plotlines and the show overall. The P&G representatives lavished Phillips and Bell with gifts, dinners, and cocktails. Not much actual story discussion came up, but Phillips always wrote up a little report, and the P&G reps would offer a few bits of feedback. Everyone won.

Phillips had a clear reputation among the P&G ranks: she was tough, a "spinster" who had had two children "under slightly mysterious circumstances," as P&G's daytime supervisor, Douglas S. Cramer, later put it. Of course, there was no real mystery at all, but that was how an unmarried woman with children looked to many others in 1952. Cramer picked up another overly dramatized belief about Phillips, which was that "she lived in Chicago because she didn't want to lose touch with the heart of America. P&G, which was in Cincinnati, loved that." Phillips probably let him believe that story. In reality, she simply felt more comfortable in her hometown.

All the hard work of Phillips and her staffers, including Bell, resulted in a hit show—but little respect from the TV industry at large. A *TV Guide* article about the popularity and power of soap operas at the time came with the condescending headline "TV Proves Housewives Do Have Time for Crying Out Loud." The publication's review of *The Guiding Light* was withering: "The first time this reviewer had the unhappy experience of seeing *The Guiding Light*, the following lines cropped up in the initial five minutes: 'The police haven't come up with anything yet?' 'There are things we can't back away from, that we have to face up to.' 'We can't continually allow ourselves to be hurt and disillusioned.' It went on like that, only worse."

The show would run on television, however, for fifty-seven years. Though Phillips struggled to raise her children on her own while she ran an empire and her empire never gained proper respect from the industry, she had cemented her status in television history.

Around that time, Phillips's son, Tom, who was approaching his teenage years, enrolled in Culver Military Academy in Indiana. He had asked to go, which had surprised Phillips. The family still lived in the sixteen-story condo building at 1335 N. Astor Street in Chicago's Gold Coast neighborhood, which had been brand-new when they had moved in three years earlier. But now Tom wanted to be 103 miles away in Culver, Indiana.

Phillips gave him what he wanted. The all-male boarding school seemed to serve him well at first. However, she wrote, "As time went on his work showed a lack of interest and he became a disciplinary problem, particularly to the chaplain of the school."

During a visit to the school for Thanksgiving, Phillips commiserated with the mother of Tom's roommate, Bill, whose grades were also low. The boys were distracting each other from their schoolwork, the mothers agreed. Bill's mother compared this distractibility with that of her husband, Bill's father. She added, "I suppose Tom is just like his father?"

"I don't know," Phillips said. "Doesn't Bill know that Tom is adopted?" When Bill's mother said no, Phillips realized that Tom was still inventing fathers. Over the years, Phillips would hear it again and again: Tom created different parents for himself at different times; what those fictional sets of parents had in common was that there was always both a father and a mother, and the mother never seemed a bit like Phillips. She wrote, "Once again the single-woman home, regardless of the opportunities I could offer my children, couldn't begin to make up in any way for the absence of a father."

Phillips had conquered daytime at last. *The Guiding Light* now a success, her radio show *The Brighter Day* made its way to television in 1954 with the same setup, the radio and TV versions running simultaneously on CBS. But she would never feel the same sense of victory in her life as a mother.

The women who invented television had survived so much in just a few years of pioneering the medium. And so far, they were still holding on to their TV dreams. Irna Phillips had her hit crossover from radio to television with *The Guiding Light*, which proved her instincts correct no matter what critics had to say about her work. Gertrude Berg emerged from her hospital stay ready to go back to work. Then she began her twenty-fifth year of playing and writing Molly Goldberg by heading to Key West, Florida, with her husband, Lewis, to recover from her health ordeal. When she returned, she'd see about getting her show a new time slot at her current network, NBC.

Even Hazel Scott, in a show of her unflagging determination, was considering a return to television. In October 1953, she was in talks to host a daytime show for the independent New York station WMGM, which had recently increased its talent budget.

And Betty White was on her way to national domination. Her sitcom *Life with Elizabeth* moved to film starting on September 25, 1953, so it could be beamed into homes across the country.

It felt so different from shooting a local show with an intimate theater audience. White and her costar, Del Moore, would shoot the same scene over and over again, from every angle: two shot, over the shoulder, close up. They left time for the eventual laughs they hoped to get. Then the edited version of what they had taped was shown to an audience, whose laughs were recorded for the final playback on television. "It was a little like doing comedy in a mortuary, and it threw our timing all off," White wrote. "Later, attending the audience screening, we would squirm to hear the people laugh in unexpected places and watch ourselves plow right on through without waiting, so that the punch line was drowned in the laugh."

She and Delsy amused themselves with the new setup in strange ways: for instance, he moved his wedding ring from one hand to the other from scene to scene. Only he and White would notice it jumping magically from hand to hand as the scenes progressed in the final, edited film version.

Moore and White didn't love doing the show as much as they used to, but they were becoming a national sensation. They aired all over the country, once or even twice a week in some areas.

And NBC executives were searching across the United States for someone who could host a national talk show to compete with radio turned TV personality Arthur Godfrey's popular CBS daytime show. They had noticed that a young woman named Betty White seemed to be doing a pretty good job with a similar show locally in Los Angeles. And now that national live broadcasting was possible, her location on the West Coast was not an impediment. Their one question: Could she handle a half-hour television show *every weekday?*

She had to laugh at that one. Then she calmly explained that she had been doing five and a half hours a day, six days a week, for four years now. But she would do her best to contain herself to a succinct thirty minutes a day instead.

They signed her, and now she had to do something she had

never imagined when she had started hosting *Hollywood on Television* in 1949. At that time, she had thought, how lucky to have such a job. How lucky to get paid to do this. Now, in December 1953, she was leaving it behind. She was leaving the station that had given her everything, KLAC.

Those years of putting her career first, of giving up the prospect of marriage and family, had paid off. Her hard work had allowed her to achieve her wildest dreams, and now she had even bigger ones. In the new year of 1954, she was preparing to host her own daily national talk show, *The Betty White Show*, on NBC. Her mentor and benefactor, producer, and business partner, Don Fedderson, had negotiated the deal. She would pull double duty on the now nationally syndicated *Life with Elizabeth*. White signed a five-year contract with NBC that made her "the most successful young woman in video," as her friend the journalist Jane Morris wrote.

Betty White was about to find out if her local Los Angeles charm would translate across time zones. But even she would not escape the hazards of the conservative groundswell taking over television, and neither would Gertrude Berg.

10

Black and White and Red

Betty White, Hazel Scott, and Gertrude Berg

Betty White felt more challenged than she had in years. Everything she did now involved so many people. She and her few close colleagues couldn't simply do what they wanted anymore, as she was used to doing on her slapdash local shows. And it was exhilarating! The nation would soon be watching her every day. All of her work and sacrifice had come down to this.

The Betty White Show would begin by shooting for a few weeks at the old NBC studios at Sunset and Vine in Hollywood and then relocate to Studio 1 at the new NBC lot in Burbank.

Things looked promising for both White and the program. She received more than two thousand fan letters per week. She produced the show and hired a female director. She had a makeup artist and a hairdresser. Her dresses were now provided by Lanz Originals, an Austrian company that had started out making traditional folk dresses in the 1920s but had come to New York and Los Angeles with more modern, on-trend dresses in the 1940s. The frocks suited White's image, as they often had high necklines but retained a flirty edge—an open back, a cute floral print, a bow accent. She thought of the wardrobe closet as her personal Hansel and Gretel cottage full of sweets—except, she hoped, without the witch to snatch her in the end.

Her life, as far as she was concerned, had turned into a dream as her show launched in January 1954, airing live across the entire country. It was her "biggest break," declared the *Los Angeles Times*. Her days took on a predictable quality, still packed with work but nothing like her five-and-a-half-hours-of-live-TV days.

On weekdays, she awoke at 4:15 a.m. in the Brentwood home she shared with her parents.

"The day starts early, but these doll-head parents of mine make it fun," she said in an interview at the time. When she had first signed on to do *The Betty White Show*, she had envisioned sneaking out of the house in the predawn hours to grab breakfast at a drive-in, but her parents insisted on getting up with her to eat and chat. As they breakfasted, their St. Bernard, Stormy; Pekingese, Bandy; and poodle, Danny, padded around the house. In fact, the early morning was the one time the family sat together to visit.

Soon White was driving her Ford convertible forty-five minutes northeast to Burbank. "It always amazed me to see how many cars were on the road at that ungodly hour," she wrote. "Where were they all *going*? They couldn't all be doing television shows."

Once there, she had her own carpeted dressing room with her name on the door, which included a private bathroom with a shower. Makeup call came at 6:00 a.m., with a musical rehearsal soon to follow. At 9:00 a.m (noon Eastern Time), she went live on air from Studio 1 at NBC, doing what she did best: interviewing guests and entertaining audiences on the fly, with little rehearsal or preparation.

The title card for the show pictured a cartoon of Betty watering flowers as an announcer declared, "*The Betty White Show*, from Hollywood!" Then Betty would appear, her smiling face filling the camera frame. Her dark, cropped hair was looped in curls and her sparkling eyes and dimples coaxed reflexive smiles from viewers. Her Lanz dress was almost always buttoned right up to the base of her neck, well above her collarbone. She began with a song, accompanied by Frank DeVol and the Little Band. "It's time to say hello again, and start our show again," she sang. Singing still made her nervous, so she focused on delivering the lyrics right to the camera "as if it were a lover," as her friend the journalist Jane Morris wrote.

It helped that DeVol and White had a warm, joking relationship. She was intimidated by all the great female vocalists of the time whom he had worked with. He proved he understood White when he began addressing his notes to her in this lighthearted way: "Dear Betty, not Dinah [Shore], not Doris [Day], not Margaret [Whiting], not Patti [Page], but Dear *Betty*." His band included Roc Hillman on guitar, Cliff Whitcomb on piano, Dick Cathcart on trumpet, Bill Hamilton on saxophone, Eddie Robinson on bass, and Jerry Kaplan on a little bit of everything. DeVol occasionally joined White on camera for some comedy or a commercial lead-in. "He had the face of a basset hound with the blues, and played everything dead straight, without a smile, so almost anything he said came out funny," White wrote. "He also had a library of toupees, and would change them without warning, depending on what mood he happened to be in that day." The band and crew would serve as something of a live audience as well, applauding numbers and laughing at Betty's jokes.

White had learned one major lesson in all those hours winging it on live local television: "If you're natural, the audience is going to like you or not, just as people anywhere would like you or not," she said. "They're certainly not going to like you any better by your pretending to be something you aren't. This isn't always easy. There were plenty of times when I was nervous and scared and the first thing you knew, I'd be six other people." Now, if nothing else, she was just one person: Betty White. Morris wrote at the time that "there's no such thing as 'on stage' and 'off stage' personality" for White: "She's the same Betty, the Betty of the quick smile, the thoughtful eyes, the strong handshake."

The thirty-minute variety show also featured White dancing, answering fan mail, and interviewing guests. Occasionally, the celebrity segments fizzled: the Western star Guy Madison stonewalled White with long, silent stares, punctuated by an occasional "Nope" or "Yup." Sometimes her interviews would have a sensational bent, such as when retired marine major Donald Keyhoe appeared on the show to accuse the air force of covering up the discovery of flying saucers. A man named Mr. Bethrem gave an interview in which he claimed to have been visited eleven times by the crew of a flying saucer.

With only thirty minutes to fill instead of five and a half hours, White began to refine her craft. Her mother watched and gave her notes. She needed to stop fidgeting, her mother said. White fidgeted no more. A fan wrote in to note her frequent use of "as a matter of fact." Acknowledged and eliminated.

After she finished with *The Betty White Show*, at around 10:00 a.m., she hit a restaurant across the street from the studio for a second breakfast. At one point she claimed she'd gained four pounds after starting work on the show because of that double morning meal. After that break, she returned to the studio to rehearse with DeVol unless he'd accompanied her to breakfast, in which case they'd go over music as they crossed the street together. They reviewed the next day's songs and camera setups and watched the day's show when it aired at noon for the West Coast.

She grabbed lunch on her way to rehearsals for *Life with Elizabeth*. If it was just a rehearsal day, she could head home by late afternoon. When she arrived at the house, she changed into comfortable clothes and, if it was early enough and she had the energy, dived into her fan mail. Then she ran through lyrics for new songs for *The Betty White Show* and lines for *Life with Elizabeth* before she got to bed by 10:00 p.m.

On filming days for *Elizabeth*, she worked until 1:00 or 2:00 a.m. As she drove home in those early-morning hours, if she was alone, she sometimes felt the comedown from the high of shooting with her costar, Del Moore, and her *Elizabeth* crew. She wondered if she was missing out on marriage and her own family and friends outside of show business. She thought about where this was all headed, if anywhere at all. "You can feel pretty sorry for yourself until you stop and realize that the dark moments are unimportant compared with the wonderful moments and that everything has its ratio," she said. "For any job worth having, you have to give a great deal."

She obsessed over her work, she had to admit. She thought about it almost every moment she was awake. "But what else can I do?" she asked in a 1954 interview, one of many in which she found herself on the defensive about her choice of work over romance and family. "Working on my NBC shows and on *Life with Elizabeth*, I *have* to concentrate to do any kind of decent job. I can't just slide through it. And that reminds me—men concentrate a lot on their work so why should they expect a woman to be any less conscientious?"

She had no time for a life outside the studio, for personal relationships or dates. Morris drafted an interview piece on White that began "Betty White, the hottest young star in the business, has found the fame and fortune, but she's found that there's a price. She has strictly . . . NO TIME FOR NOTHUN." White had tried to date sometimes since her last husband, even went with one man for a year and a half, but the schedule was just impossible. She saw only her mother and father at home, and the people at work, most of whom were happily married men. That suited her, as she wasn't interested in starting a marriage that could spoil the fruits of all her hard work. She did get lonesome, or at least she claimed so in interviews. Her social life consisted mainly of chats with friends by phone.

Sometimes, if she worked hard enough, she got a break. Because *Life with Elizabeth* was now filmed rather than broadcast live, she and the crew could bank as many as five weeks of episodes ahead of schedule, then take some time off. They could plan some actual leisure activities, such as barbecues and horseback rides, though they often still did them together. Who else did they know, really?

She thought about her radio days, when she had struggled to get any little part, and watched as other girls got great ones. She had thought them so lucky at the time. Now that she was at the top of her game, she saw how hard they must have worked. She realized now that the good jobs weren't easy.

For her, though, the hard work was paying off on both *The Betty White Show* and *Life with Elizabeth*. The sitcom, now seen in at least fifteen markets across the country and growing, got pleasant reviews, with *Variety* calling it "an amusing, wacky series based on solid Americana situation material." *Billboard* said, "It is of a type that cannot offend the most sensitive viewer, and the word wholesome might have been invented for it." *TV Guide* went even further. "Betty White and her *Life with Elizabeth* are bringing new meaning to that belabored term, 'situation comedy,'" the magazine said before it took a swipe at *I Love Lucy* without naming it: "Unlike so many other programs that bear the label but are really slapstick, *Elizabeth* builds its humor strictly on situations."

White earned a gold-standard accolade from one of the major critics of the time, *The New York Times*' Jack Gould: "A comedienne who somehow seems to have been overlooked this season is Betty White. It is a slight that should be corrected because she is an immensely personable young lady with a very real talent in a number of directions, and a high quotient of charm." He said of *Elizabeth*, "The accent is more on what's said than what's done. After Monday's 'I Love Lucy,' in which Lucille Ball was covered with honey, water, broken eggs, and cream pies, this approach of 'Life with Elizabeth' is particularly refreshing."

He made clear that that didn't mean *Elizabeth* was groundbreaking television, but "What saves the day is Miss White. She has an intuitive feel for farce and delivers her lines, many of them really witty, with an excellent sense of timing." Her agent clipped the review and sent it to Tom McAvity, the vice president of NBC, noting Gould's opinion that she should be promoted to an evening network show, which would be a step up from the syndicated *Elizabeth* and the daytime show.

Nice reviews continued for *The Betty White Show* as well. In February, *Billboard* said of her daytime show, "Attractive, charming, and talented Betty White is a bright new network personality who emsees a program that has great potential. The show is in the well-worn groove of music, singing, and chatter, a formula which nowadays has become the mainstay of daytime video entertainment." Of course, it had become that largely because of White and Al Jarvis's work on *Hollywood on Television*.

In March 1954, the *Baltimore Sun* declared, "Daytime television east of California has been considerably brightened and improved by the *Betty White Show*." And in April, *TV Guide* said she had "the disposition of a storybook heroine. She is utterly unspoiled. Furthermore, she has talent." The magazine predicted, "TV May Make Her America's Sweetheart." Her former station manager turned producer, Don Fedderson, gushed in the piece, "If this girl is the success I think she's going to be, the high neckline is going to be the next New Look."

The future looked bright, and White was thrilled, happy to fly blindly through this high-pressure, national gig while also juggling the production of *Life with Elizabeth*: "If ignorance is bliss, we were about as blissful as you can get," she wrote of herself and her production team. She didn't know then how scrutinized and tinkered with a network television show could get, given the increasing stakes of the business. This would be no *Hollywood on Television* free-for-all.

When Betty White drives up with radio announcer turned actor Paul Douglas in a cream-colored Oldsmobile convertible, it's clear that she has made it. In this advertising spot during the 1954 Academy Awards, the forty-six-year-old Douglas, wearing a tuxedo with a white vest and bow tie, explains after he exits the car, "To help us bring you the Oldsmobile story tonight, here is Betty White, bright, new, happy, television star on NBC and *Life with Elizabeth*." The beaming White gets out of the passenger side and glides up to his left side in front of the vehicle, clad in a draped gown that makes her look like a Greek goddess.

After a choreographed number featuring three female dancers twirling around the car in tulle skirts and strapless bodices and three men in white-jacketed tuxedo suits, White and Douglas, this time with announcer Bob LeMond, reappear in front of the car. "And you wait till you drive it," White says. "It's even more terrific than it looks."

Then, with little warning, she breaks into song: "So come along and take the wheel of the newest Oldsmobile . . ." She gets into the car's driver's seat, as feminist a move as one could pull off on a major broadcast at the time, and the two men close the car door for her. When Betty beams at the camera, you suddenly can't imagine *not* buying an Oldsmobile Starfire 98.

She delivered commercials, including the Oldsmobile spot, during the March Academy Awards broadcast, seen by more than 40 million viewers. This was part of a flood of national attention that came White's way that spring. Her instinct years earlier had proven right: only a husband who had otherworldly patience with an ambitious wife would have been able to withstand marriage to her when her schedule was like this. It would be asking a lot even of a modern, equal partnership. Any standard-issue 1950s husband— Gertrude Berg's husband, Lewis, being an exception—would have found White's whirlwind of professional activity not just unsuitable but untenable.

The *Los Angeles Times* followed her around on one of her busy days in April—though, comparatively, not that busy, as it was only a rehearsal day on *Elizabeth*, not a filming day. Still, it had to be a little extra trying, doing all that she did while a reporter took notes. By 2:00 p.m., "a touch of weariness creeped into her eyes," the reporter wrote, as White stood next to a piano on the set of *The Betty White Show*. She rehearsed a song as she tapped her foot, which was ensconced in a red ballet slipper. By that point, four hours after the day's live show had ended, she had smiled her famous smile a lot already.

"On the morning live show, I have to train myself to play to the camera," she explained to the reporter. "It's the only way a performer has of getting into living rooms."

The reporter remained with her through her *Elizabeth* rehearsal, which ended at about 7:00 p.m. "By that time I'm too tired for dating, so it's off to bed," she explained. "I wonder how Cinderella would have liked those apples."

This talk of her dating life—or lack thereof—constantly recurred in coverage of her newfound stardom. She was always tempering her professional success in public with sweet, folksy jokes about her failure to secure a husband. (She left her previous marriages, and her aversion to any future one, out of the discussion.) In a typical line, she explained her lack of matrimony by saying, "It wouldn't be fair to marriage, or to men. I want to get married, but not yet."

Other journalists treated White with contemptuous sexism. The syndicated television columnist John Crosby complained, "Sooner or later I knew I'd have to turn my attention to Betty White, a comparative newcomer who has mushroomed almost overnight into national prominence. Miss White is now the star of a filmed show called 'Life with Elizabeth,' which is syndicated to 87 stations and can hardly be avoided in any major city short of Chungking." The piece continued in this derisive tone, noting that White lived with her mother, railing against her "wholesomeness," and including a telling line about her being "fully dressed and well-upholstered." Translation: he objected to her high collars and implied that she was overweight for his taste. He concluded, "And now, if you'll pardon me, I'm off to stare at Jane Russell and see if some of this wholesomeness will wash off."

White saw the article. She cut it out. She cried for three days. She kept the clip for years. It had attacked her so *personally*. "He didn't like what I wore, he didn't like my laugh, he didn't like what I looked like, he certainly didn't like what I did," she later summarized the piece.

Some articles were merely patronizing. Donald Kirkley, one of White's most ardent supporters in print, wrote in the *Baltimore*

Sun, "Betty White is a charming young woman whose two-dimpled smile, depicted on a television screen, is capable of bowling over a bachelor at 1,500 miles, yet, at 28, she is unmarried." At least he was flattering.

White had wanted to be a good girl, once upon a time. So she had gotten married. Twice. But soon she had discovered that what she really wanted to do was to work. What she wanted the most, it turned out, was to work in television. And she was very good at it!

Now that she was a TV star, all anyone wanted to know in interviews was why she wasn't married. How could she play a wife on television and not be one in real life? Wasn't that sad? To have the best thing a woman could want, a good husband, but to only have him for pretend?

She couldn't bring herself to explain that she'd chosen TV instead of a husband. They wouldn't like that, and to be on TV, she needed them to like her.

Wasn't she ashamed? Nope. Not one bit. It had worked, so far.

White joked in interviews about how benign her little daytime show was, playing down any sense of power or progressiveness she might wield. "Yes, we've had one fairly serious controversy on the new morning show," she cracked to the *Christian Science Monitor.* "It was about how I should speak to dogs. I have a dreadful habit—I know I shouldn't but I do it myself with my poodle, Pekingese and St. Bernard at home—I call dogs 'baby.' So I got a—well, a pretty critical letter from a woman who felt I shouldn't talk to dogs on the program this way, and I said I'd try to do better."

White did, however, have more radical plans afoot. She invited the dancer Arthur Duncan, who had been a guest performer several times on *Hollywood on Television,* to appear on her show several times. The difference this time was that a Black tap dancer would be seen nationwide, rather than just in Los Angeles. That included the American South.

Duncan performed most days on *The Betty White Show*. White loved it when he did a number called "Jump Through the Ring."

Along with those letters that admonished her for calling dogs "baby" came far more angry ones that asked her not to feature Duncan because he was Black. Some southern stations threatened a boycott unless Duncan was removed. Several of them wrote White a letter that said they would, as she later recounted, "with deep regret, find it most difficult to broadcast the program unless Mr. Arthur Duncan was removed from the cast."

She couldn't believe what she was reading. Her response: "I'm sorry. Live with it."

She used Duncan on the show as much as she could. The network, at least, backed her decision. And, luckily in this case, not another word came of it. The southern stations continued to carry *The Betty White Show*. White was always coy about her progressive decisions, saying she chose the best people for the job, whether that was a female director or a Black performer. But she was a producer on both her sitcom and her talk show, and she understood the implications of her decisions. After all, she had hired female directors for three different shows at that point.

The "best person for the job" line has long been a go-to for Hollywood producers who want to make progressive decisions without alarming their mainstream audiences—or, more importantly, the network and advertising executives who obsessed over those mainstream audiences' sensibilities. Of course, she just happened to love Duncan and admire his work. She also knew what she was doing.

White's casting of Duncan would lead to his becoming one of the first Black regulars on a variety program, *The Lawrence Welk*

Show, from 1964 until 1982, and a major inspiration for the future tap superstar Gregory Hines.

The year Arthur Duncan joined *The Betty White Show*, 1954, coincided with a watershed moment in civil rights for Black Americans, one Hazel Scott had agitated for throughout her career: the US Supreme Court ruled against racial segregation in public schools in the case *Brown v. Board of Education*, with Chief Justice Earl Warren—a former California governor and distinguished Emmy Awards guest speaker—writing the decision. It would help ignite the movement that led to the Civil Rights Act of 1964 and the end of the Jim Crow era.

Of course, the airwaves had a long way to go before they were integrated. Scott's brief rise as a television star four years earlier was mostly forgotten just a few years after it had happened, as she toured the world with her music. Around that time, the critic Alvin "Chick" Webb wrote in the *New York Amsterdam News* that "a terrific bonanza awaits the TV company that will hire a Negro performer of the stripe of Sammy Davis Jr., or Timmie Rogers to star in a big-time variety comedy show. . . . Negro Americans await the coming of a genuine television Messiah who will make the channels of this great industry a real sounding board for a democracy that can work." Hazel Scott had not gotten a proper chance at being that Messiah.

Scott had carried on with her music career and traveled abroad with her family. In early 1954, she and her husband and son took the Panamanian ship *Cristobal* to Scott's native region, the Caribbean islands, to visit Haiti at the invitation of Haitian president Paul E. Magloire for the 150th anniversary of the country's independence. When they met the president in person, Scott spoke French, while her husband, Representative Adam Clayton Powell, Jr., spoke English. "Your husband is not an educated man?" the president joked to Scott. Powell took it gracefully and praised Magloire's "20th Century renaissance," thanks to the country's improved infrastructure. Powell also said he hoped the United States would invest in Haiti.

Ebony documented the family's trip as they swam, visited the Iron Market, attended Catholic church services, observed a voodoo ritual, and spearfished in the Gulf of Gonave. Scott wore floral dresses and silk head wraps as she purchased perfumes, a passion of hers—she had collected more than 150 bottles, $4,000 worth. She played at a state dinner at the request of Magloire, performing a few jazz tunes and singing in French and Creole, accompanied by local drummers. After five days, Scott jetted to Miami for a concert date while Powell and Skipper, now seven, stayed a little longer.

In the summer of 1954, Scott began to spend more time in Europe, urged by her European manager, Félix Marouani, who kept getting her gigs. "Okay, I'll stay one more week," she said. And then again: "Okay, next week." She sent a telegram home: "FÉLIX HAS A FEW MORE DATES FOR ME. I'LL BE ANOTHER COUPLE OF WEEKS." Skipper joined her for stretches, and she occasionally came back to the United States, but her life was increasingly centered overseas.

Time at home together had grown difficult for Powell and Scott. They fought often, with long periods of cold silence in between. Scott liked to write music in the middle of the night, an irritant to Powell, particularly on Saturday nights when he had to preach the next morning. Scott's defense: "Well, Adam, God is giving me this inspiration and what do you want me to do—tell him to come back some other time?"

Scott's absence from the United States provoked rumors. She told one interviewer, "We're America's strangest family. Nobody understands us, but we understand each other." She determined to "let them write what they want to write," as she later said.

In truth, she had long suspected her husband of having affairs. Sometimes, when she was led to believe he was in Washington, she would hear from friends who had seen him at a Manhattan night-club. Gossip columns swirled with innuendo. Powell had, after all, courted Scott while still married to his first wife. Why should things be any different this time?

At one point, he proposed that they try an "open marriage." As she recalled the era years later, she asked, "But what happens to Casanova's wife, while he's out? She should be above reproach. Why? Casanova can become the Creature from the Black Lagoon when it comes to his own wife. A man can roll in the dirt and get up and be Dr. or Mr. So-and-so. Let a woman try it. It's the old boys-will-be-boys double standard." She wanted no part of it. She quipped, "I couldn't face a marriage of convenience, especially if it was at my inconvenience."

She abandoned her hopes for her marriage, for the cozy family life in New York, and for a secure career as a television performer. The WMGM show had fallen through. And that was perhaps for the best.

When she asked for her piano to be shipped to Europe, her son remembers his father saying, "I think we need to understand that your mother's probably going to be over there for a while."

She stayed for the remainder of the 1950s. There was likely more behind her sojourn than a love of baguettes or even a desire for distance from Powell. Not only did she and several other Black American expatriates such as the writer James Baldwin feel more comfortable among Europeans, but the US government had critically injured her career and psyche. Her son remembers that after her blacklisting, he overheard a meeting with her accountant about her tour income reaching six figures, which meant a steep tax rate. He recalls her saying, "I'm never going to work this hard again for Uncle Sam."

Scott got an apartment on the Left Bank of Paris with a view of Notre Dame. She leaned on female friends in a way she never had: Mabel Howard, a longtime friend of Hazel's mother, Alma, joined her. Billie Holiday visited while she toured Europe. The pianist Mary Lou Williams split her time between London and Paris, where she frequently visited with Scott. In Scott's broken emotional state, she gave up drinking, turned to prayer, and vowed to return to the Catholicism of her youth.

Powell later wrote admiringly in his memoir about Scott's spiritual awakening: "[T]here took place in her life one of the greatest acts of faith I have ever seen. . . . One morning, accompanied by Mabel, Hazel went to Notre Dame, got down on her knees in front of the altar, and vowed she would not move until God gave her strength. She stayed there until her knees actually became bloody. When she finally did rise to her feet, she had the power and strength and the faith never again to touch or desire a drop of alcohol. She became an exceptionally religious person."

Back in the United States, the advent of color on television brought up other race issues.

In 1953, viewers who stayed up late enough in New York might have caught the silent, black-and-white image of a woman named Marie McNamara, who had porcelain skin and red hair, though they couldn't perceive it.

The NBC affiliate there, WNBT, was running color TV tests over the air. (Viewers' sets received only black-and-white transmissions, so that's what they saw; the station monitored with its own equipment how the color broadcast looked and adjusted the shades accordingly.) The station soon revealed to curious viewers who Mc-Namara was, what she was doing, and their in-house name for her: Miss Color TV.

They appeared not to see the irony in the nickname. They were calibrating all future television production to a white woman's skin tone. CBS had a (white) Miss Color TV, too, named Patty Painter. Other models followed in the race for networks to demonstrate their new color capabilities—all of them called "color girls," all of them white.

The racial implications were clear, though the color girls also represented another chapter in TV history in which unsung women would be critical to progress, only to find themselves objectified, unnamed, and then tossed aside when they were no longer useful to the men running things.

Over at the *Betty White Show* set, White's NBC bosses called her and her crew in for a meeting one day, promising a demonstration. After they had all filed into a conference room, the NBC executives cued up a TV screen in the corner. There White saw bacon and eggs frying in black and white, and then—*pow!*—it turned to color, like at the moment Dorothy lands in Oz. She heard an audible gasp among those in the room as the yolk turned from gray to bright yellow.

RCA, the network's parent company, had worked to develop color television since 1940. Now it believed it was ready for nationwide transmission. The equipment would take a while to catch up, but color television was now inevitable, and the medium's biggest leap forward yet. "It made black and white look kind-of shabby," White later recalled.

Irna Phillips thought otherwise. Commanded to make *The Guiding Light* the first daytime soap to air in color, she wrote an episode set in a gray-and-white hospital room to make the broadcast as close to monochrome as possible. A purist, she did not enjoy major changes in her creations and saw no upside to using her shows as experiments. It wouldn't appear in color regularly until 1967.

Color was only the most obvious way TV was changing and growing. ABC merged with United Paramount Theatres, which gave the network an influx of cash to invest in programming and technology. The FCC also ruled that Paramount's stake in the DuMont Network gave it a controlling interest, signaling a shift in leadership from its original founder, Dr. Allen B. DuMont, to corporate forces. A popular 1953 song recorded by Dinah Washington called "TV Is the Thing (This Year)" made it clear: television was here to stay. "If you want to have fun, come home with me/You can stay all night and play with my TV . . . Radio was great, now it's out of date/TV is the thing this year."

Television's astronomical growth and burgeoning power only encouraged anti-Communist forces to continue to target it. McCarthyism had hit yet another fever pitch when the New York couple Julius and Ethel Rosenberg, accused of stealing US atomic bomb secrets for the Soviet Union, were executed in 1953. As the Rosenbergs maintained their innocence, the case attracted international attention. Jean-Paul Sartre, Albert Einstein, Pablo Picasso, and Pope Pius XII pleaded with President Dwight D. Eisenhower to spare their lives. He refused.

Even former president Harry S. Truman, who had himself authorized screening federal employees for "totalitarian, fascist, communist, or subversive" tendencies, believed that by 1953, Eisenhower, his successor, had allowed the Communist hunters to go too far. "It is now evident that the present Administration has fully embraced, for political advantage, McCarthyism," he said. "I'm not referring to the Senator from Wisconsin—he's only important in that his name has taken on a dictionary meaning in the world. And that meaning is the corruption of truth, the abandonment of our historical devotion to fair play."

Lucille Ball sat atop the ratings charts with her series *I Love Lucy*—the episode in which her character gave birth to "Little Ricky" riveted 44 million viewers on January 19, 1953, more than the number who watched the inauguration of President Eisenhower the next day. But even she had to meet with House Un-American Activities Committee investigator William A. Wheeler in Hollywood in the fall of 1953. She gave him sealed testimony that admitted she had, indeed, registered as a Communist in 1936 at her grandfather's request. Her husband and costar, Desi Arnaz, chatted with the live studio audience before one episode taping and admitted that she had been targeted by HUAC, offering this pithy defense: "Now I want you to meet my favorite wife, my favorite redhead—in fact, that's the only thing *red* about her, and even that's not legitimate—Lucille Ball." She did such big business that in the end, she couldn't be stopped: she won the Emmy for Best Comic Actress that year and would dominate TV for years to come.

Of course, the worst of the Red Scare's damage had already been done to Hazel Scott and Gertrude Berg's careers, though Berg would continue to feel the reverberations.

Philip Loeb, *The Goldbergs*' onetime patriarch, had difficulty finding work as an actor after being accused of Communist ties. The show's creator/producer/star, Gertrude Berg, had paid him $8,775 between January and November 1953, per their severance agreement. That helped, but he was drowning in expenses to keep his mentally ill son in a home called Chestnut Lodge, which cost $11,450 for the year. To supplement his income, he appeared in a traveling production of the stage comedy *Time Out for Ginger*, about a girl who wants to try out for her school's football team.

As Loeb lived in hotel rooms throughout the Midwest and Canada, NBC dithered about where to place *The Goldbergs* on its schedule, at one point even considering moving it to daytime. By March, true to form, Berg had rebounded again. Upon her return from her vacation to Key West, Florida, she resumed deal making. Her agent, Ted Ashley, asked the DuMont Network if it would be interested in picking up *The Goldbergs*, since NBC still hadn't found the show a slot on its schedule. Her contract with NBC stipulated that she could go to another network if NBC couldn't air her series. One of DuMont's biggest stars, Bishop Fulton J. Sheen, planned to take some time off from his weekly sermon show, *Life Is Worth Living*, which opened up his time slot for a *Goldbergs* run.

The move would put her into direct competition with her friend Milton Berle's show, an intriguing setup given that, as *Variety* noted, her own appearances on Berle's program had elevated her "into a new prominent position as a TV personality." As recently as March 1954, Berg and her TV daughter, Arlene McQuade, had appeared on *The Buick-Berle Show*, as it was now called under new sponsorship, playing their characters Molly and Rosalie Goldberg. The episode-spanning sketch had Rosalie running away to become an actress, a phase Berg had faced with her real-life daughter, Harriet.

But Berg hadn't allowed McQuade to steal the show from her: in the final scene, Berg, Berle, and the forty-three-year-old screen idol Bob Cummings dance to the song "Young at Heart." As the men dutifully perform their choreography, Berg, wearing a black dress and pearls, flits from one man's arms to the other's and back again, expending one-third the effort and exuding three times as much charisma as the men. The audience applauds, and Berle kisses her on the cheek. She kisses him back, then turns to kiss Cummings on the mouth. She appears to be having the time of her life.

As usual, Berg refused to let the delays on her own show slow her down. She signed a deal to appear on comedy recordings as Molly Goldberg, the first of which would feature her together with the comedian Red Buttons. She oozed charm in an appearance on the game show *What's My Line?*, which featured a panel whose members were blindfolded asking questions to determine who a secret guest was. Wearing a fur and gloves, she arrived onstage to extended applause. She employed something that resembled a British accent, presumably to disguise her identity. One of the panel asked if she had a regular show on TV. "Depending on the sponsor's disposition," she cracked. They quickly determined who she was. Everyone knew Molly Goldberg.

In June, Berg appeared on the interview program *Person to Person*, hosted on CBS by Edward R. Murrow, the TV journalist who was most closely identified with anti-McCarthy reporting and commentary. The opportunity signified serious recognition of Berg as a cultural figure, and she seized the moment to shape her public image. In the interview piece, she answers questions in her crisp, cultivated mid-Atlantic accent while wearing a formal black dress that Molly would never choose. She shows Murrow around her Park Avenue apartment, introducing her house staff—her cook, Louise Capers, and a man in a sweater and tie named Manny Byers, as if they were family. She's gracious: "They could do without me but I couldn't do without them."

She names blintzes and borscht as her favorite dishes and explains, "I'm really Molly more hours of the day than I am Gertrude Berg." But she seems focused on distinguishing herself from her character. She says she prefers acting to writing: "Writing is work, acting is fun." She shows Murrow's cameras an opulent eighteenth-century English display cabinet and grand piano in her living room. She leads the cameras to the study to meet her husband, Lewis, who talks about typing up her scripts for her. She is careful to walk backward as they head up the stairs—a lady doesn't show her backside to Edward R. Murrow's camera.

Perhaps she was so concerned about distinguishing herself from Molly because it was becoming clear that Molly's place in pop culture was slipping. "Mrs. Berg simply is not the slim, trim contemporary matron, her successor in today's family idealization; she looks and carries herself like that matron's immigrant mother," *Commentary* magazine said. "For one thing, television audiences today do not find the portrait of a domineering, sheltering matriarch exactly comfortable."

Still, she retained enough of a following that DuMont grabbed the chance to snatch her from NBC. By April 1954, the Goldbergs were once again moving, this time to Hazel Scott's former network. DuMont sold the sponsorship to Vitamin Corporation of America, which paid $5.5 million for the chance to once again work with *The Goldbergs*. Berg could go on with her program. And DuMont, always trying to prove itself a major player, had added a bona fide star to its lineup. Though, of course, *The Goldbergs'* move from CBS to NBC to DuMont clearly marked a downward trend. And the Goldbergs' time with DuMont would last, in the end, just six months.

By now *The Goldbergs*, as a television production, ran nearly on autopilot, real family and TV family relationships mixing together behind the scenes. Berg's thirty-two-year-old son, Cherney, a balding man with apple cheeks and smiling eyes, took key backstage jobs now, doing everything from laying down blocking tape for rehearsals to writing scripts. (Cherney's younger sister, Harriet, was now married to an army physician and was not involved with the show.)

Before taking a secure position on his mother's staff, Cherney had been a music teacher. His main student, a bookie, had paid Cherney not in cash but in horse-betting tips; Cherney had also conducted for the NBC Radio Orchestra at Radio City Music Hall. He used to explain how he had decided to switch careers after Gertrude had asked him to write a script: "I made more money in one day than I made in a month of teaching music." He and his mother had a jokey rapport that kept things light on the set, and Cherney was close to Eli Mintz, who played *The Goldbergs'* uncle David.

By now, the Bergs and their team had their live broadcast production routine down to a science. What they didn't realize was that live sitcom broadcasts were on their way out, making way for the *I Love Lucy* technique, which enabled both slicker production and more flexible airing of episodes at different times and in different regions. It would also eventually allow for the syndicated reruns that would make *I Love Lucy* an enduring classic. *The Goldbergs'* DuMont rehearsals and live shows would mark the end of an era, a transition point in the way sitcoms were made.

At one rehearsal for *The Goldbergs* at the time witnessed by a reporter for *Commentary* magazine, Berg marched into the room wearing a print wrap dress, asked an actress appearing in the episode why she had arrived late, and then arranged some of the chairs to serve as the Goldbergs' living room furniture for the day's work. In the DuMont era, *Goldbergs* rehearsals took place at the Central Plaza Hotel on Second Avenue, in the ballroom. Chandeliers provided the room's dim light, and a chuppah decorated with artificial palm leaves and calla lilies might sit at one end of the room, awaiting an upcoming Jewish wedding. Rows of wooden chairs anticipated future guests while the empty expanse in the middle of the room stood in for the Goldbergs' apartment that day.

Once Berg was in the room, she took charge and became the center of attention. When she declared her intention to rehearse her lines from memory, without a script in hand, murmurs of approval swept the cast and crew. She improvised a line change, saying

"Come, rest on my Castro Convertible," instead of "sofa," as it said in the script.

When the cast reacted with, as the reporter said, "a chorus of 'hoh-hoh's,'" Berg shot back with "Why not? They gave us the couch for the set."

Berg rewrote another line on the spot to sound more Goldbergian, changing "Who made a call to Miami?" to "Who in our circle would perchance have someone in Miami to communicate with?"

After she called for a rehearsal break, Berg rushed over to the reporter, pink and pleased from her exertions. She sat down and put her hand on top of his. "Well, darling, how do you like it?" she asked. "It's going good?"

Berg continued the dance between commanding the stage and pleasing people the following Tuesday, broadcast day, at the Du-Mont Tele-Centre at 205 East 67th Street, a modern building covered in mirrored windows that the network had recently opened. DuMont had hit its peak reach, with about two hundred affiliates around the country. On the occasion of the building's June 1954 opening, the *New York World-Telegram & Sun* declared it "New York's Answer to West Coast Video Rivalry." It sat across the street from a row of narrow tenement houses not unlike the building where the fictional Goldbergs were depicted as living.

For the dress rehearsal ninety minutes before the broadcast, Berg had a new audience of about thirty to play to: the crew, admen, photographers, and assistants who hadn't been present for the earlier rehearsals that had stretched across Friday, Saturday, Monday, and earlier that afternoon. Most of them watched and laughed, which put a smile on Berg's face. One man fell asleep in a lounge chair on the set.

The *Goldbergs'* set ran along one wall of the studio floor, with three cameras and multiple microphones pointed at it, ready to beam its sights and sounds to the nation. The broadcast included its own moments of TV magic: during the second commercial, which rolled from film, Berg removed her dress to reveal another underneath—a costume change for the next scene. Four men from the crew scurried in to remove a dining room table set for dinner and swapped in an empty table.

One flight up in the control room, Cherney watched from a long table that sat in front of an equally long window overlooking the studio, the set dwarfed under the hanging lights. Next to him was the assistant director, who oversaw a panel of switches, as well as the director, a script girl, and several others. The assistant director could communicate with the three cameramen on the floor through the headphones and chest phone he wore, deciding at each moment which of their angles should appear on the broadcast. Three of the five television screens in the room showed those three angles, while the other two showed his current chosen shot.

When the broadcast wrapped, cast members and crew hugged Berg and lavished her with more praise. Her husband, Lewis, whom the reporter described as a "bald, sharp-faced gentleman"—had materialized at some point. Arlene McQuade, now a teen idol at eighteen, changed from her costume—a wool blouse, skirt, and flat shoes—into a form-fitting dress and strappy high heels. Tom Taylor, who had replaced Larry Robinson as son Sammy Goldberg now returned from military service, left in his show costume—a sports jacket and chinos. He drove off in a miniature red convertible.

The reporter who had spent the previous week with Berg and the production wrote honestly about his reaction to Berg and her assistant, Fannie Merrill: "I got the impression that the account they were offering me of Mrs. Berg's career was based on magazine and newspaper stories whose sorting and fixing of the facts they had found convenient."

No one involved knew that that would be among *The Goldbergs'* last live broadcasts.

Things were going well at the moment for Gertrude Berg and *The Goldbergs*, but not for their new network, DuMont. The network had pushed itself too far in trying to compete with ABC, CBS, and NBC. It had signed Berg to a $5 million contract that, by late 1954, it couldn't pay for. It had thrown the last of its money at expanding across the country and moving into its new headquarters. The network hoped the investment would pay off quickly. It did not. Despite strong Nielsen ratings of an estimated 10 million viewers, *The Goldbergs* had lost yet another network home.

This time, they were not canceled; their network was.

DuMont's managing director, Ted Bergmann, wrote to Berg in October 1954, "I did want to tell you how proud we were to have you on the DuMont Network even for only a short period of time. Your program has always represented the showmanship values which we strive to perpetuate on the air. If only the economies of this business would permit, 'The Goldbergs' would become a permanent feature on the DuMont Television Network."

DuMont operated with bare-bones resources through the summer of 1955 as it sold off its stations and canceled its contracts one by one. It signed off the air on October 10, 1955.

With everything in television changing—from the conservative backlash to the color invasion to the incursion of big-business interests—the women who had invented television once more had to adjust their visions for their creations and their careers to survive. The year 1955 would test them as never before.

The Scourge of 1955

Gertrude Berg, Betty White, Irna Phillips, and Hazel Scott

Gertrude Berg could not cook, but that didn't stop her from telling others how to do so.

The woman had dominated radio and television by the force of her will, charisma, and talent. She had ensured that the sitcom became a mainstay of television when she had insisted that her show, *The Goldbergs*, be given a spot on CBS just as TV took off in 1948. She had perfected the mini–living room play that had become a staple of television comedy. She had brought Jewish immigrant culture to millions of Gentiles across the United States, combating prejudices still in place in post–World War II America. She had written a parental advice column and promoted a line of housedresses modeled after her character's costumes, which extended her brand far beyond the media in which she had originally been created.

Gertrude Berg could do many extraordinary things. Cook, she could not.

Her character, Molly, was another story. Molly spent a lot of time in the kitchen, rarely getting through an episode without appearing to prepare one dish or another. In one typical 1954 scene, she rushes toward the stove in her standard apron and pearls, singing the Broadway musical song "Hernando's Hideaway" under her breath as she removes a hunk of meat from a boiling pot. Chatting with daughter Rosalie, she stirs the pot, then adds some salt and pepper.

This was a classic move for Molly: removing things from pots, salting and peppering things, stirring things, putting things into pots. On the show, she constantly worries over meals, wipes her hands on her apron, or directs Uncle David to chop vegetables. *Commentary* magazine wrote, "Molly worked away at supper—cutting up a chicken, seasoning and tasting the soup, chopping fish or herring— demonstrating at length her domestic skills." Molly even prepared the ultimate of Jewish acquired tastes, gefilte fish.

But no one who knew Gertrude Berg ever knew the woman to cook. Her hired cook, Louise Capers, was the one who made the food in the Berg residence.

That didn't stop Berg from agreeing to coauthor a cookbook. Nor did her penchant for fine dresses, furs, and pearls stop her from putting her name on a popular line of housedresses. Empire building required perpetuating such illusions at times—that is, if you were a *woman* building an empire.

In 1955, Berg agreed to coauthor *The Molly Goldberg Jewish Cookbook* with the food writer Myra Waldo. Berg, after all, knew her limitations. She would bring the name and character recognition. Waldo brought the know-how, having recently published the popular *Serve at Once: The Soufflé Cookbook*. She had also edited

The Complete Round-the-World Cookbook, which featured recipes curated by Pan American Airways.

But people would most likely buy the Berg-Waldo collaboration because of Molly Goldberg: the introduction is signed with the fictional character's name. Waldo's text plays along: "Watching Molly cook was a wonderful experience. I think the secret of her success is that she likes to cook, and she delights in having her family and friends praise her food."

Waldo provided the actual recipes—beef and sauerkraut, meat-stuffed prunes—among which Berg sprinkled Mollyisms such as "Show me someone who can make knishes and I'll show you a person." The book bursts with instructions for dishes inspired by Jewish cooking and infused with 1950s food trends: Knobl Fish and Chopped Chicken Livers, Cream of Lima Bean Soup and Cold Borscht, Fried Mackerel and Jellied Carp with Grapes, Roast Duck Pincus Pines Style (named for the fictional resort the Goldbergs frequented) and Roast Stuffed Goose, Roast Beef and Boiled Beef, Rice-Stuffed Peppers and Carrot Sticks in Honey, Schnecken and Hazelnut Rolls, Prune hamentaschen and Mohn Candy. Appendices explain kosher food and Passover.

Soon after Berg signed the cookbook deal, she set off on a summer tour of department stores across the Midwest and Northeast to promote another project that was far more Molly than it was herself: her housedress line for the "full-figured woman." As her granddaughter said, "She would never have worn a housedress. I mean *never.*" This woman had her hair done, in her classic chignon style, even when she was at home with her family. Her grandchildren never saw her hair down. In fact, they never saw her bare feet, either. She owned dozens of dress gloves, hats, fur coats, and opulent pins. She would have no use for a low-cost, simple frock meant only for a housewife to do her housework in.

But Berg did not pass by an opportunity when it presented itself to her. For the previous five years, she had capitalized on her popularity with housewives by putting her character's name on a line of casual dresses, first in partnership with a company called Suburban Cottons and then with Riverdale Frocks. She said she had helped design the plain, affordable garments (price: $3.99) based on the input she had solicited from women she had talked with during public appearances. She attracted crowds of hundreds of fans when she toured department stores on the line's behalf and even modeled a few of her own wares on those occasions. Other times, members of local women's clubs would model while "Molly" emceed the proceedings. She basked in the attention. She loved to talk to her fans. She loved to sign autographs.

Berg relished the chance to go on a tour promoting one or another of her projects. She preferred being busy to being still, and she hated to be alone. Her family believed it was a reaction to growing up the only living child of parents who had lost a son and to enduring her mother's subsequent institutionalization. After so much aloneness growing up, she wanted nothing to do with it anymore, and she had built a life of defenses against it. She always had her loyal assistant, Fannie Merrill, to follow her around wherever she went. The two spent so much time together that some people speculated that they were lovers. Most of the time, the two were also surrounded by friends, family, crew, or fans.

With all of that activity, Berg was in reality once again killing time as her show sat in TV purgatory.

When Berg wasn't on the road, Fannie and Louise were almost always with her at home. Berg also had a close friend named Mira Rostova, a famous acting coach who had worked in the Method tradition with Montgomery Clift. (She was the real-life, successful version of Madame Fagel Bagenhacher from Betty White's *Hollywood on Television* sketches.) Rostova, a petite Russian immigrant, spent Thanksgivings with the Bergs and a lot of time with Berg socially. Berg loved to play cards with her crew—she collected decks of luxe playing cards, with jeweled edges and velvet boxes, and favored canasta as her game of choice. Louise would cook them all fried chicken and apple pie. Sometimes Louise's husband would come by the house, too, to do some odd jobs for the Bergs.

On weekends, Gertrude and Lewis Berg often headed to their country home in Bedford Hills, about forty-five miles north of New York City. The historic wooden home, which predated the Revolutionary War, had two bedrooms, a bathroom, a hallway, and a sitting room they called "the sponsor room." On the rare occasions Gertrude decided to court sponsors with a social event, she did it there. At least once, she hosted a large summertime party in Bedford Hills, full of business associates. At other times, she invited her children and three young grandchildren to spend time there with her.

She busied herself with other acting work as well. She appeared on dramatic anthology shows, including ABC's *The Elgin Hour* and *The U.S. Steel Hour*. On the former, in an episode called "Hearts and Hollywood," she played a woman who moves from Pennsylvania to California to be near her son, who's working as a director in Hollywood, and seeks companionship in a newspaper's lonely-hearts column. On the latter, she starred in a segment titled "Six O'Clock Call" as a grief-stricken widow who believes she receives phone calls from her dead husband regularly.

Berg was building a reputation as a serious actress, possibly anticipating an end, after twenty-six years, to *The Goldbergs*. And she did it well. *Commentary* magazine said, "She carried off these characterizations with the skill, warmth, and plausibility—and none of the anachronisms—that she brought to Molly; as usual, she was superior to her material. . . . And she has cast away in these roles her often irritating vaudeville display of cuteness." The critic Gilbert Seldes, a longtime advocate for television and for Gertrude Berg's talent in the medium, said of her dramatic work, "She is a great force in what she does and in this, the primary business of giving life to imagined people, she is incomparable."

But she hadn't given up on *The Goldbergs* yet, despite its eviction from three of the four networks. With DuMont out of business, in March 1955 she partnered with Guild Films, the studio behind *Life with Elizabeth*'s national run, to produce *The Goldbergs* for similar national syndication. The contract came as part of what *Billboard* called "the most ambitious production program" in Guild's history.

However, a devastating blow was about to come from the show's past.

The year 1955 was not an ideal time for an empire-building woman who couldn't cook. It was the year in which the 1950s crystallized into what it would come to represent to future generations: a white, patriarchal bastion of conservatism, conformity, and consumerism that preferred the little woman in the kitchen and far away from the office. The 1950s would become the most idealized decade of the century, a standard that white men in power continue to invoke up to this day. It's what President Donald Trump means when he talks about "making America great again." He means prioritizing the supremacy of white, straight men and their ability to make money over all else. And the era's television would, curiously, become the shorthand way for future pundits and politicians to refer to the supposed realities of the time: white, suburban families such as those on *Father Knows Best* and *The Adventures of Ozzie and Harriet* standing as shining examples of a past that existed only on television screens.

This is why the year of 1955 would do its best to destroy the women who invented television. It had no use for a single, beautiful, young television host who refused to marry; a soap opera impresario who was raising two children on her own while making shows that served only female audiences; a Black woman who insisted on standing up for herself and her race; and an aging Jewish mother who thought she deserved as much screen time as anyone else.

A person's television career can surmount only so many difficulties. The turn toward a conservative ideal—a strong father figure, a beautiful and submissive housewife, sweet kids with minor problems, white Anglo-Saxon Protestants all—would soon, finally, have its way with Berg, Phillips, Scott, and White.

Though it had felt as if White's noontime talk show was going well, the small signs of trouble seemed more obvious in retrospect.

The network had begun tinkering with the show within its first few months on the air. As early as February 1954, NBC executives considered combining *The Betty White Show* with a series called *Ladies' Choice*, which had enjoyed a successful run the previous summer. A memo described that program: "*Ladies' Choice* is based on the proper blending of interesting people, as well as performing talent, and is predicated on the theme that ladies think differently than do men." It added, in parentheses, "Women effectively proved their choice in politics during the last national election." Eisenhower had won the election of 1952 with a majority of women voters on his side, a fact that would lead his reelection campaign four years later to become the first to deliberately target women. Of course, that historic and politically significant fact did not change male programmers' ideas about women. The women's clubs consulted for *Ladies' Choice* would vote on "anything pertaining to their daily life—drama, fashion, etc." Surely not politics.

242242

In March, NBC executive Sam Fuller met with White's producer, Don Fedderson. Fuller told Fedderson that the network loved White "but felt the show lacked necessary ingredient to make the people want to tune her in day after day," according to a memo from Fuller. The network suggested a regular "heart spot," a segment in which she would do good deeds that played well to the camera. The memo concluded, "At present time we feel Betty White is a singer who is nice to people. To fall into daytime formula, we feel she should be a nice person who just happens to be able to sing. In other words in our estimation the daytime field is for the most part built on emotional upsets which seem to interest dames." Irna Phillips, incidentally, had built her career on exactly that idea, though she probably wouldn't have put it quite the same way, and she had long been mocked for taking exactly that approach.

Fedderson kept his faith in White's show. He said in a telegram to Tom McAvity, "THINK THE PRESENT SHOW IS GROWING ON ORIGINAL CONCEPT THAT IS BETTY'S PERSONALITY. HOWEVER BE-LIEVE WE POSSIBLY HAVE THE GIMMICK YOU ARE LOOKING FOR TO STIMULATE A FASTER INCREASE OF HOUSEWIVES INTEREST." The "new heart gimmick" turned out to be segments in which White would reunite military men with their families after a deployment and fulfill the wishes of orphans in a nearby Los Angeles home who wanted to meet, say, a clown or a ballerina. Many major daytime talk show hosts have employed exactly this sort of gambit in the decades since, from Oprah Winfrey to Ellen DeGeneres to Kelly Clarkson.

Then Senator Joseph McCarthy came for *The Betty White Show*, though not in his traditional way. His popularity was on the decline overall and President Eisenhower didn't particularly care for him, so he made a last-ditch move to grab headlines again: he accused the US Army of being "soft" on communism. In April 1954, he presided over hearings—the first of the McCarthy hearings that were televised—to investigate his charges against the army.

The effort proved to be his undoing. His decision to attack the army turned the American public, the Republican Party, and Eisenhower against him instantly. And his performance on television, the first time large numbers of Americans saw him live in action, came across as unhinged. He interrupted those being questioned with his own unrelated commentary and yelled "Point of order!" whenever he didn't like the direction things were going. Politicians were learning about the power of television: charisma on camera could make—or its lack break—a career.

Like any good TV show, the hearings offered an indelible climax. McCarthy disparaged an associate of the man being questioned, army chief counsel Joseph Welch. Welch stared McCarthy down as only an army man could and said, "Until this moment, Senator, I think I never really gauged your cruelty or your recklessness. . . . Have you no sense of decency, sir, at long last?" The packed hearing room exploded with cheers and applause. None of McCarthy's charges against the army was upheld, and by the end of the year, the Senate voted to censure him for his conduct. The McCarthy Era had ended. And the senator was done in, fittingly, by the medium whose progressivism he had so feared. In the process, he had unwittingly produced the year's must-watch daytime programming.

His undoing, however, would not stop the larger conservative wave pushing women to the margins of television.

And unfortunately for Betty White, McCarthy self-combusted in her time slot. In late April and early May, White had to compete not only with CBS's strong soap opera lineup—which included Irna Phillips's The Guiding Light—but also with history in the making. Phillips seemed to emerge unscathed, given the immense popularity of The Guiding Light on both radio and television. But for a fledgling new series like White's, any interruption in viewers' habits could prove fatal.

Then White had to stop doing her heartrending reunion segments after a complaint from other NBC shows, *This Is Your Life* and *Truth or Consequences*, that she was infringing on their territory. Soon, in July, the network moved her show to 4:30 p.m. in the hope of attracting more viewers and thus more advertisers.

But White knew better. She understood that at that hour, women would be out shopping or picking their kids up from school. And she was right: *The Betty White Show* tanked in the afternoon. So NBC moved her back to midday in September, this time at noon, but by that time, her fans were more confused than ever about when they could find her on television.

For the first time in her TV career, White worried about losing her job. For all those years on KLAC, she had fought off jobs that piled on top of more jobs. Now her national breakthrough dangled in jeopardy. *Life with Elizabeth* had run through a lot of material and wouldn't last forever—or perhaps even much longer. Suddenly it seemed as though all her hard work and sacrifices might just leave her alone and adrift.

In November 1954, NBC executive Fred Wile threw a soiree at Romanoff's in Beverly Hills. The scene was low-key Los Angeles glamorous, expertly staged for an actress and television personality such as Betty White to be seen doing something that would land her in a gossip column. Nothing too scandalous, of course—ideally some antidote to her perpetual singleness, with a hint of romantic intrigue.

The guests included White, the gossip columnist Sheilah Graham, and Dave Garroway, the host of NBC's successful national morning show, *Today*. The *Today* show, which had launched two years earlier, was recognized as the first of its genre, with a blend of news and lighter entertainment bits—including a chimp sidekick for Garroway, J. Fred Muggs.

Graham arrived at the gathering with the stated hope of match-making for Garroway, who was distinguished by his dark-framed glasses, bowtie, and awkward smile. Her choice for Garroway, she wrote, "must be glamorous, beautiful, and intellectual."

The gossip columnist then reported overhearing Wile as he talked to a fellow executive about White. "Maybe she lacks sex appeal," he said. "I'm sure women like her, but do men?" Worry about White swirled in the air this evening: her show was down a sponsor and couldn't last much longer without one.

Wile's line of questioning was implicitly answered when Graham spotted White and Garroway "deep in intellectual conversation. Well, not too intellectual, but interesting: They are discussing their bedtimes."

"I have to exist on four or five hours' sleep a night," Garroway said.

"I get up at 5 a.m.," Betty said, "clucking sympathetically," according to Graham.

"How can you sleep so late?" he teased. He, after all, got up most days at 4:00 a.m. Graham wrote, "Commonplace words, but the way they are looking at each other I can see that something is beginning."

The pop singer Dinah Shore passed by and tried to get Garroway's attention, but to no avail. "Will you please pass the salt?" asked the dashing, dimple-chinned film star Fred MacMurray, but Betty, distracted by Garroway, passed her plate instead.

Graham concluded, "I take another look at Betty. I've never seen her look so pretty. In fact it's the first time that I've seen her at a party. That early-morning call is a date killer. And all of a sudden she has sex appeal. And a sponsor! The man from Geritol and RDX whispers to Fred Wile and it comes out a commercial."

Graham wrote that White later confided in her, "Dave left for New York the next day. But I expect to see him again very soon—in the East." White hoped to do a week of her show from New York soon; it would, remarkably, be her first trip there. Pressed for more details about her feelings for Garroway, she said, "It's terribly exciting. I really got a thrill out of meeting Dave. He's very, very nice. Also, I've never been to New York and I know I'll have a wonderful time."

It seemed everyone came out of the evening—or at least Graham's column—looking a bit sexier. Even Romanoff's: its country-club cuisine had once attracted all of Hollywood's brightest. But it had fallen out of favor in recent years as the owner, Michael Romanoff, had become friendly with the right-wing FBI director, J. Edgar Hoover, the man behind McCarthy's reign of terror.

You couldn't make up a better TV business fairy tale than the possibility of Garroway and White coupling: two affable early risers merging the East and West Coast production hubs. And for a truly happy TV business ending, White had magically landed a sponsor that same evening! NBC's Sam Fuller placed a clip of the story in his "Betty White" file—proof that at least a few people present at that soiree had done their jobs. This was the sort of thing White had to endure now as a national TV star hoping to save her show as it hung in the ratings balance: use some of her precious few hours off to keep her famous charm on full blast while proving her sex appeal, marketability, and datability to her network bosses and to the public at large via Graham.

But the column—which, let's be clear, was not likely strict journalism—may have signaled more desperation behind the scenes than any real progress for White's show. And the network and sponsor gods—as Gertrude Berg, Irna Phillips, and Hazel Scott could attest—were only growing more capricious as their economic power grew.

Four months after the Romanoff's party and a year after she signed the deal for *The Betty White Show*, White took her first trip to New York City, that trip east she'd hinted at to Graham. She went with her producer, Don Fedderson, hoping to plead for her show's life. She met with NBC executives, only to be told that there was no use; the show was over. As of January 1955, the pop singer Tennessee Ernie Ford would replace her.

She believed it was the end of her career. She had worked so hard, and now she had run out her time. Career focus and effort didn't guarantee a thing. She would never get another job. She would just walk herself out to that East Coast ocean—the Atlantic Ocean—and, as she said, never come up. "It was my first brush with the classic showbiz rejection syndrome," she wrote.

Of course, she was just being dramatic. She was Betty White, and she would handle this. Devastated, she flew home. She had to do one last episode of *The Betty White Show* to say good-bye to her viewers. The network had extended her that courtesy.

She did it on New Year's Eve, though she cried right through that opening song: "It's time to say hello again, and start our show again . . ." Only the closing song proved harder: "Till we say 'Hi' again, soooo long."

Irna Phillips had so far survived the onslaught of men into the business. But her work, her audience, and the genre she had created, the soap opera, were as disrespected as ever.

NBC tried to take down her genre from within in 1955, when it launched *NBC Matinee Theater*, an hour-long daytime anthology drama series with the stated goal of elevating the form—the implication being that it needed elevation. "We are trying to up-grade dramatic entertainment in the daytime for women," wrote Sylvester L. "Pat" Weaver, Jr., NBC's head of television. Weaver advocated using television to bring what he considered high culture to the masses. He had made his name staging TV "spectaculars," including an iconic televised stage production of *Peter Pan* starring Mary Martin, and now he was coming for daytime. He budgeted *NBC Matinee Theater* at an astounding $5 million (nearly $48 million in 2020 terms) for its first year of production.

Critics loved it, perhaps because it offered them another way to bash soap operas. "Before we had ridiculous dramas which went on and on for years about some neurotic woman's failure to capture a man," wrote Stan Anderson of the *Cleveland Press*, taking direct aim at Phillips's creations. (It of course did not occur to him that perhaps those particular shows were simply *not made for him*, which perhaps did not make them inherently useless, just *not for him*.) "This sort of abortive drama probably set our country back a century. It is, therefore, with some amount of pride that NBC can offer the adult *Matinee [Theater]* drama."

Irna Phillips had other ideas.

In 1955, after twenty-five years in the broadcast business, she began arguing for *more* soaps. She thought daytime dramas should be extended from the fifteen-minute format they'd started with in radio to a full thirty minutes now that they were prevalent on television. She felt that better plots and characters would result; those who argued against it worried the shows would get repetitive.

She worked with writer Agnes Nixon and director Ted Corday on a proposal for a half-hour soap opera. She wanted to call it *As the Earth Turns*, but that title had already been used for a book. So they would call it *As the World Turns* instead. It would follow two families, the close-knit Hugheses and the Lowells, a couple who had separated and had one daughter. Phillips wanted to explore the contrast between the two families: "I made this change because by the 1950s divorce and separation were becoming a more pronounced element in our social structure."

She also decided to make the men central to their households, a change from her previous work. "I always drew heavily on my own family experience—a family in which a widowed mother was the dominant personality," she wrote. "I also drew on my own personal life." She invoked her time with the doctor who had gotten her pregnant and abandoned her in her twenties: "My one experience with a dominant man, the doctor in Dayton, had left me with less than nothing. I came away from that experience believing that dominant men always left women with nothing. Since the beginning of my writing career I had never depended on a man. I was afraid to. There is no doubt in my mind that I transferred my deep feelings of independence to the women characters I created." Now, however, having been battered down by a society that made no room for successful working mothers to make it on their own, she had internalized the messages of the 1950s' conservative wave and come to regret it all: her own independence, and her portrayal of such.

That contradiction formed the core of Phillips's career: the more successful she became, the more she felt distanced from her children. And the more she felt distanced from her children, the more she felt inclined to believe in, and reflect, the power of patriarchy. Though her shows would populate the airwaves for years to come, she would often use her new creations to reinforce traditional values. The conservative wave hadn't wiped her out of television the way it had Scott or even sidelined her the way it did Berg and White. But in the end, it got to her, too. She did not believe in "the equality of the sexes," she said. "I wanted to be loved. I wanted to be cared for. I wanted someone to look after me, someone to turn to. I wanted a husband for me and a father for my children and I wanted him to be the head of the home." Those ideas would form the core of her next creation.

Phillips, Corday, and Nixon decided to hire an agent to help them present their half-hour serial pitch to potential sponsors and networks. They chose Herb Rosenthal from MCA, one of the biggest agents in the business.

But their relationship with Rosenthal frayed quickly. He suggested that they get a network or sponsor to pay for a pilot episode, but that seemed to defeat the point of their hiring him. Wasn't that *his* job? Then Phillips suggested that Rosenthal's company, MCA, pay at least part of the cost. His reply: "We don't believe in investing in a possible failure."

The room fell silent until he left. They knew when they looked at each other after his departure: Rosenthal was out. Once again, Phillips would have to pay to produce a pilot herself. After all that time, the industry still didn't believe in her.

Even with McCarthy himself vanquished by television, the conservative agenda of 1955 surely drew strength from the years of McCarthyism that preceded it. Berg's former TV husband, Philip Loeb, was struggling in the wake of his blacklisting. He was having problems with his eyes and difficulty paying the doctors to treat his cataracts, and that was on top of the bills from his schizophrenic son's institution. He wrote to his friend Kate Mostel, Zero's wife, in September 1954 from the road with the play *Time Out for Ginger*, saying he was "forming an anti-suicide club in the company." He added that they had a "kit" that included scotch, tape for neck wounds, splints, and the home addresses of everyone's next of kin. "I'm a bitter old man," he continued. "I never smile."

Two months later, Loeb wrote to Zero, "The only arrangements

I have made for my own funeral are to have Win Stracke"—a blacklisted children's television show host—"Sing 'With joy the impa-
tient husbandman drives forth his lusty team' from Haydn's 'The
Seasons.' Do you want to be on the bill? Next to closing, I suppose."
He joked in another letter that while Zero should speak at his funeral, it should be "under an assumed name so in case there is an
afterlife I won't have the same political troubles I had here." Zero
had been blacklisted, too.

As the Goldbergs moved toward yet another incarnation on
television with Guild, Loeb neared the end of his settlement pay-
ments from the show. The two years that had remained on his contract with *The Goldbergs* expired. At the same time, his tour with
Time Out for Ginger ended, and he faced an outstanding income tax
warrant for $964.87, his unpaid bill from 1953. He appeared for a
few weeks in a February 1955 production of Anton Chekhov's *The
Three Sisters* in New York but did not find other work. According to
the biography *Zero Dances*, Loeb could no longer pay for his son's
care at Chestnut Lodge, and his son was transferred to a state institution meant more for housing the mentally ill than for real care.

Over the Labor Day weekend of 1955, the depleted Loeb
checked into room 507 of Manhattan's Taft Hotel, in the heart of
the theater district at Seventh Avenue and 50th Street.

On September 1, he called several friends, changed into his pajamas, and took too many sleeping pills.

The next day, a maid stopped by room 507 several times, hoping
to clean it for the guest, who was registered as Fred Lang. The "do
not disturb" sign hung from the door all day. At 8:45 p.m., the maid
and the assistant manager entered the room anyway. They found
Loeb lying on the bed. On the nightstand sat a bottle of fourteen
sleeping pills and a prescription for fifty more. Loeb was dead at the
age of sixty.

His roles as an actor are largely forgotten by now. But his legacy is perhaps greater than any acting role could have been: he fought for rehearsal pay, pensions, and medical plans for actors, now all standard parts of actors' union contracts. Actors can hope to make a living from their craft in part because of Loeb's activism. His death was widely recognized as a direct result of the blacklist.

Gertrude Berg was not built to handle this sort of thing; she was built to handle the handleable, the situations that could be overcome with a little smarts and a lot of hard work, and maybe a little charm, too. She was built for solutions and action, creativity and chutzpah. She was not built for this.

There is no evidence of how she found out about his death—not in her archives, nor in her biography. She was, for certain, at a meeting with her cookbook editor, Clara Claasen, to discuss upcoming publicity plans on the day after his death, when the news was made public. According to a letter from Claasen, Berg was emotional and visibly suffering. She did not speak publicly of Philip Loeb's death afterward. Her own memoir makes no mention of it.

Just as she had learned not to speak of her deceased older brother, just as she had learned to refer to herself as an only child, and just as she had learned to lock away her own mother's decline, she found another box inside her—one imagines a suitably exquisite box, lined with velvet and trimmed in jewels—where she could place her television husband and friend. For so long, how to save him had seemed like a dilemma that might have a solution, if only she worked hard enough at it. She had believed she would win, as she had so many times before.

She had lost him now, again, twice, and forever.

Gertrude Berg dealt with the death of her former costar, Philip Loeb, the only way she knew how. She threw herself into her work.

She had just signed a deal to bring *The Goldbergs* to Guild Films, and with it came the biggest change for the TV family since Loeb had left the show three years earlier: the Goldbergs were moving to the suburbs. Berg wrote in the press release to announce the change, "The Goldbergs are now settled in a new home, with down payment made but with mortgage woes to come, in a small, average community, Haverville, which might be anywhere in the US. As author and hoverer-over of the Goldberg family, I have been asked what in the world prompted this drastic shift in locale. Well, in moving to the country, where Jake is establishing a wedding gown factory, the Goldbergs are just following a trend." She continued, "In recent years, according to surveys, more than 10 percent of Americans have forsaken urban communities for the more leisurely life and cleaner air of small towns."

The *New York Times* covered the move, noting that the quintessential New York City family, "like many other New Yorkers," was leaving town. The Goldbergs thus officially became a 1950s TV family like those in *The Adventures of Ozzie and Harriet* and *Father Knows Best*. It also went from live broadcasts to taped episodes, a change Berg resisted—she believed TV was best done live. But this switch was now unavoidable, since Guild dealt only in syndicated, filmed shows that could be broadcast whenever the stations wanted to schedule them.

Billboard gave the new *Goldbergs* what had become a standard review: "There is no question but that Guild Films has captured the essential quality of *The Goldbergs*—its warmth and humanity—in its transition from a live show to a film show. The quality stems primarily from"—where else?—"the flavorful personality of Gertrude Berg as she plays Molly Goldberg." Set in the family's new Cape Cod–style home, *Variety* said, *The Goldbergs* "maintains its innate and unique warmth and humor." But the reviewer wondered,

"As warm, wonderful, and witty a picture of family life as it is, isn't it possible that the specialized area of Jewish humor-folklore is a thing of the past?"

Haverville opened up new plotlines for *The Goldbergs*, which could be interesting at times and dark at others. Rosalie, suddenly aware of her different physiognomy, contemplated a nose job. Molly struggled to make friends and didn't quite fit in with the slim, WASPy housewives around her.

A striking 1956 episode plays like a metaphor for the public diminishment of *The Goldbergs'*, and Molly's, spirit. She is shipped off to a "milk farm"—that is, a weight loss camp—by her doctor, with a bit too strong of an endorsement from her husband, Jake, now played by Robert H. Harris. After days of eating lettuce and carrots and drinking skim milk and sauerkraut juice at the camp, Molly rebels. She pretends to have a toothache so she can go into town to visit a dentist. She returns with a knitting bag full of cured meats from the local deli. She shares them with her fellow campers during a jubilant party in her room, but she's caught and subsequently kicked out.

At the end of the episode, some of her family happily welcome her back home, none the skinnier. Rosalie assures Molly that there's no need to worry or apologize. Uncle David urges her to eat with them and says, "Be as round as you want, Molly, dear. We love you anyway."

The tearful Molly turns to Jake. "You didn't say, 'Stay as round as you are.' David said it. My uncle said it, not you."

"All right, Molly," Jake snaps. "You're a compulsive eater, and you can't help yourself." It's a breathtakingly hurtful jab. It's hard to imagine Philip Loeb's Jake saying such a thing.

"I am not!" she cries as she stands and slams the table. "I'm a human being, like you, like you, like you." She nods at each of them.

"You think going away to drink milk is the answer? It is not." She then delivers an impassioned sermon about how such a restrictive regime at the camp couldn't prepare her for the everyday world, where food choices abound.

She stalks off into the kitchen, where she shovels forkfuls of spaghetti into her mouth straight from the pot. Then she fixes herself a plate with a wedge of iceberg lettuce and a carrot and returns to the dinner table with it. "I don't need a policeman," she says. Jake smiles approvingly. The episode ends on that uncomfortably sour and sad note.

This plays in contrast to an episode just two years earlier, when the show was still set in the Bronx apartment. A neighborhood beautician recruits Molly to participate in a new local weight loss program. The flummoxed Molly is fascinated to hear about calorie counting and lured by the prospect of a "diploma" at the end of the program. A funny send-up of the contemporary weight loss culture ensues, with the women doing ridiculous calisthenics and sitting in steam boxes, their sweaty heads protruding from the top of the cabinetlike structures that hold their bodies. In the end, Molly fails to graduate—and her family, including Jake, offers her ice cream when she comes home.

The suburbs seem to have decimated the confident, meddling, happy center of attention Molly Goldberg once was. Her husband has become the embodiment of patriarchy, diminishing her spirit and disparaging her body—perhaps a reflection of how the new TV landscape felt to Berg. In the suburbs *The Goldbergs* took their last stand, but their energy was depleted and the territory was hostile. There would be no overtly Jewish main characters on TV again until the 1970s' *Bridget Loves Bernie*, about a marriage between a Catholic woman and a Jewish man.

As Berg hurried about to make the new run of shows in 1955,

she fended off calls and other social contact, with her secretary, Fannie Merrill, telling those who rang that Berg left early in the morning for the studio and returned late at night these days.

By fall, though, Berg added still more to her busy schedule as she set out to promote *The Molly Goldberg Jewish Cookbook*. She appeared on television to be interviewed by Dave Garroway and toured department stores again, this time telling the masses about her new collection of recipes in time for Hanukkah and Christmas.

Both Berg and Waldo did their share to let the world know about the book and its holiday gift potential. Waldo cooked enough beef with prunes and sweet potatoes to send to fifty-two reviewers in October. On October 21, Berg likely slipped into another of her many fine black dresses, maybe with a silk scarf and some diamond jewelry, surely a fur to ward off the chill of the approaching winter, and boarded a train to Pittsburgh with Merrill to begin another publicity tour.

The shows now dominating the airwaves were those we think of today as the heavy hitters of classic television: *The Honeymooners, The Ed Sullivan Show, I Love Lucy, The $64,000 Question, You Bet Your Life, Dragnet*. They were top-ten shows then and were preserved well enough to go into syndication, which was how future generations would learn about 1950s television. They would come to represent the era for all time.

For the moment, Gertrude Berg remained in the game. She had given everything to get there. But perhaps the cost had soared too high. Perhaps she could live without Molly after all.

The year of 1955 had so thoroughly obliterated Americans' memory of Hazel Scott that in 1956, when Nat King Cole got his own weekly prime-time variety show on NBC, he declared himself "the Jackie Robinson of television." But the show had trouble finding sponsors, who feared the reaction of southern audiences. Max Factor reps told Cole's manager, "No negro can sell lipstick." Cole snapped, "What do they think we use? Chalk? Congo paint?"

Cole spoke clearly in public about why his show was failing. He told *Ebony* magazine, "I was the pioneer, the test case, the Negro first. I didn't plan it that way, but it was obvious to anyone with eyes to see that I was the only Negro on network television with his own show. On my show rode the hopes and fears and dreams of millions of people.... After a trail-blazing year that shattered all the old bug-a-boos about Negroes on TV, I found myself standing there with the bat on my shoulder. The men who dictate what Americans see and hear didn't want to play ball."

The show lasted just thirteen embattled months. Even as the civil rights movement gained momentum under the leadership of Dr. Martin Luther King, Jr., with its bus boycotts in Montgomery, Alabama, television could not tolerate a major Black star. Cole later summed up the problem: "Madison Avenue is afraid of the dark."

While Cole's difficulties underlined how little progress had been made when it came to race on television, one flaw glared from his identification as "the Jackie Robinson of television": he seemed to have forgotten all about his friend Hazel Scott.

Scott was annoyed but not angry. *Everyone* was saying that Cole was the first Black person to have a television series. It wasn't just Cole himself. And it was simpler than adding the caveats necessary to what was, indeed, an important feat: he was the first Black TV host in this era of truly ubiquitous television, with signals that reached not just big cities but small towns, with shows you could expect most Americans to have seen and stars you could expect most Americans to know. His battle to keep his show was genuinely national news. Could you blame the guy if he wanted to tout his accomplishment?

That said, he had less reason to forget Scott's accomplishments than others did: the two were close personally. She would often visit him in Los Angeles, and their children, Skipper and Natalie, played together. "He's a good friend," she would say, then add an eye roll. "But, you know, come *on*."

Scott had moved on from her television days by now. In January 1955, she recorded *Relaxed Piano Moods* with bassist Charles Mingus and drummer Max Roach, her likely band from her TV show. Critics considered the record one of the best piano works ever and an artistic peak for Scott, well beyond swinging the classics to please the crowd. The tracks included Duke Ellington and Johnny Hodges's "The Jeep Is Jumpin,'" Gershwin's "A Foggy Day," and her own "Git Up from There."

A year after Cole's show signed off, Scott returned from her sojourn in Europe for a visit back to New York. When she got to the house, she let out a squeal of surprise when she saw the newspaper: Harry Cohn, the Columbia Pictures studio chief who had sworn she would never work in movies again as long as he was alive, had died. It felt like the start of a new era for her, whether or not she wanted to return to film.

As it happened, she did not.

Hazel Scott was finished with trying to please American show business. The other women who invented television, their spirits broken by that difficult year of 1955, would soon find their own new forms of liberation as well.

12

The World Turns

Irna Phillips wanted to tell the world what it was like to be the single mother of two adopted children—two adopted, complicated, troubled children, who might have been that way because of her own shortcomings as a mother. Still, she thought, the world should know.

So Irna knew exactly what to do when her daughter, Katherine, said, "If I ever find my real mother, I'll kill her"; she put it into her show. The Amanda Holmes character on *As the World Turns*, also adopted and troubled, threatened to murder her own birth mother. Angry mail besieged Phillips. Readers wondered: Why was she so cold and unfeeling?

Phillips picked through the pile of letters and chose four from married adoptive mothers. One by one she called them, sharing her own difficult experiences of adoption as a single working mother. She had never been able to provide the discipline and male influence she believed her son, Tom, had needed. She had never connected with Katherine the way she wished she could.

The women were surprised to hear that Phillips had adopted children herself. One of them asked: Didn't Phillips believe that love, affection, and understanding could overcome the problems of adoption?

Phillips answered, simply: No, she did not.

Story lines about adoption became her main way to work out her heartache. She hated to admit it, but she regretted adopting her children. If she could do it over again, she wrote, she wouldn't have adopted them, even though she knew she had done her best. "No, I didn't cook, dust, wash, or iron," she wrote later. "But I was at home, I did make a home for two children, I was home for meals, I arranged parties for them, I made sure they had regular medical check-ups, brushed their teeth, etc. In fact, outside of normal household chores I did everything that a normal mother could do."

But she could feel her children's resentment. "I don't believe . . . my children can possibly understand, or maybe they don't want to, that I was as unhappy in having adopted them as they were in being adopted by me," she wrote. "I adopted two children, but they never adopted me." *As the World Turns*, the second show she launched by financing her own pilot episode and dragooning sponsors, became the place she worked out her anger and grief.

It also ushered in the era of half-hour soaps—doubling the fifteen-minute standard transferred over from radio—and lasted for decades to come. But its birth was painful. When she decided in 1955 to work with writer Agnes Nixon and director Ted Corday on a new half-hour soap format, she ended up once again footing the production bill herself to prove her point. Her longtime contact at Compton Advertising, Lewis Titterton, persuaded CBS to provide the facilities and equipment to tape the pilot for a $10,000 cost to Phillips—a price break.

They held auditions and hired nine actors. The actors believed in the project enough to hold themselves available for six months, even though they had no idea if or when it would begin. The cast included Selena Royle, one of several blacklisted movie actresses who sought refuge in daytime television with sympathetic female creators such as Phillips.

Phillips had not planned to work with her longtime sponsor Procter & Gamble on the project, but in the end, she couldn't escape it: the company was looking for a series to fill the 1:30 p.m. time slot on CBS, where two shows had failed and a third was barely making it.

When P&G offered to sponsor the show, Phillips at first resisted: Didn't its quick interest indicate that others might be keen to buy it as well? She was still angry that the company had let her pay for the *Guiding Light* pilot and hadn't reimbursed her once the show had succeeded. But her *Guiding Light* supervisor at P&G, Bob Short, talked her into the deal. Procter & Gamble may have given her trouble at times, but they had proven themselves reliable over the years. She and Procter & Gamble were like a soap opera couple, destined to be torn apart and reunited over and over, forever.

In an infuriating development, Phillips's pilot proved so convincing that thirty-minute soaps suddenly transformed from an idea no one wanted into a concept worth clamoring for. The ad agency Benton & Bowles, inspired by *As the World Turns*, immediately created another half-hour show, *The Edge of Night*, to occupy the 3:30 p.m. slot on CBS. Phillips had been right, once again, though no one had wanted to bet on her; she provoked the first major evolution in the form she had created.

Still, she was happy to take the credit. In a February 1955 interview with a *Variety* reporter at the Waldorf-Astoria during one of her frequent production trips to New York, she revealed the news. The fifteen-minute conception of soaps was a vestige of the radio era, she said. Having merely ten minutes—with the other five going to commercials—to convey a compelling story just didn't work. "It's based on giving the daydreamers that nighttime 30-minute aura, with the extended time sparking such development," the article said.

The following year, *As the World Turns* officially became her second television hit. The show made its debut on April 2, 1956, with this dramatic introduction written upon a scroll that was shown on the screen: "As the world turns, somewhere the light of dawn breaks through the darkness of night. As the world turns, somewhere the sun dips into the distant horizon before the oncoming shadows of evening. . . . What is true of the world, nature, is true also of man. He too has his cycle."

With the show, Phillips said, she "fantasized as well as fictionalized my own life. For me the Hughes family represented what I imagined and believed the traditional family was at that time. The Lowells represented a fictionalized extension of my own personal life. After her husband left her, Claire Lowell raised her daughter alone. There was no man in the home. In my own mind Claire may as well have been a single woman rearing a child." (Phillips was making a distinction we likely wouldn't make now, between a divorced mother and a never-married mother.) These plotlines allowed her to share her own anguish about adoption with a wide audience. *As the World Turns* let Phillips alchemize her feelings into something that made women's days a little more interesting, a little more dramatic, a little more fun.

As the World Turns was the number one daytime soap for the next twenty years. It's hard to say in retrospect why any show is a hit, but it seems likely that Phillips's instincts proved spectacularly right in this case: the half-hour format enabled more expansive character development, the key to longevity in soap operas. Viewers fell in love with the Hughes and Lowell families at the show's center and couldn't wait to see what happened next in their hometown of Oakdale, Illinois. And Phillips's personal investment in the story lines, at least at first, must have shone through to some viewers. She was leading a daily conversation from mother to mother.

In 1958, NBC's new president, Robert E. Kintner, canceled the high-minded *NBC Matinee Theater*, which had been created to destroy soaps like Phillips's, and put two half-hour soap operas into its place. The 1960s represented a peak for Phillips's television career that surpassed her most productive years in radio: she had a hand in seven shows over the course of the next twenty years, including the long-running hit *Another World*, which she cocreated with her protégé William J. Bell.

She died on December 22, 1973, at the age of seventy-two in her hometown of Chicago. Four of her soaps were still on the air at the time, including *The Guiding Light* and *As the World Turns*.

The Guiding Light would eventually run continuously on radio and television for seventy-two years, making it not only the longest-running soap opera but also the longest running of all scripted programs in broadcast history. Phillips created the genre itself and is credited with several of its innovations: professionals such as doctors and lawyers as main characters with endless story possibilities, episode-ending cliff-hangers, organ music cues, and characters who crossed over from one serial to another. The daytime soap never truly gained the respect Phillips deserved, likely because it was associated with female audiences.

The daytime soap as she created it has been fading over the last two decades because of changing patterns in both family life and TV viewing: most adult American women are now employed full-time, and streaming services allow anyone watching TV during the day to see almost anything they want, from old sitcoms to new reality shows.

But Phillips's legacy extends far beyond daytime soaps—much of the spectacular television from the 2000s forward has built on some of these techniques. TV is now rife with heavily serialized story lines that keep viewers watching using cliff-hangers: any Netflix show that has swallowed up days of your life—*Orange Is the New Black, 13 Reasons Why*—has used Phillips's tricks. She'd be pleased to know that organ cues are not among them. The prolific producer Shonda Rhimes made her name with a soapy hospital drama, *Grey's Anatomy*, and a soapy legal drama, *How to Get Away with Murder*. And the industry *has* acknowledged the power of female audiences more in recent decades, particularly with the rise of Rhimes's empire.

Phillips's daughter, Katherine, tried to sell her mother's memoir to a publisher after her death. She wrote a dedication that indicated she understood more than Phillips may have realized: "In memory of my mother, whose life touched so many, many people—who left me a legacy of memories, some of which I would like to share with all the people who found something in her writings to make her success last until the end."

The other women who invented television found their own ways to recover from the incursion of conservatism and patriarchy that had sidelined them in the 1950s and even to thrive in surprising new ways. Their legacies would live on, whether we remembered their names or not.

By the late 1950s, Gertrude Berg was making the comeback no one had foreseen: she was being recognized as a serious actress and *not* for the role of Molly Goldberg.

On April 12, 1959, she won her first major show business award since her 1951 Emmy for playing Molly. This time it was a Tony, arguably the most prestigious of all acting awards. It recognized her performance in the Broadway drama *A Majority of One* as a Jewish American woman who, while still grieving her son's death in World War II, strikes up an unlikely romance with a Japanese man on a cruise ship. *New York Times* theater critic Brooks Atkinson raved, "Since she is on a stage, she obviously is acting. But it is difficult to remember that simple fact. For her simplicity seems to represent a native goodness that is rare and irresistible. . . . We are all children when she presides over a play."

The one person who was not surprised was Berg. She had worked for years toward this moment. Though she had played Molly onstage before, she took quite seriously the transition to playing someone else, a dramatic role she herself had not created, on the Broadway stage. She spent several years leading up to *A Majority of One* doing summer stock productions. Just as she had learned to write for radio and then for TV, and to act on the radio and then on TV, she now learned to command the stage at a Tony-winning level.

At that point, her grandchildren were old enough to understand what she did for a living. They all went to see her on Broadway, and the youngest, Annie, who was about four years old, shouted, "There's Grandma!" when the curtain came up.

In 1963, Berg starred in *Dear Me, The Sky Is Falling*—another script by *Majority of One* playwright Leonard Spigelgass—which was based on a story line she'd concocted: unsurprisingly, about a meddling mother who feels she's losing control of her husband and grown daughter.

True to character, Berg capitalized on her resurgence. In 1961, she published an autobiography, *Molly and Me: The Memoirs of Gertrude Berg*, cowritten with her son, Cherney. A delightful read, it speaks to the reader with the intimacy of the best Molly Goldberg moments. It's an inspiring tale of a girl who comes from immigrant stock and makes herself a major national star on sheer chutzpah. It never mentions World War II, Philip Loeb's firing, or his death. "I have lived and am still living a very happy life," she wrote in the opening. "Such a remark, I know, is a hopelessly unfashionable beginning for a modern autobiography, and I apologize."

Gertrude Berg knew how to give a crowd what they wanted. That is, a cheerful wife and mother, rather than what she was, a powerful, smart, ambitious businesswoman. She clearly didn't want to publicly embrace the fact that she had experienced setbacks and had made some bad decisions that led, even, to catastrophic results—even if they were not at all her fault. She was a determined woman who did her best. It turned out that her best wasn't always good enough. It turned out that she was human, not a television character.

The same year, Berg also returned to television, in yet another version of her classic role. On the CBS sitcom *Mrs. G. Goes to College*, she played a widow working to earn her degree. Even the title tried to capitalize on her former life as "Mrs. Goldberg," though this time her character was named Sarah Green. (The show was renamed *The Gertrude Berg Show* halfway through the season in an even clearer nod to her star power.) Though it didn't catch on as *The Goldbergs* had, it still earned Berg another Emmy nomination.

Her grandchildren—her daughter Harriet's daughter and two sons—traveled to Los Angeles from New York to visit her while she was making *Mrs. G*. Grandpa Lewis took them on the train across the country. Both Mr. and Mrs. Berg remained terrified of air travel, so trains were how they traveled between coasts when possible. The oldest of the three grandchildren, Josh, now a preteen, got to spend a day on the set of the show.

By this time, there was no doubt that Berg's work had made an impact on culture, for better or worse. The young Philip Roth published an essay in 1961 in *American Judaism* that derided "the new stereotype" of "Jews being warm to one another and having their wonderful family lives." Gertrude Berg's name went unsaid, but no one had done more to promote such an image of American Jews. Then again, as Molly might have said: Who says this is a bad thing?

Soon it became clear that although her impact remained, Berg herself was beginning to fade from public memory. By the mid-1960s, she became known as "the lady from the S.O.S. commercials" to kids her grandchildren's age. The scouring pads gave her one more chance to resurrect Molly Goldberg and demonstrate her knack for selling products to television audiences. In the ads, Berg leaned out an apartment window and called, "Yoo-hoo, Mrs. Bloom. Have you tried new S.O.S.? With soap it's loaded."

Berg told the *American Weekly* around that time, "When I'm by myself, sometimes I wonder—did I really become the woman I wanted to be—or am I still trying?"

Not long afterward, on September 14, 1966, Gertrude Berg died at the age of sixty-six. The official cause was heart failure, but her family blamed a lifetime of overwork. At the time, two new Broadway plays were in the works with her slated as the lead. One was a Spigelgass script based on another of her ideas, *The Playgirls*, whose opening night, set for two months later, had sold out at the time of her death. The other was an adaptation of a book that she was set to script. The satire's title: *How to Be a Jewish Mother*.

Because of the trials Berg, Loeb, and others had faced, the television industry would remain terrified of depicting Jewish characters for decades to come, even though many TV executives and creators were themselves Jewish.

"Too Jewish," in fact, became a go-to rejection note for executives. When the producers James L. Brooks and Allan Burns pitched the idea of making the main character on *The Mary Tyler Moore Show* divorced, executives threw their anti-Semitism into their rejection for good measure: "Our research says American audiences won't tolerate divorce in a lead of a series any more than they will tolerate Jews, people with mustaches, and people who live in New York." Brooks and Burns would go on to make Mary's best friend, Rhoda, Jewish anyway, and she would be such a hit that she got her own successful spin-off, *Rhoda*, who was Jewish in prime time for four highly rated seasons.

Yet the cycle continued in the 1990s. When NBC executives first saw the *Seinfeld* pilot in 1989, they dismissed its prospects: "Too New York, too Jewish." It became one of the defining shows of the 1990s and of sitcom history. And the actress Fran Drescher has said she had to fight to make her character on her 1990s sitcom *The Nanny*—which she created with her ex-husband, Peter Marc Jacobson—explicitly Jewish. Sponsors had asked that she be Italian—the Jewish New Yorker's acceptably ethnic neighbor—instead. Drescher stuck with her Jewishness and created a character who continues to live on in syndicated reruns.

But those were the exceptions. Only more recently in the late 2010s have Jewish writers felt truly free to write characters who shared their cultural experiences. The producer Amy Sherman-Palladino, after having great success with the WASPy *Gilmore Girls*, has won Emmys for *The Marvelous Mrs. Maisel*, which explores the lives of upwardly mobile Jewish families in late 1950s and 1960s New York—characters who undoubtedly never missed an episode of *The Goldbergs*. In fact, a *Mrs. Maisel* character, a successful 1950s comedian named Sophie Lennon, bears some resemblance to Gertrude Berg: Sophie's stage persona is a frowsy, working-class housewife, though Sophie herself lives in an elegant, expensive New York apartment, dresses in finery, and speaks in an impeccable, stage-neutral accent.

The producer Joey Soloway's *Transparent* broke major boundaries with its depiction of multiple trans characters, but along the way it also included one of the most Jewish TV families in history. Much of the drama centered around the family synagogue throughout the third season; its fourth season included a family trip to Israel and the Dead Sea.

There was even another hit show on ABC called *The Goldbergs* starting in 2013; though it's unrelated to Berg's creation, it depicts a Jewish family in suburban 1980s Pennsylvania. Perhaps the most striking thing about it is how much it owes to the original *Goldbergs* and how little anyone involved seems to have realized that; its title does not appear to have been a knowing homage but merely a coincidence.

Hazel Scott spent the late 1950s in Paris, away from her husband, Adam Clayton Powell, Jr. After an illness that left her bedridden for a month and worried she might die, she felt her priorities shift. As she wrote in a 1960 piece for *Ebony* magazine, "One does not look into the face of death, as I have, and come away worrying about pettiness and cattiness and gossip and conforming. . . . Love is important. Love." She added that her time away from the United States was a "much needed rest, not from work, but from racial tension."

In fact, she had enjoyed making live television appearances in other parts of the world, even if cultural differences occasionally interfered: during one performance on Italy's public broadcast station, RAI, her son recalls a last-minute dash to cover up her shoulders and cleavage, bared as always by her strapless gown, with handkerchiefs: "The pope could be watching!"

In 1960, Scott and Powell divorced, and she was free to live her European life. She married Swiss comedian Ezio Bedin in 1961.

The 1960s eventually found Scott back in the United States and fired up by Betty Friedan's revolutionary book *The Feminine Mystique*, which critiqued the pressure middle-class American women felt to become wives and homemakers and nothing else, abandoning intellect and passion. She was moved by Friedan's ideas, but she felt trapped between the civil rights movement and the nascent feminist movement. "Think about it," she told her son. "If I'm a white woman, do I feel closer to a Black man or a white woman? 'Cause that's going to be a problem." Her entire life had represented the challenge of intersectionality, later named by the scholar Kimberlé Crenshaw in 1989.

As the years passed, Scott returned to television with neither resistance nor fanfare. She appeared on *CBS Playhouse* in 1969 and the NBC drama *The Bold Ones* in 1970. Most notably, she guest starred on the sitcom *Julia* during the same period. The show starred Diahann Carroll in a groundbreaking achievement that was emotionally significant but had to be carefully worded: she was TV's first Black woman to star in a "nonservant role." (Amanda Randolph had long before notched the "first Black female lead" distinction as the maid on *The Laytons*.) Carroll played a nurse who was a widowed, single mother. Her husband had been a US Army pilot, shot down in Vietnam. The character—as a lead who was presented as a multidimensional professional woman of color—was a clear beneficiary of the image Scott had cultivated in the 1940s on film and in 1950 on television.

In the 1970s, according to legend, the last known record of Scott's television career drowned. Edie Adams, the wife of sometime DuMont host Ernie Kovacs, claimed that when ABC had bought DuMont's assets, the company had considered the entire video archive to be garbage. Adams told this story during a 1996 Library of Congress hearing on television preservation: "One of the lawyers doing the bargaining said that he could 'take care of it' in a 'fair manner,' and he did take care of it. At 2 a.m., the next morning, he had three huge semis back up to the loading dock at ABC, filled them all with stored kinescopes and 2" videotapes, drove them to a waiting barge in New Jersey, took them out on the water, made a right at the Statue of Liberty and dumped them in the Upper New York Bay. Very neat. No problem."

There's no evidence that this story is true. But it is a good story. And the fact remains that few of DuMont's shows are viewable, or remembered, because so few recordings were maintained. For instance, no recordings of *The Hazel Scott Show* have been located or properly archived, which literally erases her television legacy.

Hazel Scott landed one of her prized regular gigs in 1981, at a place called Kippy's Pier 44 in the Milford Plaza Hotel at West 44th Street and Eighth Avenue in Manhattan. She called her now-adult son, Adam Clayton Powell III, thrilled to tell him the news. "Your mother has her dream job," she said. "I can play here as many weeks as I want. I have time off if I want to go to LA and do something or if I'm going to do something else. But I can play here thirty weeks a year, thirty-five weeks a year, whatever." She paused. "Oh, no."

Her son urged her on. What?

"Oh, no. You know the show business superstition that when you have your dream job, you're about to die or something disastrous is going to happen?"

Adam countered, "But you had your dream job in 1950 with the TV show."

"Yeah," she said. "Look what happened."

Scott died of pancreatic cancer on October 2, 1981, at the age of sixty-one. But for a time, she had the perfect job.

Black female TV hosts remain a rarity outside of daytime, which speaks to the enormity of Scott's achievement in 1950. Oprah Winfrey and Wendy Williams became superstars in the female-focused realm of daytime. The comedian Wanda Sykes had a late-night show on Fox in 2009, while Mo'Nique and Robin Thede had relatively short-lived shows on BET. The white female hosts Chelsea Handler and Samantha Bee have had successful runs, though they did so on cable, not in the historically vaunted province of the major networks. In 2019, Lilly Singh, a Canadian YouTube star whose parents had immigrated from India, became the first woman of color to host a major network show since Sykes when she took over the 1:35 a.m. Eastern Time slot on NBC from Carson Daly. Clearly, progress has been glacial.

Perhaps Scott's more meaningful contribution was elevating the depiction of Black women on television, working diligently and deliberately to pull them out of that "singing maid" category. There were plenty more Black maids to come on television, some of them skillfully realized depictions, from Marla Gibbs's snippy Florence Johnston on *The Jeffersons* to Regina Taylor's Lilly Harper on the early 1990s drama *I'll Fly Away*—a period piece about the late 1950s and early 1960s, which makes Lilly a likely Hazel Scott fan. The true non-maid heirs to Scott's legacy, beyond Carroll's character on *Julia*, are those sophisticated, professional moms of 1980s sitcoms, Clair Huxtable of *The Cosby Show* and Aunt Viv of *The Fresh Prince of Bel-Air*; the polished singles of the 1990s and 2000s, such as Queen Latifah's editor character, Khadijah James, on *Living Single* and Tracee Ellis Ross's lawyer character Joan Clayton on *Girlfriends*; and the complicated leads of more recent shows such as Rhimes's as well as Issa Rae as the lead in her own creation, *Insecure*.

Hazel Scott and her onetime husband, Representative Adam Clayton Powell, Jr., were a political-cultural power couple who presaged two of the most influential couples of our time: Beyoncé and Jay-Z and Michelle and Barack Obama.

Betty White found a new tactic for survival in television after *The Betty White Show* was canceled. Her sweet demeanor and demure dress concealed an ambitious woman who had chosen a career over marriage and children. She wasn't about to sit back and let it all go to waste. So she found work as a regular guest on game shows, a growing sector of the industry.

The World Turns 273

In July 1955, she joined a panel show called *Make the Connection*, lured by the opportunity to fly to New York every week for taping. She got the New York City experience that had long eluded her, without having to move from her beloved Los Angeles. "One thing I'm still hoping to experience in the East—a big snow storm," she said in an interview at the time. "I've never seen one—had to fly back last November just one day ahead of snow." Around the time of *Make the Connection*, however, she turned down three other long-term Manhattan-based programs that would require her to establish a more permanent presence there. In 1956, she began hosting the annual Tournament of Roses parade in Pasadena, a job she would hold and cherish for the next nineteen years. Los Angeles would always remain her true home.

When she took the *Make the Connection* job, she had just finished shooting the last of sixty-five syndicated episodes of *Life with Elizabeth*. The show would keep playing in viewers' homes for years to come: as of July 1955, it had appeared on more than a hundred stations, but it would continue to cycle through many others, with occasional second runs in some locations.

By 1957, she won a similar starring role as a young wife on *Date with the Angels*, a pattern of consistent work she has continued up to the present time. While she was filming the series on the Desilu lot, she met Lucille Ball. The two struck up a friendship while talking about their work in the male-dominated TV business, and Ball became something of a mentor to White. Ball was eleven years older and had enjoyed unqualified success as a star and producer—even if White had been in front of the TV camera for longer than Ball.

The two remained close friends until Ball's death in 1989. White had become one of TV's most legendary sitcom stars on *The Mary Tyler Moore Show* and *The Golden Girls*. Both women knew by then what it was like to be a legend and how much it had taken for them to get there.

White eventually married after she met her true love, *Password* host Allen Ludden, during an appearance on his game show. The two were married from 1963 until his death in 1981. She never had children, but she became stepmother to his three children from his previous marriage.

Her career blossomed in the 1970s when she turned in an incendiary comedic performance on *The Mary Tyler Moore Show*. Her character, Sue Ann Nivens, parodied White's image from the 1950s. Sue Ann was known as "the happy homemaker" on a local cooking show, with a faux-sweet demeanor that barely hid a nasty streak—she wasn't above a withering insult, a dirty innuendo, or even an extramarital affair. She also favored high necklines. Around that time, White turned down a major opportunity to return to the kind of role that had started her TV career: she could have been an anchor on NBC's *Today* show. But that would have required daily, early-morning broadcasts and a move to New York. She was interested in neither at this point in her career.

From there she grew to become a true TV legend: she played the ditzy sexagenarian widow Rose Nylund—her sweetness out front and her real-life intelligence bubbling just underneath—on the 1980s sitcom *The Golden Girls*, which became a perennial favorite picked up by future generations in reruns. She was a rarity in television: a star who had found multiple iconic roles on multiple classic sitcoms that stood the test of time.

Men have dominated TV in every decade after these women ruled the airwaves. But they have done so in formats invented and perfected by women.

Irna Phillips's *As the World Turns* signed off the air in 2010 after more than fifty years. Throughout the 2010s, Hazel Scott experienced a resurgence thanks to video of her performances surfacing on YouTube; the pop musician Alicia Keys name-checked her during a performance at the 2019 Grammy Awards in which she played two pianos, Scott style. Betty White enjoyed a career renaissance in the past decade: she hosted *Saturday Night Live* in 2010 at the age of eighty-eight, making her the show's oldest host ever, and costarred on the sitcom *Hot in Cleveland* from 2010 to 2015. She's listed in *The Guinness Book of World Records* as the person with the longest TV career on record. In 2018, she received a Lifetime Achievement Emmy.

At the 2018 ceremony, *Saturday Night Live* star Kate McKinnon and actor Alec Baldwin introduced White. "At ninety-six years old," McKinnon said, "she still thinks about all those Emmys she didn't win. And she's still bitter." It was a joke, of course. Or perhaps losing the first Best Actress Emmy to Gertrude Berg sixty-seven years earlier really did still sting.

The radiant White took to the podium, her now golden hair cropped to her ears and as well coiffed as it was in her *Hollywood on Television* days. She wore a black jacket with sparkly aqua leaf accents. Her chunky, aqua earrings glistened. The audience stood to honor her, and she laughed with genuine modesty as the applause lingered on and on. "I'm just going to quit while I'm ahead," she said, gesturing as if to leave the stage. But she stayed, of course. You always say yes.

"Somebody said something the other day about 'First Lady of Television,'" White said. "And I took it as a big compliment. And then I heard her talking to her daughter a little later, she said, 'First lady, yes, she's that old, she was the first one, way, way back.' But little did I dream then that I would be here. It's incredible that I'm still in this business, that I'm still—and you are still putting up with me." She paused for just the right number of beats . . . one, two, three, laughter. "I wish they did that at home."

The woman knew how to play to a camera and a live TV audience. Of course she did. When you invented the whole damn thing, it just comes naturally.

It's time we remembered Betty White as more than the sassy old lady who's still got it—she was also one of television's first female producers and a foundational contributor to the medium who fought patriarchal expectations at every turn. Just as we have recently uncovered the historical importance of World War II's female code breakers and the Black female "hidden figures" whose math prowess helped launch the US space program, it's time we also remembered White's sisters who, along with her, built the medium that now dominates our lives. Just because some of their earliest contributions to the medium have been lost, erased, or (maybe, just maybe) dumped off the coast of New York City doesn't mean they're not worth remembering. It's time we realize that women invented television.

ACKNOWLEDGMENTS

A book is like a TV show: it takes a supportive and talented team to bring it into the world, even though the star (author) gets so much of the credit. Thank you, as always, to my agent, Laurie Abkemeier, for continuing to take such good care of my career. Your guidance and words of encouragement were particularly helpful this time around when we were waiting for the right book idea to come along. I'm so glad this was the one.

Sarah Haugen and Harper were so wonderfully welcoming to my little idea and *got* it from the first day. I know you're not supposed to judge a book by its cover, but this gorgeous cover, to me, shows how much you care about putting this book out into the world in the classiest way possible, honoring these women the way they deserve.

Saul Austerlitz, Andrea Bartz, and Allison Sansone, my beta readers, you are responsible for some of the best parts of this book, prompted by your keen questions and insights. Thank you especially for snapping out of any early pandemic stupor to give this your above-and-beyond attention.

Several key sources were vital to helping me understand these women and this era. Gertrude Berg's grandchildren, Adam Berg, Anne Schwartz, and Josh Schwartz, graciously lent me their memories of their grandmother and were as witty and fun to talk to as you'd expect Gertrude's grandchildren to be. Clarke Ingram shared with me his enormous expertise about all things DuMont. The Paley Center for Media in New York generously shared its stowed-away stash of early *TV Guides* and other precious resources. Jane Klain, the delightful director of research there, went above and beyond. And it was an honor to speak with Adam Clayton Powell III, who shared his memories of his true hero of a mother, Hazel Scott, and even let me rifle through her papers and memorabilia.

Shout out to the V.I.P. Club text chain, and Erin Carlson, who made me an inspiring drawing of my four women that hovered over my desk as I wrote. Thank you to my family, as always, for your support. Dena Davis, thank you for sparking my interest in the Mc-Carthy Era and sharing your vast knowledge about it with me.

And, of course, thank you to my quarantine teammate, partner, love, meticulous editor, and, now, coworker, A. Jesse Jiryu Davis.

NOTES

Epigraph

v Epigraph: James L. Baughman, *Same Time, Same Station: Creating American Television, 1948–1961* (Baltimore: Johns Hopkins University Press, 2007), 8.

Introduction: Bold Claims

ix Five feet five: Publicity questionnaire, ca. 1936, Box 57, Gertrude Berg Papers, Syracuse University, Syracuse, NY (hereafter referred to as Berg Papers).

xi longest-running scripted program: Bill Carter, "CBS Turns Out 'Guiding Light,'" *New York Times*, April 1, 2009, https://www.nytimes .com/2009/04/02/arts/television/02ligh.html.

xiii reached 1 million: *The New York Times Guide to Essential Knowledge* (New York: St. Martin's Press, 2004), 412.

xiii The C. E. Hooper Company had just begun: Hugh Malcolm Beville, Jr., *Audience Ratings: Radio, Television, Cable, Revised Student Edition* (Hillsdale, NJ: Lawrence Erlbaum Associates, 1988), 63.

xiii past fourteen years: Ibid., 8.

xiii had debuted in May: "Looking Back 60 Years on the 'CBS TV News,'" CBS News, May 2, 2008, https://www.cbsnews.com/news/looking -back-60-years-on-the-cbs-tv-news/.

xiii WTVR in Richmond: "WTVR-TV, South's First Television Station, Celebrates 70 years," WTVR, April 22, 2018, https://wtvr.com /2018/04/22/souths-first-television-station-celebrates-70-years/.

xiv a dismal 6.5 percent: Miranda J. Banks, "Unequal Opportunities: Gender Inequities and Precarious Diversity in the 1970s U.S. Television

Industry," *Feminist Media Histories* 4, no. 4 (Fall 2018): 109–29, https://online.ucpress.edu/fmh/article/4/4/109/91947/Unequal -OpportunitiesGender-Inequities-and.

xiv when women made up 21 percent: Dr. Martha M. Lauzen, "Boxed In 2016–17: Women on Screen and Behind the Scenes in Television," Center for the Study of Women in Television & Film, San Diego State University, September 2017, https://womenintvfilm.sdsu.edu /wp-content/uploads/2017/09/2016-17_Boxed_In_Report.pdf.

xiv In 2018–2019: Joe Otterson, "Women Reach Historic Highs in On-Screen, Behind the Scenes TV Roles," *Variety*, September 4, 2019, https://variety.com/2019/tv/news/women-reach-historic-highs-in -on-screen-behind-the-scenes-tv-roles-1203323057/.

xv only if her real-life husband: Madelyn Pugh Davis, *Laughing with Lucy: My Life with America's Leading Lady of Comedy* (Cincinnati: Clerisy Press, 2005), 50.

Chapter 1: Yoo-Hoo, Gertrude Berg!

2 "she spent money faster": Author's interview with Anne Schwartz, April 30, 2019.

2 urging him to sign Berg: *Yoo-Hoo, Mrs. Goldberg!*, DVD, directed by Aviva Kempner (Docurama, 2010).

3 "didn't believe it was fair": Glenn D. Smith, Jr., *"Something on My Own": Gertrude Berg and American Broadcasting, 1929–1956* (Syracuse, NY: Syracuse University Press, 2007), 114.

3 nervous breakdown: Smith, *"Something on My Own,"* 12.

3 carried the telegram: "Anything but Average," *Tablet*, January 18, 2008, https://www.tabletmag.com/jewish-arts-and-culture/1291/anything -but-average.

3 "We lived a life": Gertrude Berg and Cherney Berg, *Molly and Me: The Memoirs of Gertrude Berg* (New York: McGraw-Hill, 1961), 53.

3 "Grandpa Mordecai": Ibid., 16.

4 "I think in that whole Edelstein": Author's interview with Adam Berg, May 8, 2019.

4 fourth-floor walk-up: Ibid., 45.

4 "When I was in the country": Ibid., 79.

4 she implied that she had graduated: Smith, *"Something on My Own,"* 83.

4 "I went to Columbia": Morris Freedman, "From the American Scene:

The Real Molly Goldberg," *Commentary*, April 1956, https://www
.commentarymagazine.com/articles/morris-freedman/from-the
-american-scene-the-real-molly-goldberg/.

5 "When I was a very advanced thirteen": Berg and Berg, *Molly and
Me*, 134.

5 "Well, we would walk": Author's interview with Adam Berg, May 8,
2019.

5 invented instant coffee: Smith, *"Something on My Own,"* 20.

5 He then got a job: Ibid., 21.

5 burned down: *Yoo-Hoo, Mrs. Goldberg!*

5 "Jewish art theaters": Marjorie Ingall, "Remembering the Emmys'
First Best Actress Winner," *Tablet*, September 17, 2018, https://www
.tabletmag.com/sections/community/articles/gertrude-berg-best
-actress-emmy.

6 typed up her scripts: Smith, *"Something on My Own,"* 102.

6 CBS canceled it: Ibid., 29.

6 planned the whole thing: Dan Senseney, "The Heart of the Goldbergs," *TV-Radio Mirror*, August 1954, 40–43, 91–93.

6 "My sense of Jewishness": Freedman, "From the American Scene:
The Real Molly Goldberg."

7 ran without a sponsor: Christopher H. Sterling, ed., *The Concise Encyclopedia of American Radio* (New York: Routledge, 2010), 327.

7 NBC executives suggested: David Zurawik, "Made-for-TV History,"
Baltimore Sun, April 28, 2002, https://www.baltimoresun.com/news
/bs-xpm-2002-04-28-0204280385-story.html.

7 "The show would be nothing": Ibid.

7 "plump, dark, and motherly": "Anything but Average," *Tablet*.

7 Ten million listeners: Freedman, "From the American Scene: The
Real Molly Goldberg."

7 Berg got sick: Sterling, *The Concise Encyclopedia of American Radio*,
327.

7 "It's hard to say": Freedman, "From the American Scene: The Real
Molly Goldberg."

8 "Although the program": Harlow P. Roberts, "The Radio Audience,"
Broadcast Advertising, April 1932, 36.

8 "We love Mollie!": Letter from Mary E. Kelly to Berg, August 5,
1932, Oversize Box 1, Berg Papers.

9   "I didn't set out": Berg and Berg, *Molly and Me*, 191.

9   keeping politics off the airwaves: Michael J. Socolow, "American Broadcasting Has Always Been Closely Intertwined with American Politics," The Conversation, April 5, 2018, https://theconversation.com/american-broadcasting-has-always-been-closely-intertwined-with-american-politics-94392.

9   "You see, darling": Freedman, "From the American Scene: The Real Molly Goldberg."

10   second most respected woman: Ingall, "Remembering the Emmys' First Best Actress Winner."

10   "Not in a long time": John Chapman, "Gertrude Berg's 'Me and Molly' an Amusing Play," *Chicago Daily Tribune*, March 7, 1948, F9.

11   "As a play": John Beaufort, "Life with Mommele," *Christian Science Monitor*, March 6, 1948, 10.

11   nearly led to a film version: Synopsis by Florence Soman of playscript *Me and Molly*, November 5, 1947, Box 644, folder M740, Paramount Pictures Scripts, Margaret Herrick Library, Beverly Hills, CA.

12   "It was during the time": Berg and Berg, *Molly and Me*, 206.

12   "a two-hour gala": Smith, *Something on My Own*, 111.

12   "exactly right for television": Ibid.

12   had attended camp: Ernest Kinoy, interview with Sunny Parich, Television Academy Foundation, October 29, 1998, video, https://interviews.televisionacademy.com/interviews/ernest-kinoy.

13   more than five thousand: James W. Roman, *From Daytime to Primetime: The History of American Television Programs* (Westport, CT: Greenwood Press, 2005), 83.

13   They all turned her down: *Yoo-Hoo, Mrs. Goldberg!*

14   "Mrs. P. had only one fault": Gerald Clarke, "Bye Society," *Vanity Fair*, April 1988, https://www.vanityfair.com/news/1988/04/truman-capote-198804.

14   multimillionaire cigar magnate: Jeremy Gerard, "William S. Paley, Who Built CBS into a Communications Empire, Dies at 89," *New York Times*, October 28, 1990, https://www.nytimes.com/1990/10/28/obituaries/william-s-paley-who-built-cbs-into-a-communications-empire-dies-at-89.html?pagewanted=all.

14   more than a hundred affiliates: David Halberstam, *The Powers That Be* (New York: Alfred A. Knopf, 1979), 25.

14 turned down a chance: David Halberstam, "The Power and the Profits," *The Atlantic*, January 1976, https://www.theatlantic.com/ideas tour/media/halberstam-full.html.

16 she at last got the call: Smith, *"Something on My Own,"* 115.

16 On Thanksgiving Day 1948: "Television: 'Goldbergs' Definitely Set for CBS Tele Series," *Variety*, December 8, 1948, 26.

16 "I just wanted to let you know": Letter from C. M. Underhill to Berg, December 6, 1948, Box 57, Berg Papers.

17 "frantic conferences": Smith, *"Something on My Own,"* 116.

20 "a warm, human, humorous show": Smith, "Something on My Own," 119.

20 "an immediate hit on television": Ibid.

21 "The Goldbergs came to television": Ibid.

21 "While *we* know *what* to say": Letter from Joseph A. Moran to Berg, Box 35, folder 519, Thelma Ritter and John Aloysius Moran Papers, Margaret Herrick Library, Beverly Hills, CA (hereafter referred to as Ritter and Moran Papers).

22 "Or what do you think": Ibid.

22 "In effect, we have": Ibid.

23 increased by 57 percent: NBC ad sales brochure, ca. 1952, Box 1, Berg Papers.

24 "The studio was being built": Berg and Berg, *Molly and Me*, 209.

Chapter 2: Predicament, Villainy, and Female Suffering

25 "Now we add": Marcy Carsey and Tom Werner, "Father of Broadcasting David Sarnoff," *Time*, December 7, 1998, http://content.time .com/time/magazine/article/0,9171,989773,00.html.

26 wrote 2 million words per year: "Irna Phillips, 72, Serials Writer," *New York Times*, December 30, 1973, https://www.nytimes.com /1973/12/30/archives/irna-phillips-72-serials-writer-created-as -the-world-turns-dr-brent.html.

26 "We're beginning to get really active": Letter from Bill Ramsey to Irna Phillips, June 24, 1948, Box 62, Irna Phillips Papers, Wisconsin Historical Society, Madison, WI (hereafter referred to as Phillips Papers).

27 "The intriguing angle": Letter from Phillips to Ramsey, September 7, 1948, Box 62, Phillips Papers.

28 "To my way of thinking": Letter from Ramsey to Phillips, September 23, 1948, Box 62, Phillips Papers.

28 youngest of the ten children: Joanne Passet, "Irna Phillips, 1901–1973," Jewish Women's Archive, https://jwa.org/encyclopedia/article/phillips-irna.

28 The family lived above: Barbara Sicherman and Carol Hurd Green, eds., *Notable American Women: The Modern Period: A Biographical Dictionary* (Cambridge, MA: The Belknap Press of Harvard University Press, 1980), 542.

28 Betty provided for the family: Passet, "Irna Phillips, 1901–1973."

28 "a plain, sickly, silent child": Sicherman and Green, *Notable American Women*, 542.

28 graduated from Senn High School: "Phillips, Irna (1901–1973)," Encyclopedia.com, April 15, 2020, https://www.encyclopedia.com/women/encyclopedias-almanacs-transcripts-and-maps/phillips-irna-1901-1973.

28 longed to find a reliable husband: Phillips autobiographical drafts, 22–41, Box 12, Phillips Papers.

29 When Phillips returned to Chicago: Christopher H. Sterling, *The Biographical Encyclopedia of American Radio* (New York: Routledge, 2011), 288.

29 Someone at WGN thought: Phillips autobiographical drafts, 46–50, Phillips Papers.

30 aired six days a week: Sterling, *The Biographical Encyclopedia of American Radio*, 289.

30 "I've never worn that shade": Robert Clyde Allen, *Speaking of Soap Operas* (Chapel Hill: University of North Carolina Press, 1985), 187.

30 voiced Mother Moynihan: John Dunning, *On the Air: The Encyclopedia of Old-Time Radio* (New York: Oxford University Press, 1998), 531.

30 Her pay rose to $100 per week: Marilyn Lavin, "Creating Consumers in the 1930s: Irna Phillips and the Radio Soap Opera," *Journal of Consumer Research*, June 1995, 75–89.

30 refused to try to take her show national: Sterling, *The Biographical Encyclopedia of American Radio*, 289.

31 "work for hire": Dunning, *On the Air*, 531.

31 chose to end it: Phillips autobiographical drafts, 73–74, Phillips Papers.

31 took comfort afterward: Phillips autobiographical drafts, 77, Phillips Papers.

31 "A soap opera is": James Thurber, "Soapland I—O Pioneers!," *New Yorker*, May 15, 1948, 34, https://www.newyorker.com/magazine /1948/05/15/soapland-i-o-pioneers.

32 up to six scripts per day: Sterling, *The Biographical Encyclopedia of American Radio*, 290.

32 an elaborate chart system: "Phillips, Irna (1901–1973)," Encyclopedia .com.

32 An average nonfarm family: Bureau of the Census, "Income of Non-farm Families and Individuals," *Current Population Reports: Consumer Income*, January 28, 1948, https://www2.census.gov/prod2/popscan /p60-001.pdf.

32 "America's highest-paid": "Script Queen," *Time*, June 10, 1940, 66–68.

33 began the show: Phillips autobiographical drafts, 98, Phillips Papers.

33 socially significant issues: Passet, "Irna Phillips, 1901–1973."

33 joined the army in 1944: "Arthur Peterson; TV and Stage Character Actor," *Los Angeles Times*, November 6, 1996, https://www.latimes .com/archives/la-xpm-1996-11-06-mn-61872-story.html.

33 When Phillips noticed: Phillips autobiographical drafts, 50, Phillips Papers.

33 "In time my use of women": Ibid., 146.

34 "without missing a word": "Phillips, Irna (1901–1973)," Encyclopedia .com.

34 After Agnes Eckhardt graduated: Erin Karter, "Remembering Agnes Nixon: 'Queen of Soaps,'" *Northwestern Now*, September 29, 2016, https://news.northwestern.edu/stories/2016/09/obituary-agnes -nixon/.

34 She had managed it: Agnes Nixon, interview with Connie Passalaqua, Television Academy Foundation, October 21, 1997, video, https:// interviews.televisionacademy.com/interviews/agnes-nixon.

34 "heard like one hears": Ibid.

35 In 1943: Cary O'Dell, *Women Pioneers in Television: Biographies of Fifteen Industry Leaders* (Jefferson, NC: McFarland, 1997), 186.

35 Phillips began craving: Phillips autobiographical drafts, 117, Phillips Papers.

36 "During the time I was there": Ibid., 120.

37 "keep my eyes closed": Ibid., 121.

38 "It was well-known": Ibid., 122.

38   visited Page Military Academy: Ibid., 126–27.

39   "For the first time": Ibid.

39   "as the weeks went by": Ibid.

39   "Miss Phillips, you're making": Ibid.

39   She threw an Easter party: Ibid., 156.

40   she decided to move: Ibid., 124–25.

40   "It was difficult": Ibid.

40   "the death knell": Ibid.

41   had to pay him $250,000: Garren Waldo, "Law and Order Revisited: Irna Phillips vs. Emmons Carlson," *Soap Hub*, September 23, 2019, https://soaphub.com/general-soap-operas/soap-opera-history/law -and-order-revisited-irna-phillips-vs-emmons-carlson/.

41   General Mills threatened: Phillips autobiographical drafts, 127–29, Phillips Papers.

41   a high of more than $300,000: Ibid., 129.

41   Phillips was contending: Letter from Phillips to Evelyn Peirce, May 20, 1948, Box 62, Phillips Papers.

42   "I choose to think": Ibid.

42   "Spasmodic turmoil": Letter from Phillips to Dr. Friedman, June 10, 1948, Box 63, Phillips Papers.

42   Phillips and her secretary: Phillips autobiographical drafts, 130–31, Phillips Papers.

42   "Apartments in Chicago": Ibid.

43   at a $20,000 loss: Unsent letter from Phillips to Ramsey, February 14, 1948, Box 62, Phillips Papers.

43   "Yes, the grass is green": Letter from Phillips to Ramsey, May 20, 1948, Box 62, Phillips Papers.

43   "Back in her beloved": Jack Hellman, "Light 'n' Airy," *Variety*, June 10, 1948, n.p., Box 63 Phillips Papers.

44   enrolled them in Blackhawk Day Camp: Phillips autobiographical drafts, 132–33, Phillips Papers.

44   "But I was too much": Ibid.

44   "going to couch": Letter from Phillips to Ramsey, March 8, 1949, Box 62, Phillips Papers.

45   She shopped for a new apartment: Phillips autobiographical drafts, 136–38, Phillips Papers.

45   expressed interest: Ibid., p. 137.

45 "Of course one couldn't": Letter from Phillips to Ramsey, September 7, 1948, Box 62, Phillips Papers.

46 "To me": Letter from Ramsey to Phillips, March 1, 1949, Box 62, Phillips Papers.

46 "even more dialogue": Letter from Phillips to Ramsey, September 7, 1948, Box 62, Phillips Papers.

47 "The TV Department": Letter from Phillips to Ramsey, October 6, 1948, Box 62, Phillips Papers.

47 had to reenvision soap operas: Phillips autobiographical drafts, 138, Phillips Papers.

47 "Television also brought": Ibid., 138.

48 "New show will be eagle-eyed": "Irna Phillips' Video Soaper," *Variety*, December 22, 1948, 27.

48 "I hope Irna does not": Letter from Lewis H. Titterton to Ramsey, 1949, Box 62, Phillips Papers.

48 promising rehearsals: "TV 'Soap Opera,'" *Broadcasting-Telecasting*, February 7, 1949, 57.

48 "Last week television": "Soap Comes to TV," *Pathfinder*, February 9, 1949, 51.

48 they scrawled key lines: Jack Gould, "Television in Review: First Soap Opera Starts—'The Broadway Revue,'" *New York Times*, February 6, 1949, 242.

48 "Television dived into the corn": Ibid.

49 *These Are My Children*: "These Are My Children," *Variety*, February 9, 1949, 34.

49 "my temporary": Letter from Phillips to Ramsey, March 8, 1949, Box 62, Phillips Papers.

50 "Was it only yesterday": Letter from Phillips to Ramsey, April 22, 1949, Box 62, Phillips Papers.

51 "superbly produced": Letter from Phillips to Ramsey, March 8, 1949, Box 62, Phillips Papers.

51 her new proposal for a TV soap: "Irna Phillips Pens 'Challenge' Soaper," *Billboard*, March 19, 1949, 13.

51 an elaborate dinner: Letter from Ramsey to Phillips, April 5, 1949, Box 62, Phillips Papers.

51 "I may be wrong": Letter from A. H. Morrison to Phillips, September 27, 1949, Box 62, Phillips Papers.

52 country's first all-day schedule: David Weinstein, *The Forgotten Network: DuMont and the Birth of American Television* (Philadelphia: Temple University Press, 2004), 40.

52 suggested she visit: Letter from Ramsey to Phillips, September 23, 1948, Box 62, Phillips Papers.

52 first Black woman to star: Henry Louis Gates, Jr., and Evelyn Brooks Higginbotham, eds., *Harlem Renaissance Lives from the African American National Biography* (New York: Oxford University Press), 418.

52 may have made her: Tim Brooks and Earle F. Marsh, *The Complete Directory to Prime Time Network and Cable TV Shows, 1946–Present* (New York: Ballantine, 2007), 776.

52 "Yessir, it sure is the truth!": Margaret R. Weiss, *The TV Writer's Guide* (New York: Pelligrini & Cudahy, 1952), 96.

52 "actress, singer": "Radio and Television: Writers Guild to Strike at 12:01 A.M. Tomorrow over Contract Terms," *New York Times*, October 25, 1948, 46.

53 "television can help rid": "Leaders Guestar on Video," *Pittsburgh Courier*, April 30, 1949, 18.

53 "For eight dollars a week": S. W. Garlington, "Hymn Time to Swing Time," *New York Amsterdam News*, April 2, 1949, 17.

53 "Amanda Randolph is herself": Ibid.

Chapter 3: Women's Realm

55 "a chunky man": White, *Here We Go Again: My Life in Television* (New York: Scribner, 1995), Apple Books/iPad, 55.

55 as close as they'd get to rehearsing: Ibid., 60.

56 "Let's talk about how": Betty White, interview with Tony Fantozzi, Television Academy Foundation, June 4, 1997, video, https://interviews.televisionacademy.com/interviews/betty-white.

57 thought she wanted to be a writer: White, *Here We Go Again*, 24.

57 her class had studied Japan: White, Television Academy Foundation interview.

57 she sang "Spirit Flower": White, *Here We Go Again*, 25.

58 an investor in the fledgling technology: Brooks Barnes, "Betty White's Sitcom Solution," *Wall Street Journal*, May 4, 2007, https://www.wsj.com/articles/SB117824705381591915.

58 established his own radio station: "A Landmark's Storied and Color-ful History," Packard Lofts, https://packardloftsla.com/p/history/.

58 A small crowd gathered: White, *Here We Go Again*, 25–27.

59 "a fluffy white tulle number": Ibid., 26.

59 opera singer Felix Hughes: Ibid., 25.

59 bout of strep throat: Tess White, "My Daughter, Betty White," *TV Radio Mirror*, February 1955, 30.

59 "I had been studying": White, *Here We Go Again*, 24.

60 American Women's Voluntary Services: Ibid., 27–28.

60 a young man named Paul: White, *Here We Go Again*, 30.

60 Dick Barker: Kristy Puchko, "15 Fun Facts About Betty White," Mental Floss, January 17, 2019, https://www.mentalfloss.com/article/61054/15-things-you-didnt-know-about-betty-white.

60 "Back in those days": Betty White, interview with Piers Morgan, *Piers Morgan Tonight*, April 17, 2012, video, https://www.youtube.com/watch?v=rayQ1y8Up1I, https://www.youtube.com/watch?v=vSUpYuwyyOc.

60 Bliss-Hayden Theatre: White, *Here We Go Again*, 31–35.

61 going to the beach: Jane Morris, "No Time for Nothun," article draft, ca. 1954, Box 27, folder 16, Jane Ardmore Papers, Margaret Herrick Library, Beverly Hills, CA (hereafter referred to as Ardmore Papers).

61 fifth floor of the Taft Building: White, *Here We Go Again*, 35–39.

62 "Listen, I know": Ibid., 36.

63 "There are some outstanding examples": Ibid., 54.

63 break up with Allan: Ibid., 39–42.

63 a little bit of everything: Ibid., 55–61.

64 went out of business: Ibid., 44–45.

64 On one of her casting rounds: Ibid., 45–50.

66 "It must have looked": Ibid., 49.

66 "Betty, I must ask you": Ibid.

67 Park La Brea: Ibid., 60.

67 recognized Jarvis's voice: Ibid., 51–53.

67 It turned out: Ibid., 63.

67 "I should have heard": Ibid., 53.

68 "All you have to do": Ibid., 55.

69 "Mrs. Allan, your tail is wagging": Ibid., 61.

71 "For whatever reason": Ibid., 66.

71   Herb Jeffries: Ibid., 69.
71   "That girl in the green suit": White, Television Academy Foundation interview.
72   "As our audience multiplied": White, *Here We Go Again*, 74.
73   nearly sixty: White, *Here We Go Again*, 79.
73   refused to read off a script: Ibid., 76.
73   "You put the soap": Ibid., 81.
73   hired pitchmen performed: Ibid., 76–79.
74   Saint Bernard: Ibid., 117.
74   White dressed as a young girl: Ibid., 119.
74   riffed on local news stories: Ibid., 61–62.
74   Mary Sampley dressed: Ibid., 80–82.
74   "loved doing the show": Ibid., 82.
75   "Never to talk down": Ibid., 84–85.
75   "all the good things": Ibid., 34.
75   "I love working": Jane Ardmore, "Look at the Girl Who Was Never Going to Marry!," article draft, ca. 1971, Box 27, folder 16, Ardmore Papers.
76   A three-year-old girl: "Mother Recalls 1949 Well Accident That Ended in Tragedy with AM-Well Rescue," Associated Press, October 17, 1987, https://apnews.com/53498a86a7733cff398986f30fa5c4f9.
76   "ONE LITTLE GIRL": Photo, Find a Grave, https://www.findagrave.com/memorial/10679/kathy-fiscus#view-photo=160824971.
76   first televised cooking show: "Monty M. McDonald; Early TV Show Host," *Los Angeles Times*, March 5, 1997, https://www.latimes.com/archives/la-xpm-1997-03-05-mn-35064-story.html.
76   she didn't know how to cook: Mary Beth Haralovich and Lauren Rabinovitz, *Television, History, and American Culture: Feminist Critical Essays* (Durham, NC: Duke University Press, 1999), 37.
76   Viewers delighted: Ibid., 43.
77   "conform rapidly": Quoted in Gilbert Seldes, *The Great Audience* (New York: Viking Press, 1950), 182.
77   "The extraordinary sense": Ibid., 192.

Chapter 4: A Holy Terror

80   threw a garden party: "Socially Speaking," *New York Amsterdam News*, June 18, 1949, 13.

80   "to cook or play sports": Author's interview with Adam Clayton Powell III, May 11, 2019.

80   "After three years": Adam Clayton Powell, Jr., "My Life with Hazel Scott," *Ebony*, January 1949, 42–50.

81   "You understand": Author's interview with Adam Clayton Powell III, May 11, 2019.

82   only surviving child of six: Karen Chilton, *Hazel Scott: The Pioneering Journey of a Jazz Pianist from Café Society to Hollywood to HUAC* (Ann Arbor: University of Michigan Press, 2008), 1.

82   her father left the family: Ibid., 5.

82   with four-year-old Hazel: Ibid., 8.

82   She discovered the piano: Ibid., 6.

82   She improvised on the instrument: Donald Bogle, *Prime Time Blues: African Americans on Network Television* (New York: Farrar, Straus and Giroux, 2001), 15.

83   By the time she was eight: Chilton, *Hazel Scott*, 22.

83   By age fifteen: Joanna Scutts, "This Piano Prodigy Was the First African-American Woman to Host Her Own TV Show," *Time*, September 27, 2016, https://time.com/4507850/hazel-scott/.

83   She played gigs at night: Chilton, *Hazel Scott*, 48.

83   she began to perform solo: Lorissa Rinehart, "This Black Woman Was Once the Biggest Star in Jazz. Here's Why You've Never Heard of Her," Narratively, August 1, 2018, https://narratively.com/this-black-woman-was-once-the-biggest-star-in-jazz-heres-why-youve-never-heard-of-her/.

83   she hosted her own radio show: Grant Jackson, "Hazel Scott on Piano Jazz," NPR, June 10, 2011, https://www.npr.org/2011/06/10/137107329/hazel-scott-on-piano-jazz.

83   "But where others murder": "Music: Hot Classicist," *Time*, October 5, 1942, http://content.time.com/time/subscriber/article/0,33009,773793-1,00.html.

84   performed at the 1939 World's Fair: Scutts, "This Piano Prodigy Was the First African-American Woman to Host Her Own TV Show."

84   Scott made $4,000 a week: Chilton, *Hazel Scott*, 77.

85   "Scott was about as elegant": Donald Bogle, *Brown Sugar: Eighty Years of America's Black Female Superstars* (New York: Da Capo Press, 1980), 106.

85 She turned down: Chilton, *Hazel Scott*, 73.

86 "Am I to understand": Ibid., 83.

86 Harry Cohn swore: Ibid., 85.

86 "I've been brash": Ibid., xiv.

86 just weeks after: Rinehart, "This Black Woman Was Once the Biggest Star in Jazz."

86 he had admired her: Powell, "My Life with Hazel Scott."

86 "We both were tired of leeches": Ibid.

87 *Life* magazine photo spread: Scutts, "This Piano Prodigy Was the First African-American Woman to Host Her Own TV Show."

87 He agitated for: "POWELL, Adam Clayton, Jr., 1908–1972," History, Art & Archives, United States House of Representatives, https:// history.house.gov/People/Detail/19872.

87 disagreed with civil rights leader: "Powell, Adam Clayton, Jr.," King Encyclopedia, The Martin Luther King, Jr. Research and Education Institute, Stanford University, https://kinginstitute.stanford.edu /encyclopedia/powell-adam-clayton-jr.

87 A few months after their wedding: Scutts, "This Piano Prodigy Was the First African-American Woman to Host Her Own TV Show."

88 Powell sent a telegram: Telegram from Powell to Truman, October 12, 1945, "Harry S. Truman to Adam Clayton Powell, Jr., with Attached Telegrams and Press Releases, October 12, 1945," Harry S. Truman Library & Museum (hereafter referred to as Truman Library), https://www.trumanlibrary.gov/library/research-files/harry-s -truman-adam-clayton-powell-jr-attached-telegrams-and-press-releases ?documentid=NA&pagenumber=9.

88 "in the management or policy": Letter from Truman to Powell, October 12, 1945, Truman Library, https://www.trumanlibrary.gov/library /research-files/harry-s-truman-adam-clayton-powell-jr-attached -telegrams-and-press-releases?documentid=NA&pagenumber=2.

88 When Truman's wife: "POWELL, Adam Clayton, Jr., 1908–1972," History, Art & Archives, United States House of Representatives.

88 Powell told a story: Powell, "My Life with Hazel Scott."

89 "This is for being": Ibid.

89 "She is a great help": Ibid.

90 she made $85,000: "Hazel Pays Tax on Income of $85,000," *Cleveland Call and Post*, March 13, 1948, 10B.

90 She signed: Otto Mack, "Record Parade," *Cleveland Call and Post*, March 6, 1948, 8B.

90 2,500 at St. Louis's Auditorium Opera House: "2500 Hear Miss Hazel Scott at St. Louis," *New Journal and Guide*, January 17, 1948, A 18.

90 more than 14,000 at New York City's Lewisohn Stadium: "14,000 at Stadium Hear Hazel Scott," *The New York Times*, June 20, 1948, 53.

90 "seemed unintimidated": Arthur V. Berger, "Hazel Scott: Pianist Performs Beethoven Concerto at Stadium," *New York Herald Tribune*, June 21, 1948, 12.

90 The hometown crowd mobbed her: "15,000 Applaud Scott at Stadium," *New York Amsterdam News*, June 26, 1948, 4.

91 "If this happens again": Chilton, *Hazel Scott*, 138.

91 refused to play a scheduled concert: "Hazel Scott Says Segregation Rule Surprise to Her," *The Austin Statesman*, November 16, 1948, 1.

91 when she saw: Chilton, *Hazel Scott*, 138.

91 set her back $2,000: "Jimcro Dealt Telling Blow by Artist in Texas," *New Journal and Guide*, November 20, 1948, E2.

91 "Why would anyone": Chilton, *Hazel Scott*, 138.

91 "Oh, don't tell the boy": Author's interview with Adam Clayton Powell III, May 11, 2019.

92 "I want the following things": Chilton, *Hazel Scott*, 139.

92 she filed a $50,000 lawsuit: "Hazel Scott Sues Café for $50,000," *Afro-American*, February 26, 1949, 7.

93 Scott got the call: Chilton, *Hazel Scott*, 140.

95 Leon openly identified: John S. Wilson, "Barney Josephson, Owner of Café Society Jazz Club, Is Dead at 86," *New York Times*, September 30, 1988, https://www.nytimes.com/1988/09/30/obituaries/barney-josephson-owner-of-cafe-society-jazz-club-is-dead-at-86.html.

Chapter 5: One of Us

99 "Visuality has made": Larry Wolters, "The Goldbergs Move in for a Long Stay on TV," *Chicago Daily Tribune*, February 14, 1949, B7.

99 "I can truthfully say": Letter from Mrs. Libby to Berg, ca. 1951, Box 57, Berg Papers.

99 "A shut-in who wants": Letter from Mrs. W. J. MacInerney, ca. 1951, Box 57, Berg Papers.

100 "I have been resisting": Letter from Alfred H. Morton to Berg, June 20, 1949, Box 57, Berg Papers.

100 "pick up dialect and color": James Poling, "I'm Molly Goldberg," *Redbook*, August 1949, n.p., Berg Papers.

100 "For years radio": Jerry Franken, "Radio and Television Program Reviews: The Goldbergs," *Billboard*, January 29, 1949, 8.

101 "When I first heard": Letter from Carrie Welch to CBS, October 24, 1949, Box 57, Berg Papers.

101 "MRS. SCHUSTER AND I": Telegram from M. Lincoln Schuster to Berg, October 4, 1949, Box 57, Berg Papers.

102 "the Motion Picture Industry": Carol A. Stabile, *The Broadcast 41: Women and the Anti-Communist Blacklist* (London: Goldsmiths Press, 2018), 165.

102 Washington plays a cook/maid named Louise: Fredi Washington, script for *The Goldbergs*, January 24, 1949, folder 24, Fredi Washington Papers, Amistad Research Center, New Orleans.

102 sales representatives had secured: SWIG, "Hazel Scott Gets Own TV Show," *New York Amsterdam News*, February 11, 1950, B2.

104 It was likely located: I've deduced this with the help of Clarke Ingram, a Pittsburgh radio personality and programming executive who maintains an archive of DuMont materials and information. Because Scott was broadcasting in the same studio as *Captain Video and His Video Rangers* in 1950, Ingram says, it's likely that she was in the Wanamaker Building.

104 Wanamaker's shoppers could sometimes: DuMont–John Wanamaker Television Studio announcement, September 3, 1945, http://eyesof ageneration.com/teletales-2-1945-dumont-to-open-worlds-largest -tv-studios-the-location-o/.

105 The set looked like a living room: Donald Bogle, *Primetime Blues: African Americans on Network Television* (New York: Farrar, Straus and Giroux, 2001), 16.

106 "Pianist Hazel Scott": June Bundy, "Radio and Television Program Reviews: The Hazel Scott Show," *Billboard*, March 25, 1950, 13.

106 Mondays, Wednesdays, and Fridays: Bogle, *Primetime Blues*, 15.

107 "a neat little show": "Television Reviews: Hazel Scott," *Variety*, April 19, 1950, 34.

107 "Negro performers win better roles": "Television," *Ebony*, June 1950, 22–24.

108 "The thinking": "Negro Talent Coming into Own on TV, Without Use of Stereotypes," *Variety*, May 3, 1950, 30.

108 Five million sets were sold: "1950s: TV and Radio," Encyclopedia.com, https://www.encyclopedia.com/history/culture-magazines/1950s -tv-and-radio.

108 almost 90 percent: "The Fifties," The Gilder Lehrman Institute of American History AP US History Study Guide, https://ap.gilderlehrman .org/history-by-era/fifties/essays/fifties.

108 Lazy Bones: "Six Decades of Channel Surfing," Zenith, https://zenith .com/heritage/remote-background/.

108 "Complete automatic program selection": 1950 ad, Television History—the First 75 Years, http://www.tvhistory.tv/1950_Zenith _Wired_Remote.JPG.

108 owners kept tripping: "Six Decades of Channel Surfing," Zenith.

109 "Without prejudice": Gilbert Seldes, *The Great Audience* (New York: Viking Press, 1950), 173.

109 Videotape wasn't widely available: Wesley S. Griswold and Martin Mann, "TV Goes to Tape," *Popular Science*, February 1960, 101–03, 236–37.

110 Albert Einstein warned: Albert Einstein, "Atomic War or Peace," *The Atlantic*, November 1947, https://www.theatlantic.com/magazine /archive/1947/11/atomic-war-or-peace/305443/.

110 found out from a fellow musician: Karen Chilton, *Hazel Scott: The Pioneering Journey of a Jazz Pianist from Café Society to Hollywood to HUAC* (Ann Arbor: University of Michigan Press, 2008), 143.

110 titled *Red Channels*: Andrew Glass, "Counterattack Publishes 'Red Channels,' June 22, 1950," Politico, June 22, 2012, https://www .politico.com/story/2012/06/this-day-in-politics-077707.

110 Many major advertisers subscribed: "Blacklisting," AdAge, September 15, 2003, https://adage.com/article/adage-encyclopedia/black listing/98533.

111 The group behind both: Nancy Bernhard, *U.S. Television News and Cold War Propaganda, 1947–1960* (Cambridge, UK: Cambridge University Press, 1999), 56.

111 "Several commercially sponsored dramatic series": American Business Consultants, *Red Channels* (New York: Counterattack, 1950), 2–3.

112 Scott's listing included: Ibid., 129–30.

112 put on a benefit concert: E. Taubman, "Swing Feature Soviet Benefit: Café Society Assures at Least a Thousand Watches for the Russian Fighting Forces," *New York Times*, April 12, 1943, 28.

114 Ironically, it was Scott: Hazel Scott FBI File.

115 "The set looks like nothing": Jo Coppola, "Tele-Tales," *Newsday*, June 26, 1950, 34.

116 "television's father of the year": Joseph Dorinson, *Kvetching and Shpritzing: Jewish Humor in American Popular Culture* (Jefferson, NC: McFarland & Company, 2015), 162.

116 "have marked down": Letter from Schuster to Berg, February 27, 1950, Box 57, Berg Papers.

117 In March 1950: Summary of agreement, March 31, 1950, Box 2, folder 193, Paramount Pictures Contract Summaries, Margaret Herrick Library, Beverly Hills, CA.

117 The script: MOLLY, script, 1950, Paramount Pictures Scripts, Box 644, folder M740, Herrick Library.

118 The final film: MOLLY, script, 1950, Paramount Pictures Scripts, Box 644, folder M741, Herrick Library.

119 "Anybody in the world": Author's interview with Barbara Rush, September 19, 2019.

119 Berg threw a wrap party: Mike Connolly, "Just for Variety," *Variety*, ca. September 1950, n.p., Berg Papers.

120 five nights a week: "Radio-Television: Hazel Scott," *Variety*, June 28, 1950, 36.

120 "Miss Scott is a lively performer": Ibid.

120 even the museum: Stabile, *The Broadcast 41*, 175.

120 Ethel Waters was: Ni'Kesia Pannell, "15 Monumental Moments in Black Hollywood History," *Essence*, October 24, 2017, https://www.essence.com/entertainment/timeline-black-hollywood-firsts/#25179.

121 "Hazel Scott had carried": Bogle, *Primetime Blues*, 18.

121 "There sat the shimmering Scott": Ibid., 16.

121 "Here is a gal": Sam Chase, "Radio and Television Program Reviews: Hazel Scott Show," *Billboard*, August 12, 1950, 14.

121 Just a month later: "Defense vs. Getting Muirized," *Billboard*, September 9, 1950, 4.

122 appealed to the FBI: Carol Stabile, "The Typhoid Marys of the Left: Gender, Race, and the Broadcast Blacklist," *Communication and Critical/Cultural Studies*, September 2011, 266–85.

122 told Berg she had two days: Thomas Doherty, *Cold War, Cool Medium: Television, McCarthyism, and American Culture* (New York: Columbia University Press, 2005), 43.

123 "run-of-the-play": Glenn D. Smith, Jr., *"Something on My Own": Gertrude Berg and American Broadcasting, 1929–1956* (Syracuse, NY: Syracuse University Press, 2007), 157.

123 She asked to go before: Scutts, "This Piano Prodigy Was the First African-American Woman to Host Her Own TV Show."

123 "Your mother cannot": Author's interview with Adam Clayton Powell II, May 11, 2019.

Chapter 6: What Are You Going to Do About Your Girl?

125 called a press conference: "Gypsy, Scott, and Wicker in Red Denials," *Billboard*, September 23, 1950, 3.

126 "This is the day": "Hazel Scott's Anti-Communist Statement," *Billboard*, September 23, 1950, 4.

126 "I call upon my colleagues": Ibid., 93.

126 "House Un-American Activities Committee's pussyfooting": "High-Low Democracy," *Chicago Defender*, September 23, 1950, 6.

127 the committee didn't have time: "Hazel Scott Denies Any Red Sympathies," *New York Times*, September 16, 1950, 5.

127 "A method must be found": "Call for United Industry," *Billboard*, September 23, 1950, 3–4.

127 At 10:40 a.m.: Testimony of Hazel Scott Powell, Hearing before the Committee on Un-American Activities, House of Representatives, Eighty-first Congress, second session, September 22, 1950, https://babel.hathitrust.org/cgi/pt?id=uiug.30112042685518&view=1up&seq=5, 3611.

128 "guilt-by-listing": Ibid., 3620.

128 "a lie": Ibid., 3618.

128 "vile and un-American": Ibid., 3620.

128 "I am not": Ibid., 3619.

128 "headline-seeking superpatriots": Ibid., 3625.

128 "The actors, musicians": Ibid., 3626.

128 "by direction of my employer": Ibid., 3612.

128 "Did the publishers": Ibid., 3613.

128 "What I am getting at": Ibid., 3617.

129 "I don't agree with you": Ibid.

129 "They make no bones": Ibid.

129 "As often and expertly": Lester B. Granger, "On 'Red Channels,'" *New York Amsterdam News*, September 23, 1950, 8.

129 "Hazel Scott Assails": Karen Chilton, *Hazel Scott: The Pioneering Journey of a Jazz Pianist from Café Society to Hollywood to HUAC* (Ann Arbor: University of Michigan Press, 2008), 147–48.

129 HUAC appeared to regret: "Wood Closes Door on HUAC Appearances," *Billboard*, September 30, 1950, 4.

130 "It was just that we felt": Merle Miller, *The Judges and the Judged: The Report on Blacklisting in Radio and Television* (New York: Doubleday & Company, 1952), 112.

130 "Why did Hazel": Chilton, *Hazel Scott*, 149.

130 with her husband joining her: J. T. Gipson, column, *Los Angeles Sentinel*, November 2, 1950, B4.

131 had to cancel: Harry Levette, "Gossip of the Movie Lots," *Philadelphia Tribune*, November 28, 1950, 12.

131 "It's so wonderful": Author interview with Adam Clayton Powell III, May 11, 2019.

131 Accompanied by her son: "Latch On," *Chicago Defender*, January 13, 1951, 6.

131 pulled in an impressive: Glenn D. Smith, Jr., *"Something on My Own": Gertrude Berg and American Broadcasting, 1929–1956* (Syracuse, NY: Syracuse University Press, 2007), 194.

131 She began meeting regularly: Ibid., 157.

132 "appear on every available platform": Ibid.

132 "Discussions are now": Ibid., 158.

133 A typical headline: Hedda Hopper column, "Gertrude Berg More like Her Amiable Molly Than She Is Herself," *Providence Sunday Journal*, November 12, 1950, n.p., Berg Papers.

133 "Dear Molly": Letter from Bill Ramsey to Berg, December 21, 1950, Box 57, Berg Papers.

133 Another typical article: "Molly Goldberg Tells How to Make Blintzes," marked "*Bulletin*, 12/28/50," n.p., Berg Papers.

134 "She was always": Author's interview with Adam Berg, May 8, 2019.

134 "This egg is cold": Ibid.

135 Henry James's *The Bostonians*: Morris Freedman, "From the American Scene: The Real Molly Goldberg," *Commentary*, April 1956, https://www.commentarymagazine.com/articles/morris-freedman /from-the-american-scene-the-real-molly-goldberg/.

135 a print of Raphael's: Smith, "*Something on My Own*," 55.

135 twelve hours a day: "Anything but Average," *Tablet*, January 18, 2008, https://www.tabletmag.com/jewish-arts-and-culture/1291/anything -but-average.

137 about eight hundred people: "'Emmy' Awards," *Broadcasting-Telecasting*, January 29, 1951, 64.

137 Dr. Ross's Dog Food: Thomas O'Neil, *The Emmys: Star Wars, Showdowns, and the Supreme Test of TV's Best* (New York: Viking Penguin, 1992), 27.

137 "Just like one book": "Alan Young, Gertrude Berg Win TV Honors for 1950," *Los Angeles Times*, January 24, 1951, 2.

138 "I've been a good father": Todd Van Luling, "10 Super Weird Things You Didn't Know About the Emmys," HuffPost, August 25, 2014, https://www.huffingtonpost.ca/entry/emmys-facts_n_5699168.

138 added the actor and actress categories: O'Neil, *The Emmys*, 27.

138 "heartwarming": "Film Reviews: The Goldbergs," *Variety*, November 22, 1950, 8.

139 "great fun": "Feature Reviews: The Goldbergs," *Boxoffice*, December 2, 1950, B15.

139 the first property: "On the Air," *The Hollywood Reporter*, September 7, 1950, n.p., Berg Papers.

139 received a summons: Congressional summons from W. J. Jones to Philip Loeb, April 20, 1951, Reel 1, Box 1, folder 1.5, Philip Loeb Papers, New York Public Library Manuscripts and Archives Division, New York City (hereafter referred to as Loeb Papers).

139 TV's number nine show: "'Fireside,' 'Philco' in Lead," *Billboard*, May 26, 1951, 7.

139 had a sit-down conversation: Smith, "*Something on My Own*," 158–60.

139 It cost about $11,000: "'Fireside,' 'Philco' in Lead," *Billboard*.

140 "The Columbia Broadcasting System": Quoted in Smith, *Something on My Own*," 60.

140 her first in twenty-two years: "Studio Sidelights: CBS," *Tele-Talent*, June 25, 1951, n.p., Berg Papers.

140 "I'm going to find": Quoted in Smith, *Something on My Own*," 163.

140 was back in Los Angeles: "Angelenos Awaiting Hazel Scott Concert," *Los Angeles Sentinel*, April 19, 1951, A4.

141 first US TV series: Nicole Chung, "The Search for *Madame Liu-Tsong*," *Vulture*, September 2017, vulture.com/2017/09/the-search -for-the-gallery-of-madame-liu-tsong.html.

141 had been in the works: Donald Roe, "Childress, Alvin," *Encyclopedia of African American History* (New York: Oxford University Press, 2009), 372.

141 who would lip-sync: Si Steinhauser, "Amos 'n' Andy Chose Negro Stars for TV Film," *The Pittsburgh Press*, December 13, 1950, https://news .google.com/newspapers?id=sXgbAAAAIBAJ&sjid=ak0EAAAAI BAJ&pg=1581,6710228&dq=spencer+williams&hl=en.

142 *Pittsburgh Courier* had encouraged: "Courier Seeks 5,000 Ministers to Talk on Self-Respect," *Pittsburgh Courier*, September 12, 1931, 7.

142 issued a clear bulletin: "Why the Amos 'n' Andy Show Should Be Taken Off the Air," *NAACP Bulletin*, August 15, 1951.

142 The call for a boycott: Joshua K. Wright, PhD, "Reflections on Black Image in Amos 'n' Andy," *Abernathy*, March 1, 2017, https://abernathy magazine.com/reflections-on-black-image-in-amos-n-andy/.

143 took her act from Los Angeles to London: "Gypsy, Scott Score at London Palladium," *Variety*, September 12, 1951, 2.

143 a tour of Europe: "Hazel Scott Set for 40 Weeks, May Hit 100G," *Billboard*, February 10, 1951, 41.

143 "We share each other's glory": Chilton, *Hazel Scott*, 154.

143 "A person needs to": Ibid., 156.

144 she recorded a new album: Ibid., 155–56.

144 "All right, we're going": Ibid., 156.

144 he later wired: Richard Cohen, "Tear Down J. Edgar Hoover's Name," *Washington Post*, November 20, 2017, https://www.washingtonpost .com/opinions/j-edgar-hoover-not-just-robert-e-lee-should-go/2017 /11/20/26f3ce26-ce2f-11e7-81bc-c55a220c8cbe_story.html.

144 her moods swung: Chilton, *Hazel Scott*, 157.

145 a standard treatment: Edward Shorter, "The History of ECT: Un-solved Mysteries," *Psychiatric Times*, February 1, 2004, https://www.psychiatrictimes.com/schizophrenia/history-ect-unsolved-mysteries.

145 She showed little improvement: Chilton, *Hazel Scott*, 157–58.

Chapter 7: Aren't You Ashamed?

147 checked into the hospital: Phillips autobiographical drafts, 141–42, Phillips Papers.

149 The idea had struck her: Ibid., 139–42.

151 "In my opinion": Ibid., 139-140.

151 "No one seemed overly enthusiastic": Ibid.

152 "unusually talented and photogenic": Ibid., 141.

152 added an afternoon movie: White, *Here We Go Again: My Life in Tele-vision* (New York: Scribner, 1995), 90.

153 "Had we overextended": Ibid., 93.

154 visit Western Costume Company: Ibid., 96.

154 "Oh, you like": Ibid.

154 Jarvis had often mentioned: Ibid., 100.

154 "On a few occasions": Ibid.

155 "Whether Al was using": Ibid.

156 more than a hundred: Pat Saperstein, "Longtime Thesp Eddie Al-bert Dies," *Variety*, May 27, 2005, https://variety.com/2005/scene/markets-festivals/longtime-thesp-eddie-albert-dies-1117923612/.

156 extraordinary record in World War II: "Famous Veteran: Eddie Al-bert," Military.com, https://www.military.com/veteran-jobs/career-advice/military-transition/famous-veteran-eddie-albert.html.

157 "You've attracted a large following": David C. Tucker, *The Women Who Made Television Funny* (Jefferson, NC: McFarland & Company, 2007), 159.

157 Fedderson called another meeting: White, *Here We Go Again*, 105.

158 "had delicious senses of humor": Robert Moritz, "Life Is a Scream for Betty White," *Parade*, October 31, 2010, https://parade.com/132208/robertmoritz/betty-white-goes-wild/.

159 whom Tibbles knew: White, *Here We Go Again*, 109.

159 "Both Alvin and Elizabeth": Ibid., 108.

159 "Incident number one": Ibid., 109.

159 "a little anecdote": Tucker, *The Women Who Made Television Funny*, 160.

159 skip around in time: White, *Here We Go Again*, 111–13.

161 "I started having": Betty White, interview with Tony Fantozzi, Television Academy Foundation, June 4, 1997, video, https://interviews
.televisionacademy.com/interviews/betty-white.

161 Moore jabbed at White: White, *Here We Go Again*, 114.

161 "That monster knew me": Ibid.

161 At the end of a broadcast: Ibid., 112.

161 "mayor of Hollywood": Ibid., 120.

161 felt glamorous: Ibid., 123.

162 "For a lovely girl": Ibid.

162 "Zsaz": White, Television Academy Foundation interview.

162 "I don't know which": Ibid.

162 "You're wasting your talent": Tucker, *The Women Who Made Television Funny*, 161.

163 Liberace had become a friend: White, *Here We Go Again*, 125.

163 had dreamed of that moment: Ibid., 127.

Chapter 8: A Note of Sadness

165 "has had, and does have": Memo from Robert W. McFadyen to Fred Wile, July 5, 1951, Box 567A, folder 13, National Broadcasting Company Records, Wisconsin Historical Society, Madison, WI.

166 "Because of the nature": Ibid.

166 a ten-year contract: Memo from Thomas McAvity to Folsom, February 19, 1953. Box 368, folder 61, NBC Records (hereafter referred to as NBC Records).

166 "Molly Goldberg, a well-known": Letter from Loeb to Zero Mostel, September 15, 1951, Box 5, folder 15, Zero and Kate Mostel Papers, New York Public Library, Bill Rose Theatre Division, New York (hereafter referred to as Mostel Papers).

167 "Mrs. Berg is getting ready": Letter from Loeb to Zero Mostel, September 21, 1951, Mostel Papers.

167 "Would more analysis": Letter from Loeb to Zero Mostel, October 14, 1951, Mostel Papers.

167 an appeal to Cardinal Francis Spellman: Glenn D. Smith, Jr., *"Something on My Own": Gertrude Berg and American Broadcasting, 1929–1956* (Syracuse, NY: Syracuse University Press, 2007), 164.

167 Spellman had exonerated: Ibid., 168.

167 "She said she never": Ibid., 167.

168 "He said he could fix": Jeff Kisseloff, *The Box: An Oral History of Television* (New York: Penguin Books, 1995), 412.

168 "Things coming to a head": Letter from Loeb to Zero Mostel, October 18, 1951, Mostel Papers.

168 as a companion: Madelyn Pugh Davis, *Laughing with Lucy: My Life with America's Leading Lady of Comedy* (Cincinnati: Clerisy Press, 2005), 53.

169 the nation's number one show: "How 'I Love Lucy' Dominated Ratings from Its Start," *Hollywood Reporter*, August 15, 2011, https://www.hollywoodreporter.com/news/how-i-love-lucy-dominated-222960.

169 insisted on shooting: Davis, *Laughing with Lucy*, 55–56.

170 via Karl Freund: Leigh Allen, "Filming the *I Love Lucy* Show," *American Cinematographer*, https://ascmag.com/articles/filming-the-i-love-lucy-show.

170 whom Arnaz challenged: Ibid., 57.

170 agreed to a pay cut: Davis, *Laughing with Lucy*, 59.

171 worked as a magazine journalist: "Rountree, Martha (1911–1999)," Encyclopedia.com, https://www.encyclopedia.com/women/encyclopedias-almanacs-transcripts-and-maps/rountree-martha-1911-1999.

171 created a radio spin-off: Sharon Shahid, "60 Years Ago in News History: America Meets the Press," Newseum, November 14, 2007, Internet Archive, https://web.archive.org/web/20081117170923/http://www.newseum.org/news/news.aspx?item=jn_MTP071114&style=f.

171 longest-running show: David Uberti, "Who's Hosted Meet the Press?," *Columbia Journalism Review*, November–December 2014, https://archives.cjr.org/currents/whos_hosted_meet_the_press.php.

171 In one of his appearances: "Joseph McCarthy on Communism in the State Department," *Meet the Press*, NBC, July 2, 1950, NBC Learn, https://archives.nbclearn.com/portal/site/k-12/browse?cuecard=1790.

172 toting a gun: "MTP at 70: Martha Rountree Blazes a Trail," NBC News, November 6, 2017, https://www.nbcnews.com/storyline/meet-the-press-70-years/mtp-70-martha-rountree-blazes-trail-n817941.

172 first standard contract: J. E. Smyth, "When a Woman Called the Shots at the Screen Writers Guild," Women and Hollywood, March 14, 2017, https://womenandhollywood.com/guest-post-when

-a-woman-called-the-shots-at-the-screen-writers-guild-bbdb72e
2984f/.

172 Harry Warner of Warner Bros. and Paramount's Y. Frank Freeman: J. E. Smyth, "The Mary C. McCall Years: When a Woman President Called the Shots at the Guild, Part Two," *Written By*, October 2017, 38–42, 63, https://www.bluetoad.com/publication/?i=437002&article _id=2884825&view=articleBrowser.

173 "Is Y. Frank Freeman": Ibid.

173 she was indignant: Letter from Gustav Margraf to Sydney N. Kiges, November 12, 1951, Box 567A, folder 13, NBC Records.

173 "'silent conspiracy' against": "Sponsor Standoff Bewilders NBC in 'Goldbergs' Bid," *Variety*, October 31, 1951.

174 "I am hopeful": Letter from Loeb to Zero Mostel, December 3, 1951, Mostel Papers.

174 "sticking to" him: Letter from Loeb to Zero Mostel, undated, Mostel Papers.

174 "Will Gertrude really stick": Ibid.

174 Berg called Loeb: Thomas Doherty, *Cold War, Cool Medium: Television, McCarthyism, and American Culture* (New York: Columbia University Press, 2005), 44.

175 "twenty people depending": Smith, *"Something on My Own,"* 163.

175 "At no extra cost": Memo from Rud Lawrence to TV Network Sales Staff, September 7, 1951, Box 567A, folder 13, NBC Records.

175 "So recently": NBC sales brochure for *The Goldbergs*, ca. 1951–1952, Box 1, Berg Papers.

175 NBC was now trying: Various contracts, 1952, Box 567A, folder 13, NBC Records.

175 the American Civil Liberties Union responded: Letter from Patrick Murphy Malin to Berg, January 22, 1952, Box 920, folder 5, item 813, American Civil Liberties Union Records, Mudd Library, Princeton University, Princeton, NJ.

176 "Despite the fact": Doherty, *Cold War, Cool Medium*, 45.

176 "commend Gertrude Berg": Ibid., 45–46.

176 "most appreciative of the fight": Letter from Bill Prince to Loeb, January 14, 1952, Reel 1, Box 1, folder 1.5, Loeb Papers.

176 "It is hard to find words": Letter from Stryker to Loeb, January 17, 1952, Reel 1, Box 1, folder 1.5, Loeb Papers.

177 "It developed that": "If You've Missed These Faces . . . ," *Who's Who in TV & Radio*, 2, no. 1 (1952): 2, http://www.otrr.org/FILES/Magz _pdf/Misc%201/Who%27s%20Who%20in%20TV%20&%20 Radio%201952.pdf.

177 the Television Authority negotiated: "Loeb Settles Contract with 'The Goldbergs,'" *Billboard*, February 2, 1952, 6.

177 As a result of the deal: "45G Loeb Payment Won't Deter TVA in 'Blacklist' Fight," *Variety*, January 30, 1952, 24.

178 NBC also received: Letter from Luba Aronoff to Berg, January 28, 1952; letter from Bill Ross to George Heller, ca. 1952; letter from Charlotte A. Christner to NBC, February 11, 1952, Reel 1, Box 1, folder 1.5, Loeb Papers.

178 "I have been pained": Letter from Luba Aronoff to Berg, January 28, 1952, Loeb Papers.

180 Some actors refused: Smith, *"Something on My Own,"* 173.

180 She saw thirty-five actors: Unattributed news clipping, Oversize Box 17, Berg Papers.

180 She called the actor George Tobias: News clipping, *World Telegram Sun*, February 1, 1952, Oversize Box 17, Berg Papers.

181 offered the role: Arthur Sainer, *Zero Dances: A Biography of Zero Mostel* (New York: Limelight Editions, 1998), 165.

181 just forty-eight hours before: News clipping, *Gazette & Daily*, February 6, 1952, Oversize Box 17, Berg Papers.

181 "The New Jake Goldberg": John Crosby, *New York Herald Tribune*, "Radio and Television: The Goldbergs Return," February 10, 1952, n.p., Berg Papers.

182 "may detect a note": Eric Burns, *Invasion of the Mind Snatchers: Television's Conquest of America in the Fifties* (Philadelphia: Temple University Press, 2010), 172.

182 "Have I given up": Loeb notes, February 6, 1952, Reel 1, Box 1, folder 1.5, Loeb Papers.

182 "It does not make": Letter from H. Graham Morison to Barbara Ziegler, March 28, 1952, Reel 1, Box 1, folder 1.4, Loeb Papers.

183 did win a $3.5 million lawsuit: Ken Tucker, "The Man Who Beat the Blacklist . . . John Henry Faulk," *Entertainment Weekly*, July 27, 1990, https://ew.com/article/1990/07/27/man-who-beat-blacklistjohn -henry-faulk/.

183 well-received Passover episode: News clipping, *East Side News*, April 19, 1952, Oversize Box 17, Berg Papers.

183 featured thirty-four seder guests: News clipping, *Pittsburgh Press*, April 17, 1952, Oversize Box 17, Berg Papers.

183 an internal NBC memo: Memo from Robert E. Button to Edward Hits, May 26, 1952, Box 567A, folder 13, NBC Records.

183 "as a friend": Sainer, *Zero Dances*, 165.

183 Loeb and Berg rarely saw each other: Smith, "Something on My Own," 181.

183 Loeb was compelled to testify: United States Senate, Subcommittee to Investigate the Administration of the Internal Security Act and Other Internal Security Laws of the Committee on the Judiciary, *Subversive Infiltration of Radio, Television and the Entertainment Industry*, Washington, DC, April 23, 1952.

184 The cost of a black-and white television set: Christopher H. Sterling and John Michael Kittross, *Stay Tuned: A History of American Broadcasting* (Mahwah, NJ: Lawrence Erlbaum Associates, 2002), 317.

184 With 15.3 million TVs in use: Ibid., 864.

184 The new union set: Betty White, *Here We Go Again: My Life in Television* (New York: Scribner, 1995), 87.

185 sales of Hazel Bishop lipstick: "1950s TV Turns on America," *Ad Age*, March 28, 2005, https://adage.com/article/75-years-of-ideas/1950s -tv-turns-america/102703.

185 "Stays on YOU": Mary Tannen, "Hazel Bishop, 92, an Innovator Who Made Lipstick Kissproof," *New York Times*, December 10, 1998, https://www.nytimes.com/1998/12/10/nyregion/hazel-bishop-92 -an-innovator-who-made-lipstick-kissproof.html.

185 placed television's first political ad: Chapman Rackaway, *Communicating Politics Online* (New York: Palgrave Macmillan, 2014), 20.

185 108 stations in sixty-five cities: Gary R. Edgerton, *The Columbia History of American Television* (New York: Columbia University Press, 2007), 103.

185 was lifted in April 1952: *Eighteenth Annual Report: Federal Communications Commission* (Washington, DC: US Government Printing Office, 1952), 107.

185 allowed for 1,875 new commercial stations: *The Television Inquiry: Allocations Phase, Interim Report of the Committee on Interstate and*

Foreign Commerce (Washington, DC: US Government Printing Office, 1956), 2.

185 on a twenty-five-acre lot: Patrick Shanley, "CBS Sells Iconic Television City Property for $750 Million," *Hollywood Reporter*, December 10, 2018, https://www.hollywoodreporter.com/news/cbs-sells -television-city-property-750-million-1168095.

186 Movie ticket sales dropped: Jim Callan, *America in the 1960s* (New York: Facts on File, 2006), 19.

186 Motion Picture Association of America prohibited: Susan Murray, *Hitch Your Antenna to the Stars: Early Television and Broadcast Stardom* (New York: Routledge, 2005), 43.

186 "theater television": Janet Wasko, "Hollywood and Television in the 1950s: The Roots of Diversification," Encyclopedia.com, https://www.encyclopedia.com/arts/culture-magazines/hollywood-and -television-1950s-roots-diversification.

188 She tried to soothe herself: Karen Chilton, *Hazel Scott: The Pioneering Journey of a Jazz Pianist from Café Society to Hollywood to HUAC* (Ann Arbor: University of Michigan Press, 2008), 158.

188 "No matter what": Martin Chilton, "Billie Holiday: The Wild Lady of Jazz Who Adored England," *The Independent*, July 17, 2019, https://www.independent.co.uk/arts-entertainment/music/features/billie -holiday-anniversary-death-jazz-age-cause-a8997656.html.

188 "she is believed": Chilton, *Hazel Scott*, 158.

188 "were delighted by the way": Ibid., 159.

189 filed a complaint: ACLU, Complaint before the Federal Communications Commission, April 2, 1952, Box 920, folder 11, item 911, ACLU Papers.

189 "probably because of": Ibid.

189 "both unfounded and lacking in responsibility": Letter from William A. Roberts to T. J. Slowie, May 29, 1952, Box 920, folder 11, item 911, ACLU Papers.

190 Duke Ellington praised Scott: Duke Ellington, "The Most Exciting Women I've Known," *Ebony*, April 1952, 23–30.

Chapter 9: Dramatic Pause

192 had traveled to Chicago: Phillips autobiographical drafts, 142, Phillips Papers.

192 "I know for a certainty": Ibid., 81, Phillips Papers.

193 "Please let me repeat": Letter from Phillips to "Charley," ca. 1950, Box 37, Phillips Papers.

193 "You've got to have": "Magnificent Corrosive," *Time*, March 8, 1954, 61.

194 first soap to successfully transition: David Bianculli, *The Platinum Age of Television: From I Love Lucy to The Walking Dead, How TV Became Terrific* (New York: Anchor Books, 2017), 130.

194 Phillips was paid: Phillips autobiographical drafts, 143, Phillips Papers.

194 "While it's difficult": "Television Reviews: Guiding Light," *Variety*, July 2, 1952, 29.

195 "I had also come": Phillips autobiographical drafts, 147, Phillips Papers.

196 "I know of a group": Committee on Un-American Activities, United States House of Representatives, *Investigation of Communist Activities in the New York City Area—Part 1*, May 4, 1953 (Washington, DC: US Government Printing Office, 1953), 1352–53.

196 inspired civil rights organizations: Dwayne Mack, "Hazel Scott: A Career Curtailed," *The Journal of African American History*, Spring 2006, 153–70.

197 told the network she needed: Memo from Rud Lawrence, March 19, 1952, Box 567A, folder 13, NBC Records.

197 boarded the *Queen Mary*: Steward's list of first-class passengers on *Queen Mary*, July 7, 1952, Oversize Box 17, Berg Papers.

197 in the fall of 1952: "'Goldbergs' Back to ½-Hr. Format," *Variety*, June 11, 1952, 22.

197 not enough stations: "NBC-TV to Co-op 'Goldbergs,' 'Jury,'" *Variety*, November 19, 1952, 25.

197 "I realize now": Milton Berle, *Milton Berle: An Autobiography* (New York: Delacorte Press, 1974), 294.

199 to do a music-based show: "Gertrude Berg 'Kinnies' New Program for TV," *Variety*, May 27, 1953, 54.

199 Her appearances drew: "NBC-TV's Chant: 'We Want Mollie,'" *Variety*, February 4, 1953, 27.

199 she had turned down: Glenn D. Smith, Jr., *"Something on My Own": Gertrude Berg and American Broadcasting, 1929–1956* (Syracuse, NY: Syracuse University Press, 2007), 194.

199 The cast would convene: *Goldbergs* schedule, July 3, 1953, Oversize Box 8, Berg Papers.

200 "The new Jake Goldberg": Leon Morse, "Goldbergs Back for Summer TV with Old Familiar Charm," *Billboard*, July 11, 1953, 2, 10.

200 "Robert H. Harris segued": "Television Reviews: The Goldbergs," *Variety*, July 8, 1953, 35.

200 "open-faced warmth": Morse, "Goldbergs Back for Summer TV with Old Familiar Charm."

201 "After the dose": "TV Previewers Recommend," *Philadelphia Bulletin*, July 3, 1953, n.p., Oversize 8, Berg Papers.

201 the same old problem: "Orphans of the TV Storm," *Variety*, September 23, 1953, 28.

201 "re-established itself": Ibid.

201 carried from her Park Avenue home: Smith, *"Something on My Own,"* 195.

201 gastric hemorrhages: "Gertrude Berg Seriously Ill; Daughter Also in Hosp," *Variety*, December 9, 1953, 2.

201 in critical condition: "Gertrude Berg Out of Hosp; to Rest in Fla.," *Variety*, January 27, 1954, 30.

201 more than 10,000 fan letters: Smith, *"Something on My Own,"* 195.

201 read some of the notes: Note from Fannie Merrill to Joseph A. Moran, December 13, 1953, Box 35, folder 519, Ritter and Moran Papers.

201 "I can only do two": Letter from Moran to Berg, December 10, 1953, Box 35, folder 519, Ritter and Moran Papers.

202 had been given at least: "Gertrude Berg Seriously Ill; Daughter Also in Hosp," *Variety*.

203 "I just figured": William Bell, interview with Alan Carter, Television Academy Foundation, July 15, 1998, video, https://interviews.televisionacademy.com/interviews/william-bell.

204 "spinster": Douglas S. Cramer, interview with Henry Colman and Jenni Matz, Television Academy Foundation, May 22, 2009, video, https://interviews.televisionacademy.com/interviews/douglas-s-cramer.

204 "TV Proves Housewives": "Sobs and Suds," *TV Guide*, June 5, 1953, 8.

204 "The first time this reviewer": "Guiding Light," *TV Guide*, ca. 1953, n.p. Snapshot of magazine on file at the Paley Center for Media, New York, June 7, 2019.

205 enrolled in Culver Military Academy: Phillips autobiographical drafts, 158, Phillips Papers.

205 "As time went on": Ibid., 167.

205 commiserated with the mother: Ibid., 159.

206 "Once again the single-woman home": Ibid., 167.

206 heading to Key West: "Gertrude Berg Out of Hosp; to Rest in Fla.," *Variety*.

206 she was in talks: "Hal (Gildersleeve) Peary, Hazel Scott into WMGM New Daytime Lineup," *Variety*, October 28, 1953, 22.

206 starting on September 25, 1953: Betty White, *Here We Go Again: My Life in Television* (New York: Scribner, 1995), 128–29.

207 "It was a little like doing": Ibid., 128.

207 to compete with: Mary Cremmen, "TV Notebook," *Boston Globe*, February 11, 1954, 3.

207 Could she handle: White, *Here We Go Again*, 130.

208 in December 1953: "Betty White Leaving KLAC Day Program; Linkletter in the Dough," *Los Angeles Times*, December 15, 1953, 24.

208 Her mentor and benefactor: White, *Here We Go Again*, 130.

208 "the most successful young woman": Jane Morris, "No Time for Nothun," article draft, ca. 1954, Box 27, folder 16, Ardmore Papers.

Chapter 10: Black and White and Red

209 involved so many people: Betty White, *Here We Go Again: My Life in Television* (New York: Scribner, 1995), 132–33.

209 more than two thousand fan letters: Jane Morris, "No Time for Nothun," article draft, ca. 1954, Box 27, folder 16, Ardmore Papers.

209 produced the show: *Betty White: First Lady of Television*, DVD, directed by Steven J. Boettcher and Michael J. Trinklein (Boettcher + Trinklein Television, 2018).

209 a makeup artist and a hairdresser: White, *Here We Go Again*, 133.

209 Her dresses were now provided: Morris, "No Time for Nothun."

210 "biggest break": Walter Ames, "Betty White Signed by NBC for Network Show; Gleason Mishap Filmed," *Los Angeles Times*, February 2, 1954, 22.

210 she awoke at 4:15 a.m.: White, *Here We Go Again*, 140.

210 "The day starts early": Morris, "No Time for Nothun."

210 "It always amazed me": White, *Here We Go Again*, 140.

210 her own carpeted dressing room: Ibid., 133.

210 Makeup call came: Ibid., 140.

211 "as if it were a lover": Morris, "No Time for Nothun."

211 "Dear Betty": White, *Here We Go Again*, 135.

211 "He had the face": Ibid., 136.

212 "If you're natural": Morris, "No Time for Nothun."

212 Western star Guy Madison: White, *Here We Go Again*, 134–35.

212 retired marine major Donald Keyhoe: "Keyhoe to Tell All on Betty White Seg," *Billboard*, April 10, 1954, 3.

212 A man named Mr. Bethrem: Thomas Morrow, "Man on TV Tells of Visiting Crew of a Flying Saucer," *Chicago Daily Tribune*, April 4, 1954, 40.

212 She needed to stop fidgeting: Morris, "No Time for Nothun."

213 watched the day's show: White, *Here We Go Again*, 141.

213 She grabbed lunch: Morris, "No Time for Nothun."

213 "You can feel pretty sorry": Ibid.

213 "But what else": Jack Holland, "Can I Ever Be a Wife?," *TV Star Parade*, December 1954, 38.

214 "Betty White, the hottest young star": Morris, "No Time for Nothun."

214 in at least fifteen markets: "'Life with Elizabeth' Sold in 15 Markets," *Variety*, September 23, 1953, 31.

214 "an amusing, wacky series": "Life with Elizabeth," *Variety*, October 21, 1953, 33.

214 "It is of a type": Sam Chase, "TV Film: Life with Elizabeth," *Billboard*, November 7, 1953, 19.

214 "Betty White and her": "Life with Elizabeth," *TV Guide*, April 30, 1954, 21.

215 "A comedienne who somehow": Jack Gould, "Television in Review; Betty White's Comic Antics Deserving of Better Spot," *New York Times*, March 24, 1954, 37.

215 Her agent clipped: Letter from MCA Artists Ltd. to Thomas McAvity, March 26, 1954, Box 380, folder 23, NBC Records.

215 "Attractive, charming": Leon Morse, "The Betty White Show," *Billboard*, February 20, 1954, 12.

215 "Daytime television east of California": Donald Kirkley, "Look and Listen," *The Sun*, March 9, 1954, 10.

216 "the disposition of a storybook heroine": "Betty White's Life with Elizabeth," *TV Guide*, April 23, 1954, 15–17.

216 "If ignorance is bliss": White 130.

217 She delivered commercials: Walter Ames, "'Cinderella Never Worked This Hard,'" *Los Angeles Times*, April 11, 1954, D1.

218 "It wouldn't be fair": Donald Kirkley, "Betty White Varies Give-Away Style," *The Sun*, October 3, 1954, L11.

218 "Sooner or later": John Crosby, "Radio and Television: 'Wholesome' Routine and Big Sister Acts," *Hartford Courant*, May 24, 1954, 12.

218 "He didn't like": Kliph Nesteroff, "The Early Betty White 1947–1973," WFMU's Beware of the Blog, April 4, 2010, https://blog .wfmu.org/freeform/2010/04/the-early-betty-white.html.

219 "Betty White is a charming young woman": Kirkley, "Betty White Varies Give-Away Style."

219 "Yes, we've had one": Richard Dyer MacCann, "Television's Betty White," *Christian Science Monitor*, May 11, 1954, 11.

219 She invited the dancer Arthur Duncan: White, *Here We Go Again*, 137.

220 "with deep regret": *Betty White: First Lady of Television*, DVD.

220 one of the first Black regulars: Brian Seibert, "Dance: This Week; All the Tap Dancers in New York," *New York Times*, May 30, 2004, https://www.nytimes.com/2004/05/30/arts/dance-this-week-all -the-tap-dancers-in-new-york.html?n=Top%2FReference%2F Times+Topics%2FPeople%2FH%2FHines%2C+Gregory.

221 "a terrific bonanza": Quoted in Murray Forman, *One Night on TV Is Worth Weeks at the Paramount* (Durham, NC: Duke University Press, 2012), 261.

221 took the Panamanian ship: Karen Chilton, *Hazel Scott: The Pioneering Journey of a Jazz Pianist from Café Society to Hollywood to HUAC* (Ann Arbor: University of Michigan Press, 2008), 161–65.

222 "Okay, I'll stay": Author's interview with Adam Clayton Powell III, May 11, 2019.

222 "Well, Adam, God is giving": Chilton 163.

222 "We're America's strangest family": Ibid.

223 "But what happens": Ibid., 164.

223 "I think we need to understand": Author's interview with Adam Clayton Powell III, May 11, 2019.

224 "I'm never going to work": Ibid.

224 "[T]here took place": Adam Clayton Powell, Jr., *Adam by Adam: The*

Autobiography of Adam Clayton Powell, Jr. (New York: Dafina Books, 1971), 228.

224 viewers who stayed up late enough: Benjamin Gross, "Living Test Patterns: The Models Who Calibrated Color TV," *The Atlantic*, June 28, 2015, https://www.theatlantic.com/technology/archive/2015/06/miss-color-tv/396266/.

225 White's NBC bosses: White, *Here We Go Again*, 141–42.

225 had worked to develop color television: "Pioneering in Electronics, Chapter Nine—Television: Monochrome to Color," The David Sarnoff Library, http://www.davidsarnoff.org/kil-chapter09.html.

225 "It made black and white": Betty White, interview with Tony Fantozzi, Television Academy Foundation, June 4, 1997, video, https://interviews.televisionacademy.com/interviews/betty-white.

225 Commanded to make *The Guiding Light*: Allison J. Waldman, "'GL' Through the Years," *Television Week*, January 22, 2007, 36–37.

226 ABC merged with United Paramount Theatres: Harold L. Erickson, "American Broadcast Company," Encylopaedia Britannica, https://www.britannica.com/topic/American-Broadcasting-Company#ref 167751.

226 Julius and Ethel Rosenberg: "Julius and Ethel Rosenberg Executed for Espionage," History, https://www.history.com/this-day-in-history/rosenbergs-executed.

226 Jean-Paul Sartre: "Rosenbergs convicted of espionage," History, https://www.history.com/this-day-in-history/rosenbergs-convicted-of-espionage.

226 Albert Einstein: Tim Ott, "Julius and Ethel Rosenberg: Their Case, Trial and Death," Biography, https://www.biography.com/news/julius-ethel-rosenberg-espionage-trial-death.

226 Pablo Picasso: David S. Martin, "Art Exhibit About Rosenbergs Tours Country," AP, March 18, 1989, https://apnews.com/7879 e93a3174b5573390d5a6a29a40cf.

226 Pope Pius XII: Joe Heim, "Sons of Executed Spies Julius and Ethel Rosenberg Ask Obama to Exonerate Their Mother," *Washington Post*, December 1, 2016, https://www.washingtonpost.com/local/education/sons-of-executed-spies-julius-and-ethel-rosenberg-ask-obama-to-exonerate-mom/2016/12/01/a654c7ca-b7e6-11e6-b8df-600bd9d38a02_story.html.

226 "totalitarian, fascist": Thomas I. Emerson and David M. Helfeld, "Loyalty Among Government Employees," *Yale Law Journal* 58, no. 1 (December 1948): 1–143, https://digitalcommons.law.yale.edu/cgi /viewcontent.cgi?article=4746&context=ylj.

226 "It is now evident": "Text of Address by Truman Explaining to Nation His Actions in the White Case," *New York Times*, November 17, 1953, 26.

227 riveted 44 million viewers: Tim Page, "Desi Arnaz, TV Pioneer, Is Dead at 69," *New York Times*, December 3, 1986, D26.

227 she had to meet with: Lucille Ball, *Love, Lucy* (New York: Berkley Boulevard, 1996), Apple Books/iPad, 242–43.

227 "Now I want you": Ibid., 250.

227 had paid him $8,775: Document of Earnings 1953 from January 1 to November 1, Reel 1, Box 1, Folder 1.7-1.8. Loeb Papers.

227 which cost $11,450: Letter from V. E. Korns to Loeb, November 3, 1954, Reel 1, Box 1, folder 1.6, Loeb Papers.

228 considering moving it to daytime: "'Goldbergs' May Become Strip," *Billboard*, October 3, 1953, 3.

228 Her contract with NBC stipulated: "Molly Vice Sheen in DuMont Deal with NBC Blessing," *Variety*, March 3, 1954, 1.

228 "into a new prominent position": Ibid.

229 She signed a deal: "Buttons and Berg," *Variety*, July 28, 1954, 108.

230 "Mrs. Berg simply is not": Morris Freedman, "From the American Scene: The Real Molly Goldberg," *Commentary*, April 1956, https:// www.commentarymagazine.com/articles/morris-freedman/from -the-american-scene-the-real-molly-goldberg/.

230 DuMont sold the sponsorship: "General Foods Switches $3.3 Million to Y&R, B&B; P&G in Record CBS-TV Buy," *Broadcasting-Telecasting*, March 29, 1954, 29.

230 took key backstage jobs: Freedman, "From the American Scene: The Real Molly Goldberg."

231 "I made more money": Author's interview with Adam Berg, May 8, 2019.

232 about two hundred affiliates: "DuMont Television Network," Encyclopaedia Britannica, https://www.britannica.com/topic/DuMont -Television-Network.

232 June 1954 opening: David Weinstein, *The Forgotten Network: DuMont*

and the Birth of American Television (Philadelphia: Temple University Press, 2004), 46.

232 "New York's Answer": Muriel Fischer, "DuMont's Tele-Centre Is New York's Answer to West Coast Video Rivalry," *New York World-Telegram & Sun*, June 12, 1954, n.p., Berg Papers.

232 dress rehearsal: Freedman, "From the American Scene: The Real Molly Goldberg."

234 a $5 million contract: Smith, *"Something on My Own,"* 198–99.

234 "I did want to tell": Letter from Ted Bergmann to Berg, October 27, 1954, Box 57, Berg Papers.

234 DuMont operated: Smith, *"Something on My Own,"* 199.

Chapter 11: The Scourge of 1955

236 "Molly worked": Morris Freedman, "From the American Scene: The Real Molly Goldberg," *Commentary*, April 1956, https://www.commentarymagazine.com/articles/morris-freedman/from-the-american-scene-the-real-molly-goldberg/.

237 the introduction is signed: Gertrude Berg and Myra Waldo, *The Molly Goldberg Jewish Cookbook* (Bala Cynwyd, PA: Ivyland Books, 2008), 7.

237 "Watching Molly cook": Ibid.,

237 beef and sauerkraut: Ibid., 97–98.

237 "Show me someone": Ibid., 185.

237 "full-figured woman": Joyce Antler, ed. *Talking Back: Images of Jewish Women in American Popular Culture* (Hanover, NH: Brandeis University Press, 1998), 97.

237 "She would never": Author's interview with Anne Schwartz, April 30, 2019.

238 For the previous five years: "Yoo-Hoo, Mrs. Newark—Molly Goldberg's Coming to Bam's," Bamberger's press release, April 30, 1953, Box 62, Berg Papers.

238 hundreds of fans: "Molly Goldberg Is Just What Milwaukee Had Expected," *Milwaukee Journal*, circa 1952, n.p., Box 62, Berg Papers.

238 members of local women's clubs: "Molly Goldberg to Introduce Her Own Dress Designs Here," *Columbus Dispatch*, September 5, 1952, n.p., Box 62, Berg Papers.

238 who had worked in the Method tradition: Eric Grode, "Mira Rostova,

Coach to Montgomery Clift, Dies at 99," *New York Times*, February 6, 2009, https://www.nytimes.com/2009/02/06/movies/06rostova.html.

239 "She carried off": Freedman, "From the American Scene: The Real Molly Goldberg."

240 "She is a great force": "Anything but Average," *Tablet*, January 18, 2008, https://www.tabletmag.com/jewish-arts-and-culture/1291/anything-but-average.

240 partnered with Guild Films: "Guild Films to Shoot Massey TV Series Here," *Radio Television Daily*, March 16, 1955, 1.

240 "the most ambitious production program": "Guild Production Sked Embraces Six Shows," *Billboard*, July 23, 1955, 12.

241 As early as February 1954: Memo from Sam Fuller to Thomas McAvity, February 11, 1954, Box 380, folder 23, NBC Records.

241 successful run the previous summer: Letter from Wilbur Stark to Fuller, February 12, 1954, Box 380, folder 23, NBC Records.

241 "*Ladies' Choice* is based on": Memo from Sam Fuller to Thomas McAvity, February 11, 1954.

241 Eisenhower had won: "Women in Politics," CQ Researcher, https://library.cqpress.com/cqresearcher/document.php?id=cqresrre1956022000.

241 "anything pertaining to their daily life": Memo from Sam Fuller to Thomas McAvity, February 11, 1954.

242 NBC executive Sam Fuller met: Memo from Fuller to Fred Wile, March 26, 1954, Box 380, folder 23, NBC Records.

242 "but felt the show lacked": Ibid.

242 "THINK THE PRESENT SHOW": Telegram from Fedderson to McAvity, March 21, 1954, Box 380, folder 23, NBC Records.

242 His popularity was on the decline: Myles Hudson, "Why Did Joseph McCarthy's Influence Decline?," Encyclopaedia Britannica, https://www.britannica.com/story/why-did-joseph-mccarthys-influence-decline.

242 didn't particularly care for him: Jesse Greenspan, "How Eisenhower Secretly Pushed Back Against McCarthyism," History, https://www.history.com/news/dwight-eisenhower-joseph-mccarthy-red-scare.

242 he accused the US Army: "Joseph McCarthy Begins Hearings Inves-

tigating U.S. Army," History, https://www.history.com/this-day-in
-history/mccarthy-army-hearings-begin.

243 turned the American public: "Joseph McCarthy Condemned by Senate," History, https://www.history.com/this-day-in-history/mccarthy
-condemned-by-senate.

243 He interrupted: "Joseph McCarthy Begins Hearings Investigating U.S.
Army," History.

243 "Until this moment, Senator": Ibid.

243 McCarthy self-combusted: *The Betty White Show* ratings memo for
April 26, 27, 28, 1954, from Sam Fuller; memo from Jim Cornell to
Fuller re "Betty White Trendex," May 6, 1954, Box 380, folder 23,
NBC Records.

243 had to stop: Letter from Wile to Pat Kelly, August 9, 1954, Box 380,
folder 23, NBC Records.

244 after a complaint: Letter from Wile to Mickey Rockford, July 19,
1954, Box 380, folder 23, NBC Records.

244 moved her show: "Betty White Unsold, Shifts to New Time," *Variety*,
June 30, 1954, 31.

244 moved her back to midday: Letter from McAvity to Louis G. Cowan,
September 9, 1954, Box 380, folder 23, NBC Records.

244 threw a soiree: Sheilah Graham, "A Date for Garroway," syndicated
column, November 1954.

246 had fallen out of favor: Martin Turnbull, "Spotlight on . . . Romanoff's," Martin Turnbull, https://martinturnbull.com/hollywood
-places/spotlight-romanoffs/.

247 first trip to New York City: Betty White, *Here We Go Again: My Life
in Television* (New York: Scribner, 1995), Apple Books/iPad, 144.

247 "It was my first brush": Ibid.

248 "We are trying": James L. Baughman, *Same Time, Same Station: Creating American Television, 1948–1961* (Baltimore: Johns Hopkins
University Press, 2007), 103.

248 "spectaculars": Jack Slater, "Sylvester L. 'Pat' Weaver: Hall of Fame
Tribute," Television Academy, 1985, https://www.emmys.com/news
/hall-fame/pat-weaver-hall-fame-tribute.

248 $5 million: Baughman, *Same Time, Same Station*, 103–05.

248 "Before we had ridiculous dramas": Ibid.

248 she began arguing: Phillips autobiographical drafts, 144–46, Phillips Papers.

249 "I made this change": Ibid., 145.

249 "I wanted to be loved": Ibid., 146.

250 "We don't believe in": Ibid., 148.

250 having problems with his eyes: Letter from Loeb to IRS, October 4, 1954, Reel 1, Box 1, folder 1.6, Loeb Papers.

250 "forming an anti-suicide club": Letter from Loeb to Kate Mostel, September 3, 1954, Box 5, folder 15, Mostel Papers.

250 "The only arrangements": Letter from Loeb to Zero Mostel, November 5, 1954, Box 5, folder 15, Mostel Papers.

251 "under an assumed name": Letter from Loeb to Zero Mostel, undated, Box 5, folder 15, Mostel Papers.

251 outstanding income tax warrant: Letter from Philip D. Greenspan to Loeb, March 15, 1955, Reel 1, Box 1, folder 1.6, Loeb Papers.

251 Loeb could no longer pay: Arthur Sainer, *Zero Dances: A Biography of Zero Mostel* (New York: Limelight Editions, 1998), 174.

251 checked into room 507: "Philip Loeb Dead; Prominent Actor," *New York Times*, September 2, 1955, 38.

251 called several friends: Glenn D. Smith, Jr., *"Something on My Own": Gertrude Berg and American Broadcasting, 1929–1956* (Syracuse, NY: Syracuse University Press, 2007), 180.

251 changed into his pajamas: "Philip Loeb Dead; Prominent Actor," *New York Times*.

252 he fought for : Smith, *"Something on My Own,"* 180.

252 Berg was emotional: Letter from Claasen to Berg, September 2, 1955, Box 62, Berg Papers.

253 moving to the suburbs: J. P. Shanley, "TV: 'Goldbergs' Move; Shift to Suburbs Seen on Opening Show," *New York Times*, September 23, 1955, 49.

253 "The Goldbergs are now settled": Press release, ca. 1955, Box 62, Berg Papers.

253 "Like many other New Yorkers": Shanley, "TV: 'Goldbergs' Move."

253 "There is no question": Leon Morse, "'Goldbergs' Moves to Film with Ease," *Billboard*, May 28, 1955, 8.

253 "maintains its innate and unique": "The Goldbergs," *Variety*, September 28, 1955, 38.

255 would be no overtly Jewish: Vincent Brook, "The Americanization of Molly: How Mid-Fifties TV Homogenized 'The Goldbergs' (and Got 'Berg-larized' in the Process)," *Cinema Journal*, Summer 1999, 45–67.

256 telling those who rang: Letters from Claasen to Berg, March 14 and July 28, 1955, Box 62, Berg Papers.

256 She appeared on television: Letter from Claasen to Berg, October 26, 1955, Box 62, Berg Papers.

256 Waldo cooked enough beef: Letter from Claasen to Berg, October 11, 1955, Box 62, Berg Papers.

256 to send to fifty-two reviewers: Letter from Louise Thomas to Berg, October 18, 1955, Box 62, Berg Papers.

256 On October 21: Letter from Janet Gleason to Fannie Merrill, October 18, 1955, Box 62, Berg Papers.

256 They were top-ten shows: Tim Brooks and Earle F. Marsh, *The Complete Directory to Prime Time Network and Cable TV Shows, 1946–Present* (New York: Ballantine, 2007), 1681.

256 "the Jackie Robinson of television": David Johnson, "'The Jackie Robinson of Television': The Nat King Cole Show," Indiana Public Media, February 10, 2020, https://indianapublicmedia.org/nightlights/nat-king-cole-show.php.

257 "I was the pioneer": Ibid.

258 "He's a good friend": Author's interview with Adam Clayton Powell III, May 11, 2019.

Chapter 12: The World Turns

259 "If I ever find": Phillips autobiographical drafts, 157, Phillips Papers.

259 The Amanda Holmes character: Ibid., 165–66.

260 "No, I didn't cook": Ibid., 158.

260 persuaded CBS to provide: Ibid., 148–49.

260 one of several blacklisted: Carol A. Stabile, *The Broadcast 41: Women and the Anti-Communist Blacklist* (London: Goldsmiths Press, 2018), 159.

261 In a February 1955 interview: "Irna Weeps for the Weepers," *Variety*, February 9, 1955, 33.

262 "As the world turns": Phillips autobiographical drafts, 151, Phillips Papers.

262 "fantasized as well as fictionalized": Ibid., 147.

262 the number one daytime soap: Sam Ford, "Growing Old Together: Following *As the World Turns'* Tom Hughes Through the Years," in *The Survival of Soap Opera: Transformations for a New Media Era*, edited by Sam Ford, Abigail de Kosnik, and C. Lee Harrington (Jackson: University Press of Mississippi, 2011), 87.

263 put two half-hour soap operas: James L. Baughman, *Same Time, Same Station: Creating American Television, 1948–1961* (Baltimore: Johns Hopkins University Press, 2007), 296.

263 had a hand in seven shows: "Phillips, Irna (1901–1973)," Encyclopedia .com, https://www.encyclopedia.com/women/encyclopedias-almanacs -transcripts-and-maps/phillips-irna-1901-1973.

263 longest running of all scripted programs: Bill Carter, "CBS Turns Out 'Guiding Light,'" *New York Times*, April 1, 2009, https://www .nytimes.com/2009/04/02/arts/television/02ligh.html.

264 "In memory of my mother": Dedication by Katherine L. Phillips, Phillips autobiographical drafts, Box 12, Phillips Papers.

264 "Since she is on a stage": Brooks Atkinson, "Theatre: 'Majority of One,'" *New York Times*, February 17, 1959, 28.

265 She spent several years: "Anything but Average," *Tablet*, January 18, 2008, https://www.tabletmag.com/jewish-arts-and-culture/1291/any thing-but-average.

265 "I have lived": Gertrude Berg and Cherney Berg, *Molly and Me: The Memoirs of Gertrude Berg* (New York: McGraw-Hill, 1961), ix.

266 "the new stereotype": Marjorie Ingall, "Remembering the Emmys' First Best Actress Winner," *Tablet*, September 17, 2018, https://www .tabletmag.com/sections/community/articles/gertrude-berg-best -actress-emmy.

267 "Yoo-hoo, Mrs. Bloom": Stuart Elliott, "The Media Business: Advertising; Animated Pots and Pans Clamor to Be Scrubbed Clean in a New Commercial for S.O.S. from Clorox," *New York Times*, August 19, 1994, D16.

267 "When I'm by myself": Glenn D. Smith, Jr., *"Something on My Own": Gertrude Berg and American Broadcasting, 1929–1956* (Syracuse, NY: Syracuse University Press, 2007), 217.

267 The official cause: "Gertrude Berg, Molly of 'The Goldbergs,' Dead," *New York Times*, September 15, 1966, 43.

267 opening night: Smith, *"Something on My Own,"* 215.

267 *How to Be a Jewish Mother*: Ingall, "Remembering the Emmys' First Best Actress Winner."

267 "Our research says": Jennifer Keishin Armstrong, *Mary and Lou and Rhoda and Ted: And All the Brilliant Minds Who Made the Mary Tyler Moore Show a Classic* (New York: Simon & Schuster Paperbacks, 2013), 36.

269 "One does not look": Quoted in Karen Chilton, *Hazel Scott: The Pioneering Journey of a Jazz Pianist from Café Society to Hollywood to HUAC* (Ann Arbor: University of Michigan Press, 2008), 177.

269 "much needed rest": Lorissa Rinehart, "This Black Woman Was Once the Biggest Star in Jazz. Here's Why You've Never Heard of Her," Narratively, August 1, 2018, https://narratively.com/this-black -woman-was-once-the-biggest-star-in-jazz-heres-why-youve-never -heard-of-her/.

269 "The pope could be watching!": Author's interview with Adam Clayton Powell III, May 11, 2019.

270 "Think about it": Ibid.

270 "nonservant role": David K. Li and Diana Dasrath, "Diahann Carroll, First Black Woman to Star in Nonservant Role in TV Series, Dies at 84," NBC News, October 4, 2019, https://www.nbcnews.com/pop -culture/pop-culture-news/diahann-carroll-first-black-woman-star -non-servant-role-tv-n1062511.

270 "One of the lawyers": "Hearing Before the Panel of the Library of Congress, Hotel Sofitel Ma Maison, Los Angeles, California, March 6, 1996," National Film Preservation Board, https://www.loc.gov/pro grams/national-film-preservation-board/preservation-research /television-videotape-preservation-study/los-angeles-public-hearing/.

271 Hazel Scott landed: "Hazel Scott, Jazz Pianist, Singer Dies," *Washington Post*, October 4, 1981, https://www.washingtonpost.com /archive/local/1981/10/04/hazel-scott-jazz-pianist-singer-dies /a6a2da7e-afc2-424c-af56-dac992e729e0/.

271 "Your mother has her dream job": Author's interview with Adam Clayton Powell III, May 11, 2019.

273 In July 1955, she joined: Donald Kirkley, "Betty White Connects," *The Sun*, July 10, 1955, FA12.

273 "One thing I'm still": Ibid.

273 she met Lucille Ball: "Betty White and Lucille Ball Had Quite the

Special Friendship: 'They Considered Each Other Family,'" *Closer Weekly*, November 1, 2017, https://www.closerweekly.com/posts /betty-white-lucille-ball-friendship-145598/.

274 White eventually married: *Betty White: First Lady of Television*, DVD, directed by Steven J. Boettcher and Michael J. Trinklein (Boettcher + Trinklein Television, 2018).

INDEX

ABOUT THE AUTHOR

JENNIFER KEISHIN ARMSTRONG is the New York Times bestselling author of *Seinfeldia*; *Mary and Lou and Rhoda and Ted*; and *Sex and the City and Us*. She worked at *Entertainment Weekly* for a decade and has written for many publications, including BBC *Culture*, the *New York Times Book Review*, *Vice*, *New York* magazine, and *Billboard*. She also speaks about pop culture history and creativity. Armstrong lives in New York City.